UNCORRECTED BOOK PROOF

ON DUTY

REFLECTIONS ON A LIFE IN THE GUARDS

JOHN O'DRISCOLL

Gill Books

Gill Books
Hume Avenue
Park West
Dublin 12
www.gillbooks.ie
Gill Books is an imprint of M.H. Gill and Co.
© John O'Driscoll 2024

978 18045 8102 5

Designed by Typo•glyphix, Burton-on-Trent, DE14 3HE
Edited by Jane Rogers
Proofread by Sally Vince
Printed by xxxx
This book is typeset in 12 on 20pt, Sabon.

*The paper used in this book comes from the wood pulp
of sustainably managed forests.*

A CIP catalogue record for this book is available from the
British Library.

5 4 3 2 1

[to follow]

CONTENTS

ACRONYMS AND ABBREVIATIONS

AC   assistant commissioner
CAB   Criminal Assets Bureau
CBP   Customs and Border Protection (US)
CTA   common travel area
CTF   Crime Task Force
DEA   Drug Enforcement
               Administration (US)
DFA   Department of Foreign Affairs
DOJ   Department of Justice
DPP   Director of Public Prosecutions
DVI   Disaster Victim Identification
EEA   European Economic Area
ERU   Emergency Response Unit
ESDA   electrostatic detection apparatus
GIM   Garda Information Message
GNBCI   Garda National Bureau of
               Criminal Investigation
GNCCB   Garda National Cyber Crime Bureau
GNDOCB   Garda National Drugs and Organised Crime
               Bureau
GNDU   Garda National Drug Unit

GNECB	Garda National Economic Crime Bureau
GNIB	Garda National Immigration Bureau
GNPSB	Garda National Protective Services Bureau
GRA	Garda Representative Association
GSOC	Garda Síochána Ombudsman Commission
GTB	Garda Technical Bureau
IADP	Inter-Agency Drugs Project
ICON	Inner City Organisations Network
IFPC	International Fraud Prevention Centre
IPO	International Protection Office
NCDDU	National Central Division Drug Unit
OCG	Organised crime gang
OFAC	Office of Foreign Assets Control
ORAC	Office of the Refugee Applications Commissioner
PSNI	Police Service of Northern Ireland
RIC	Royal Irish Constabulary
RUC	Royal Ulster Constabulary
SOC	scene of crime
TTVIIMC	Thai Tsunami Victim Identification Information Management Centre

PROLOGUE

A DUTY TO SERVE

I wasn't supposed to be here.

From the moment I walked into Templemore, back in 1981, my retirement date was set in stone: 30 June 2020. The mandatory retirement age at that time was set at 60. There was no career beyond 2020, I had always known that. And yet, here I was, on 15 May 2022, dressed in the uniform of the Garda Síochána and bearing the insignia assigned to the rank of Assistant Commissioner, standing on the National Mall in Washington DC, preparing to mark the lives and deaths of those who had died on duty. Mine had been an extraordinary career and it wasn't over yet. In my final weeks I was still experiencing 'firsts', and this was one of huge significance.

I had travelled to Washington with Seamus Boland, head of the Garda National Drugs and Organised Crime Bureau (GNDOCB), and a team of detectives. Seamus and I had been colleagues since our days in the North Central Division Drug Unit in Store Street in the 1990s, where our team had changed the approach to drugs policing. We had come to attend a meeting on 13 May at the Department of the Treasury, a building once only familiar to me from the back of the US ten dollar bill. The meeting was a debriefing after the unprecedented law enforcement event at City Hall a month earlier, when the US Department of the Treasury had announced sanctions on the Kinahan organised crime group (OCG), the first time the US had imposed such restrictions on a European drug cartel. I had choreographed the announcement extremely carefully, and the fallout was still sending shockwaves across the global drug trafficking networks. At the Department of the Treasury, the Under Secretary of the Office of Terrorism and Financial Intelligence, Brian E. Nelson, had handed me a letter thanking me for being a trusted partner and friend to the Department and for helping to 'protect the national security, foreign policy and economy of the United States from transnational organised crime'. That was another first, to be sure, and it was mind-boggling to me.

As Seamus and I descended the steps of the Treasury building after the meeting, I turned to him and said, 'Well, this is a long way from the streets of the north inner city.' We could only shake our heads. It was an extraordinary moment, coming off the back of a number of extraordinary events. I wasn't sure that I was ready for my career to end, but I certainly felt I was going out on a high. If I had pictured my retirement when I was a young garda, I probably would have imagined tea and cake in Fitzgibbon Street or Store Street, a farewell pint in Phil Ryan's around the corner, perhaps. A quiet emptying of the locker and a lonely walk to the car, as the station got on with its raucous busyness without me. The route my life in policing had followed had not led to that moment, and I was grateful for that.

Now, at the National Mall, I gave an interview to Sean Whelan, RTÉ News's Washington correspondent, and he questioned me about the Treasury visit. Later, I accompanied those who had travelled with me to the west front of Capitol Hill, one of the most architecturally impressive and symbolically important buildings in the world. It stands for independence and democracy and human rights, all the things that a public servant such as myself believes in upholding and protecting. There, we gathered to honour law enforcement officers who had died in the course of carrying out their duty. The event was organised by the US Annual National Peace Officers' Memorial Service, and they had bestowed upon me the honour of laying a wreath to commemorate the memory of those who had made the ultimate sacrifice. It was one of the greatest privileges of my career to participate in that ceremony and to lay a wreath while wearing the uniform of the Garda Síochána.

My mind turned to my father, who had risen to the rank of chief superintendent and head of the Central Detective Unit, and who had also served for over forty years. At first, he had not understood my decision to join the force, but when he saw how I tackled my job and how I enjoyed it, he soon realised it was the right choice for me. By the time my younger brother expressed a wish to join the ranks, he had no reservations and was proud to see us carrying on the family tradition of public service. We were living according to the strong sense of duty our father had believed in too, passing on his legacy of serving with dedication and the highest ethical standards.

When my last day as a garda arrived, I donned my uniform for the final time and walked through the wrought iron gates, with their Celtic-inspired spirals, that lead from the Chapel Royal and State Apartments in Dublin Castle to the Garda Memorial Garden. In a mirroring of my Washington visit, I wanted to pay my respects to those who had died on duty. It was quiet in the memorial garden and I walked among the stone scrolls, on which were inscribed the names of all those colleagues who had been killed in uniform, some of whom I had known. They never got the opportunity to retire. Some were murdered by terrorists, particularly the IRA; others died while protecting the public or pursuing criminals. As I recalled them and their sacrifices, I felt immensely grateful that their fate had not befallen me.

For my part, I could count myself among the very luckiest ones. We had all signed up as eager young recruits, making it through Templemore; then we were out on the streets and laneways of Ireland, wanting to make a difference. We knew there were dangers, of course. The death of each one of those 89 gardaí had affected the entire force, every single member, because they spoke of the threats we spent most of our time deliberately not thinking about. But we were driven by an ideal of serving the public, protecting people and upholding the law for the greater good. For me, that impetus had found expression in a career that had been long and enjoyable, with all those 'firsts' that were so gratifying to experience. My work took me from the back streets of Dublin to places like Bermuda, Copenhagen, Cairo, Kuala Lumpur, Thailand, Warsaw and The Hague, and from the needle-strewn rundown flats of society's forgotten people to the opulence of ambassadors' residences. I am lucky indeed to be able to say that my 41 years on duty were an incredible adventure.

PART 1
EARNING THE UNIFORM
(1977–1994)

CHAPTER 1

THE FAMILY BUSINESS

'*Where did the bomb hit?*'

My father rushed to the telephone. He snatched up the receiver and dialled a number. When the call was answered he said tersely: 'Where did the bomb hit?' My mother and I, who were standing close by, went still, shocked to hear those words. At the other end of the line, his garda colleague was shocked, too, asking what bomb my father was talking about. Nothing had been called in. What did he mean?

My father returned the phone to its cradle. Almost immediately, the phone started ringing, sounding louder in our silence. He picked it up again, and listened as he was told that three bombs had just gone off in Dublin's city centre, at

Parnell Street, Talbot Street and South Leinster Street. From the higher ground of our house in Santry, he had heard the reverberation of the explosion and understood what it was before those unfortunate enough to be in the vicinity fully knew what was happening.

It was Friday 17 May 1974. Three car bombs had been detonated on the streets of inner-city Dublin – claimed years later by the UVF. They had taken the lives of 27 people and injured hundreds more. I exchanged a look with my brother – because of a bus strike, our father had collected us from near Parnell Street just 90 minutes earlier. The no-warning bombs had been set to coincide with the evening rush hour, around five-thirty. Buildings were ravaged, windows blown out, debris strewn across the streets and cars left as skeletal wrecks as the emergency services raced to the scene.

My father got the details, as far as they were known, then he left to go and play a role in the Garda investigation. He was a detective superintendent in the Garda Síochána's Central Detective Unit and to me it seemed he met every situation, no matter how frightening or tragic, calmly and coolly. His work fascinated me and I was intrigued by the stories he told us about it. From childhood I had a deep interest in Irish history, politics and public affairs, and the policing of the state was very much part of that. My father's daily return from work, with the *Irish Independent* under his arm, was eagerly awaited. I would wait impatiently for him to read it and complete the crossword, when finally I could enter the fray to be the next family member to read it. Even at 12 years of age I would read it with great concentration from first column to last.

So I knew about the Troubles in Northern Ireland; I knew about bombs going off there. But this was a first for me. It wasn't for my father, though. I knew why he had so quickly recognised the sound and sensation of the bombs going off. He was a fairly new recruit, about eighteen months in uniform, when the German Luftwaffe bombed Dublin on 31 May 1941. It was an event that would have a lasting impact. That attack killed 28 people, injured 90 and destroyed about three hundred houses. It was an unprecedented attack on Irish soil. But this bombing, to which I was now bearing witness, replaced it as the greatest loss of life in a terrorist attack in Ireland. An hour and a half after the bombs exploded in Dublin, another device was detonated in Monaghan, claiming seven lives. In all, 34 people were killed that day.

The bombings and their aftermath left a deep impression on me. I think they played a role in my life choices later, as a young adult. Although my family was steeped in the ideals of public service, my father did not push me or my siblings towards joining the ranks of the Garda Síochána. He had joined out of necessity and, even though he enjoyed his work and was wholly dedicated to it, I think he felt that there were easier ways for his children to earn a living. He had joined in 1939, when wartime Ireland was bleak, with high unemployment and widespread deprivation. His mother had encouraged him because the family believed in the vocation and because jobs were scarce.

He joined not as a member of the Garda Síochána, but as a garda in what was known as the Taca Síochána, in effect a temporary police force. This was a wartime measure, when new recruits were needed but the public purse was light on funds. In fact, my father once told me that the Guinness brewery at St James's Gate had subsidised the wages bill of the Garda Síochána at times during the war years when the government didn't have enough to pay the guards. Guinness had stepped in to help to keep the country running. The financial difficulties facing the Garda Síochána during 'The Emergency', as World War II was known in Ireland, led to the creation of the Taca Síochána. It allowed for recruits to play a full role in policing, but with lower wages, lesser conditions and no guarantee of permanency. Four hundred men were hired on this basis, and my father was one of them. He wore the same uniform and had the same powers as his colleagues, but he was on a temporary contract and had to live on the reduced sum of £2.10s. Gardaí were being paid £3.10s per week at that time. In 1942, the Taca recruits were finally inducted into the ranks of the Garda Síochána and my father became a fully paid-up member from that moment on.

When it came to Leaving Cert exams in 1977 and the time to make my own choices, I didn't apply to the Garda

Síochána. Even if I had been serious about it, I was too young. I was only 16 years old when I sat the exams, turning 17 a few days after they finished, and the age threshold for the guards was 19 years. I didn't want to follow my two older brothers into college, so that wasn't an option either. I would have happily spent my time at my mother's homeplace down in West Cork, where I whiled away every summer holiday of my childhood, but my mother ensured I took a more realistic approach to my future. I applied for various jobs and was offered a position with Texaco oil company, at its head office in Ballsbridge.

Texaco House was a landmark building in south Dublin, renowned for its striking architecture. It was just down the road from the American Embassy and its curved window openings echoed that iconic building. It was designed by David Keane and Partners and was unusual at the time for being built of pre-cast concrete. Built in 1971, it was still a new building when I joined Texaco and it was like a breath of fresh air on the streetscape – unashamedly modern and unique – and I enjoyed the walk towards it each morning, watching as more of the structure was revealed as I got closer.

What really struck me on my walks around Ballsbridge was the huge queue at the American Embassy down the road. There wasn't a working day when there wasn't a snaking queue of people at its gates. In 1970s Ireland, youth unemployment stood at around 25 per cent and many of my generation simply couldn't see a future ahead of them. They did what so many Irish people had done before them – they set their sights on America. Those thousands of youngsters were lining up to get a US visa, a passport to a brand new life in a country they were promised was teeming with jobs and opportunities. Ireland felt stagnant by comparison. We were a country of emigration stretching back a hundred years or more, and it seemed impossible to believe that would ever change. Walking past those hopeful young people, I felt very glad for my permanent job in Texaco (Ireland) Ltd. I was one of the lucky ones, skirting the queue and never joining the back of it.

Inside the Texaco building, I was busy learning a whole new set of skills, meeting some wonderful people and forging the first of many life-long friendships. My first boss was Tony Farrell, who played for Bohemians and Drumcondra football clubs. I worked with him in administration for my first two years with Texaco. One of the highlights of that time was being seconded to work with Simon Behan, who had earned an All-Ireland medal playing for Dublin, in the public relations department. Texaco ran two huge annual events – the art competition and the sports stars awards – and Simon needed extra help with the workload on those.

The Texaco Children's Art Competition is almost a national institution. It was first run in 1955 and since then thousands of children have entered drawings and paintings in different categories and age groups. Back at the start, children were invited to illustrate a particular slogan or idea that was linked to Texaco's business or products, but it has branched out hugely since then and encourages artworks of every type. It has become a prestigious competition and a serious achievement for any child who gets picked from the deluge of entries.

In the 1970s the competition was in full swing and every year Texaco rented a house in nearby Sandymount, a few minutes' walk from the office, where the children's artworks were stored and assessed. A judge came over from the UK to go through them and whittle them down to the winners. My job was to help the judge – even though I was really only a kid myself, with very little experience of the art world. I helped store and sort all the entries and propped them up all around the house for the judge to peruse them and make his choices. Every single room was filled with colourful drawings and you couldn't help smiling as you walked among them.

My other work with Simon Behan was on the Texaco Sportstars of the Year awards. It was a huge event at that time, then the only one of its kind. It culminated in a black-tie event at the Burlington Hotel, where the great and the good of Ireland gathered to toast the winners who were awarded the coveted trophies. It was said that it was the only occasion in the year, other than Cabinet meetings, when the whole government Cabinet would gather together. People from the worlds of sports, politics, the media – they all wanted to be there.

The long list of VIPs invited to attend the event, in 1978, included the Garda Commissioner, Ned Garvey, a name familiar to me because he had joined the Taca Síochána with my father and they knew one other. Before the event had even kicked off, a bombshell scandal engulfed the government. Commissioner Garvey was unceremoniously sacked from his job. It was only the second time this had ever happened in the history of the state, the first being the sacking of General Eoin O'Duffy in 1933 by Éamon de Valera. On this occasion there was a Jack Lynch-led Fianna Fáil government in power and the impression was that Garvey was not 'one of their own'. This was at a time when the government tended to appoint sympathetic allies into key positions, including the head of the Garda Síochána.

Needless to say, Ned Garvey did not attend the Sportstars awards as planned – his seat was conspicuously empty as all around the government ministers raised their glasses and toasted the winners. It wasn't the end of the matter, though. The former Commissioner took a case against his former employers for summary dismissal. He won the case – and it quickly became famous, ultimately leading to the legal requirement that there must be reasonable process in place before a person can be dismissed from their post. It felt very exciting to me, as a young man, to be so close to the biggest news story of the day.

My final position at Texaco was in the computer department. I was one of two who manned the computer room where payrolls and customer accounts were produced. I was accompanied by Dessie Fitzgerald, who was an Ireland rugby international in the days before professionalism. Dessie would be capped 34 times for his country. Another colleague who became a great friend was Peter Cullen. He was my own age and we both had a love of adventure. We engaged in a wide range of sporting activities, including parachuting and open-sea rowing. We joined a rowing club based at Bulloch Harbour and we were out rowing after work five or six days a week. It was that time of life when you have energy to burn and everything is hard work and good fun. The truth was, though, I was becoming restless in that little two-man computer room and had begun to wonder what else might be out there for me. I had been with Texaco for over three years and I felt I would prefer a career that was less office-based.

In the years before I left school, as I followed the daily news, I was fascinated by Ireland's decision to join the European Economic Community (EEC), now the European Union (EU). In 1972, when I was twelve, the country voted 83 per cent in favour of joining the EEC. I followed the campaigns and the vote very closely, and what struck me even then was the level of cross-party support the pro-EEC campaign garnered, with Jack Lynch, Seán Lemass, Liam Cosgrave and Garret FitzGerald all singing from the same hymn sheet. This was amazing to see after the Treaty divide that had dominated Ireland for decades and that I would have been very aware of through my own family in West Cork. For a long time, people were known by which side their family had chosen; it was a deep seam that ran through the Irish psyche. Now, I was seeing a sense of cohesion that seemed exciting and full of promise. I distinctly remember thinking how positive it was for the nation, and also how positive it was that we joined the same day as the UK. Again, it suggested a sweeping change – our old and bitter rival was now standing beside us, as equals, and that gave a great sense of unity and possibility for the future. I was very impressed with the leadership of Garret FitzGerald, who was our first Minister for Foreign Affairs with a seat at the table of the Community. He succeeded Liam Cosgrave as leader of Fine Gael and one of his first reforms of the party involved the creation, in 1977, of Young Fine Gael.

Those interests naturally led me towards political participation. While working at Texaco, I attended meetings of the Irish Council of the European Movement, whose purpose was to inform the Irish people about Europe and the status of Ireland's EEC membership. In 1978, I pinned my colours to the mast and joined Young Fine Gael. They asked me to help establish a branch in what was then called the Dublin Artane constituency, which I did. I organised our first public meeting, which focused on a discussion of pirate radio stations and made the next day's headlines. At the first meeting of the new branch of Young Fine Gael I was elected branch chairperson. I felt a sense of pride in that because it echoed my grandfather

Brian O'Driscoll's life – he was at the inaugural meeting of the Kilbrittain branch of the United Irish League party and was elected as branch honorary secretary and later as chairperson. I was taking up the baton for the family, taking on the belief in public service for the public good.

There was another echo in that meeting, although I could have no knowledge of it then. The location chosen for Young Fine Gael Artane's first meeting was the Crofton Airport Hotel, which was later renamed the Regency Hotel. As you get older, you realise there are certain coincidences patterning your life.

My political career was very short-lived, as it happened. Both Peter Cullen and I conceded that our work in Texaco was not holding our interest and we had a longing for something completely different. We realised that we shared a common interest in joining the Garda Síochána. I quietly applied for the entrance exam, as did Peter, and I sat it on 4 September 1980. The exam took place in Matt Talbot Hall, off Parnell Square – another echo, I would later discover – and featured papers on Irish, English, maths and general knowledge. There were around two thousand candidates and I think I placed about sixtieth overall. There was a high failure rate that year, which was primarily due to candidates performing badly in the general knowledge paper. I remember the *Sunday Journal* published the paper to show the public what had tripped up the candidates.

I received a letter telling me that my application had been successful and I duly presented myself for a medical and fitness exam at Garda HQ in Phoenix Park on 14 February 1981. While there, I bumped into an old pal from secondary school, Sean Cullen – he was no relation to Peter, and it would be years before we met up again. My father was at Garda HQ later that evening, as it happened, attending a retirement event. We met up at home, and then watched with a sense of dread as the night sky over Santry lit up orange and the air boomed with intermittent explosions. It was Valentine's night, and the Stardust dancehall in Artane had gone up in flames, trapping hundreds of young people inside. The scale of the tragedy only became apparent the following morning, as the hall smouldered – 48 people of my own age dead and 214 injured. It was horrific.

The next day, I issued a press release on behalf of the Artane branch of Young Fine Gael, of which I was PRO (public relations officer), expressing sympathy for the dead, the surviving and the bereaved. I also postponed a scheduled meeting as a mark of respect. That was the last act of my life as a politician. I had been offered a place in Garda Training Centre (now Garda College), where I would start on 29 April 1981. Once that was confirmed, I immediately resigned from Young Fine Gael – a garda cannot have political affiliations. Peter Cullen had made the cut, too, so we would soon both end our careers with Texaco. At home, my father could not believe that I was ditching a marvellous job in the private sector and urged me to stay put in Texaco. He genuinely couldn't understand my desire to join the force. Indeed, he wasn't alone – when people realised that Peter and I were taking a drop in salary to become gardaí, they thought we were mad. But we were not to be dissuaded.

I arrived at Templemore for my Phase 1 six-month training programme in April. (It was supposed to be followed by a Phase 2 six-week programme, but my class of recruits never got Phase 2. We did the initial training and that was it – we were out on the streets as uniformed gardaí.) One of my abiding memories of that first day adjusting to the 'boarding school' of Templemore was seeing everyone in the centre glued to the radio for news on the Troubles. This was at the time of the H-Block protests and there was much social unrest in Dublin; gardaí were protecting UK-owned shops like BHS in the city centre to ensure the buildings weren't attacked. The British Embassy had fallen victim to an arson attack in 1972 and the new building was in danger of suffering a similar fate. It meant that any and all gardaí – including the green recruits – could be shunted on to the frontlines to lend manpower. Those huddled around the radio were waiting to hear if this might happen for us.

At Templemore we lived three to a room and the walls between the rooms were just partitions, so you could converse with your neighbours. The recruits came from all over the country, which lent a great sense of camaraderie to the organisation. I can still remember the first people I went for a pint with in Templemore town – John Foudy and Eugene Corcoran, both from Longford. We had a curfew of 10 p.m. and woe betide anyone who wasn't signed in at curfew. The hierarchy and authority were apparent from your first moment through the door. You were given your number and you became that number. After my experience working in private enterprise, it was a bit of a culture shock.

It was important to adapt quickly, however, so I focused on doing just that. We had some 'macho' characters, of course, the sort who would shout and roar at us like you'd see in films about the army. Likewise, we had room inspections where we had to stand to attention on our highly polished floor with all our belongings stacked and stored just so. There was one incident when one of the macho sergeants announced a room inspection and we three took up our positions, standing to attention at the foot of our beds. He opened my locker – perfect. Then he opened Eugene Corcoran's locker – perfect. Then he opened the third chap's locker and what did he find only a picture of the Pope. It was strictly forbidden to have any personal items or photographs, so my heart sank a little for my roommate, but then I thought that there wasn't a garda alive who could take issue with the Pope. The sergeant stared at the photo for a long minute, then turned and roared: 'Look at this! A picture of the Pope today, God only knows what it will be tomorrow!' Myself and Eugene were biting back our smiles at that one. Although it went badly for our roommate – he had to clean the ceiling as punishment – I can only suppose that he offered it up.

We had classes in a wide range of topics, including first aid and anatomy. In one first aid class, the instructor pulled down two big charts, one showing the muscular system, the other a photograph of a human skeleton. As we all studied them, one lad got up quickly and headed for the door at a trot. There were long, heavy curtains hanging down in front of the door and as he reached them, he swooned into a faint and grabbed hold of the curtains. He crashed to the floor, bringing the whole curtain down on top of him. There was a bemused silence in the room. I remember thinking to myself that squeamishness didn't seem an ideal disposition for a garda. Templemore was grand if you were robust, but some did find it very difficult. It was a challenging environment and it was sink or swim. Overall, I enjoyed the experience and made some long-lasting friendships.

After six months, we passed out as gardaí. While my father had reservations, I felt proud and pleased to have taken this decision and to be embarking on a new career. I again had that sense of the family connection, of working towards fulfilling my duty. Both my father's and mother's families – the O'Driscolls and the O'Briens – stretched back many generations in West Cork. My grandfather Brian O'Driscoll was an energetic and disciplined man, captain of the first Kilbrittain hurling team, member of the Land League, Officer in Command of the local battalion of the old IRA and member of the local circle of the IRB. In fact, a significant proportion of earliest recruits to the Garda Síochána had been former members of the old IRA. On the O'Brien side, my mother was a relation of Michael Collins, who was of course involved in the establishment of the Garda Síochána. My mother and Michael Collins's mother both hailed from the O'Brien family of Sam's Cross, Clonakilty. We had Royal Irish Constabulary (RIC) officers on both sides of the family and relatives who had fought in World War I. Michael Collins himself had two uncles in the RIC. Prior to the War of Independence, many members of the RIC were well respected and even popular in the communities they served.

When controversy erupted in 2020 over the government's planned commemoration of the RIC, it pained me to see the level of total misunderstanding of the history of that organisation. The event was eventually cancelled amidst a storm of protest.

I felt huge pride in my O'Driscoll and O'Brien, and, by extension, Collins family members who had provided a public service to the nation. They had a loyalty to Ireland and her people that coloured their whole lives and directed their actions. I had that blood running through my veins and it was a proud day to stand in Garda uniform, joining the ranks of all those who had gone before me in working towards the betterment and safety of all citizens. It felt right to me to become a member of the Garda Síochána.

CHAPTER 2

LEARNING THE BEAT IN
FITZGIBBON STREET STATION

When we had completed our initial training, we were given our first assignment. On 5 October 1981, I would report for duty at Fitzgibbon Street Garda Station. It is an imposing building of redbrick and Portland stone in north inner-city Dublin. When I first walked through its doors, it rose up taller than any building around it, dwarfing the residential houses nearby. It's a nineteenth-century, three storey-over-basement building that was built around 1912. That was during the final decade of the British administration in Ireland, after which the building was handed over to the Garda Síochána and the organisation's crest was cast into the fanlight above the door. It was my first posting as a newly minted garda, and it was a homecoming of sorts because it had been my father's 'home' when he was posted in nearby Store Street station. In earlier years unmarried members were required to live in barracks – living-in accommodation was still available, but optional, in 1981 – and my father had been resident in Fitzgibbon Street when the German bombs fell nearby.

During my father's time at the station, there were washrooms in the basement, but when I arrived in October 1981, the washrooms were long gone and the basement had been converted into a gym. It was nothing like the gyms of today. There were two treadmills and you had to put fifty pence in the metre to get a 20-minute run. That led to an ongoing competition to see who could run furthest in 20 minutes. One colleague, Pat Kelly, regularly ran 5km in 20 minutes, and this became the distance to beat. I did manage it, but rarely.

The other big difference was the teleprinters. They were a feature of every garda station back then. It was an important communications machine in the days long before mobile phones. A tape was fed into it, and it typed out the incoming information on incidents throughout the country. The sound of its constant rat-a-tat-tatting was the soundtrack in every station; you couldn't escape it. But the rest of the building hadn't changed much since my father's day. We paraded for duty at the start of each shift in front of a big, ornate fireplace that was original to the building. The entire uniformed shift, usually a dozen officers, lined up in front of the fireplace and the sergeant assigned the beats for that shift, reading from the Allocations Book. There were three shifts: 6 a.m.–2 p.m., 2 p.m.–10 p.m. and 10 p.m.–6 a.m. We were assigned to foot or mobile (car) patrol. Usually a senior colleague would be the driver of the mobile patrol, but one of us might be assigned to accompany him as an observer. It was always welcome to get a break from the walking beats, especially if your driver was a proactive type and you might see some action. Often, I came in earlier than my colleagues in the hope of getting assigned to a mobile patrol.

One bank holiday, I was first in for the 2 p.m. shift, hoping to get assigned to the patrol car. I was too early, however, and the sergeant from the previous shift was waiting for an oncoming member to arrive, to take over scene preservation duties from one of his unit. A car had been burnt out and the scene was being preserved by a uniformed garda. The sergeant caught sight of me then, loitering with intent, and immediately instructed me to take over scene preservation duties. I was annoyed, but I didn't let that show, of course. I simply nodded and headed straight off, on foot, to Charleville Mall.

I arrived at the scene a few minutes later and my predecessor was very happy to see me coming along to relieve him. We exchanged a few words and then he hurried off to the station, and no doubt home to bed for some rest. I took up my position, standing beside the burnt-out wreck of a car, and inwardly I sighed deeply – this was about the most boring duty I could have landed for the day. Talk about drawing the short straw. But at the same time, I knew it was important. If someone took the trouble to burn out a car, it might be because they had used it to commit a crime. Around Dublin's inner city in the early 1980s there was a constant flow of lower-level crime, like handbag-snatching, car and bicycle theft and joyriding, so this wrecked vehicle might lead us to something else; it might contain clues or information, and for that reason my very boring watching job was valuable.

I'd been standing there for thirty long minutes when something entirely unexpected happened. A passing bus driver spotted me, stopped the bus, opened the doors with a hiss of hydraulics and urgently called out to me. I walked towards him and he shouted excitedly that a man had just been shot outside Cusack's pub on North Strand. Well, a shooting trumps a burnt-out car, so I left my minding post and quickly made my way over there. Would I find the victim of an attempted murder, maybe a trail of blood and the victim gone? I had no idea what to expect. I had never witnessed the aftermath of a gun crime.

I was the first garda on the scene at North Strand. The first responder has a major responsibility – if they fail to manage the scene correctly, evidence can be lost or compromised. I had learned that from a book in Templemore, but now I was facing the abrasive reality of being in uniform at a serious crime scene, with a victim and a crowd of onlookers.

All eyes turned to me as I surveyed the scene. Before me, on the footpath, lay a man, flat on his back. He was dead. There was a scatter of empty bullet shells around his body. Without preamble or warning, I had just encountered my first murder scene. I had received basic scene of crime training at this point, but common sense tells you not to touch anything, to leave everything exactly as you found it. And yet over the course of the next minutes, I would pick up those bullet shells and secure them in my shirt pocket.

The knot of people around the crime scene was my first thought, so I straightened my back and with nervous authority asked everyone to step back and create space. But the crowd kept growing as word spread and people ran to the location to have a look. A group of young lads raced over and I could see that things were quickly taking a turn for the worse. The young lads were unruly and rough, pulling and grabbing, darting about and generally running amok. I was still the only garda, vastly outnumbered, and I knew those young lads had mischievous intent. I reassessed the scene and I knew with certainty that the young fellas would snatch those bullet shells and they'd be lost to us. Again, I employed common sense, picking up the shells from around the man's lifeless body and dropping them in my pocket.

Finally, assistance arrived. I helped set a cordon and we pushed the crowd right back. The detectives took over, and I was glad to hand over responsibility to them. I talked to one of the detectives, explained what I had found and what I had done and why I had done it. I gave him the bullet shells and described where they had been lying when I first arrived. I had gone against my Templemore book learning, but I explained that I felt it was more important to have the bullets in our possession than to try to preserve a scene in those circumstances.

That experience taught me a valuable lesson. You can reel off all the theory you want and get A-plus for your knowledge, but when you are in a real-life situation and you are the only garda present, you must be able to think on your feet and trust your instincts. I realised that I would face many unexpected and largely unpredictable situations, so it was important to be able to adapt to what was in front of you. I had learned, too, that the location can affect a crime scene and how you deal with it. It was clear to me from that first murder scene that a good garda had to have flexibility, common sense and good instincts in equal measure.

It turned out that the dead man, Jimmy Flynn, had been killed as a result of a feud within the Irish Republican Socialist Party. The incident room for the murder investigation was set up in Fitzgibbon Street, and I would be required to visit the incident room to provide whatever assistance I could to the investigation. I was in this room in advance of the first case conference. Among the senior officers and investigating detectives who attended was the detective chief superintendent from the Central Detective Unit – my father. This was the only time our work lives overlapped. It was the only time we were in the same room on the same case.

That was June 1982, and my father was in the final stages of his career, although he continued to be involved in some extraordinary cases right up to the end of his time as a detective. One day, 4 August 1982, he came home and said to us, 'You won't believe where I've just been.' He told us that he had been out to Bulloch Harbour, a place I knew like the back of my hand. But he wasn't walking or rowing, he was on Garda business. He had been called to the apartment at Pilot View of the Attorney General, Patrick Connolly, where Malcolm McArthur had been arrested on suspicion of committing two murders. This was the famous GUBU incident that rocked Irish politics, so called because it was described by Charles Haughey as 'grotesque, unbelievable, bizarre and unprecedented'.

It was a sensational crime – the eccentric McArthur had murdered two completely innocent people, one because he wanted to steal her car and the other because he wanted to steal his shotgun. It truly was unprecedented and the nation was hooked on the drama as it unfolded. When it was discovered that McArthur could not be found because he was a guest in the home of the Attorney General, there was uproar. Some saw it as the wealthy and privileged shielding the wealthy and privileged – especially when the Attorney General headed off on a planned holiday instead of giving an interview to the gardaí. It was heady stuff to be so close, via my father, to a seismic political upheaval.

My father retired in October 1982. He had been due to retire at the beginning of April 1983, when he would reach compulsory retirement age. However, John Joy, his predecessor in the role of detective chief superintendent at CDU, who had retired a number of years earlier, and had taken up a security-related consultancy role with the AIB, died suddenly. While my father had been determined to continue working until he had to retire, he was encouraged by colleagues to accept an offer from the AIB to fill John Joy's role.

He had to complete a medical test in advance of taking up employment with AIB. He was the type of man rarely to darken a doctor's doorway and hadn't had a medical consultation for years, but he passed the fitness test with flying colours. My father was still mulling it all over and I remember him saying to me, 'If I retire now, six months earlier than I need to, then your mother won't be as well provided for if I die before compulsory retirement age.' He and my mother had plans for a long retirement they saw stretching out ahead of them, but it didn't turn out like that. In January 1983, my grandfather Michael O'Brien died and we went to West Cork for his funeral. My father had what we thought was the flu and did not travel with us to the funeral. However, his illness was soon after diagnosed as cancer. He died in March 1983.

After my father died, a garda from the local station turned up at the front door, looking to collect his Garda ID. We carry the Garda badge at all times; it identifies us as serving members and verifies our police powers. It must be handed back when you leave the Garda Síochána. It's often the case that members want to keep it, which I understand because it does become part of you, but that is not permitted. I had to tell the garda at the door that we couldn't put our hands on it right at that moment and I promised to find it. Eventually, our searching uncovered it and I put my father's ID badge in my pocket and walked up to the station and handed it over on his behalf. There was grief in that gesture, too.

By 1984 I had been moved on to a Crime Task Force (CTF). These operated citywide, so you weren't confined to your own station district, and we worked in pairs. My partner, Jim Fox, and I spent our shifts out on mobile patrol all around the city, observing and responding in an unmarked car. One particular day turned out to be memorable. We were driving up North Circular Road, in the direction of the Phoenix Park. I was behind the wheel on that occasion and as we crept along in the heavy traffic, my eye was caught by a man to our right whose movements suggested a jerky wariness. I watched him for a few moments, then I turned to Jim and said, 'Look at that fella on the footpath, he looks like he's up to something.'

As the patrol car was stopped in traffic, Jim got out to approach him. He walked around the front of the car just as the man started to cross the road towards us. His attention was fixed on the Credit Union office behind Jim, but suddenly his eyes focused on us and he twigged that our attention was very much fixed on him. As I watched, he reached behind his back and pulled out a sawn-off shotgun that had been concealed under his coat. It was like watching a movie. I went very still and calm. The man roared at Jim to get on the ground and Jim lay down flat on his stomach, hands over his head. Then the man turned his gaze and his shotgun towards me, sitting motionless in the car. He pointed the gun directly at me for a second or two, then he turned suddenly and sprinted off.

I put the car in gear while yelling at Jim, 'Get in! Get in!' He leapt up and threw himself back into the passenger seat and we took off, tyres squealing. I saw the man duck down a side street on the left, and after him I went. We swung into the turn and there he was, jumping onto the back of a waiting motorcycle. It tore off and us right after it. But unfortunately for me, I was driving a Garda standard-issue Ford Granada and it was heavy and had poor acceleration. The motorbike was pulling away, weaving nimbly through the traffic and out onto Dorset Street. Then it veered sharply up a footway beside the Grand Canal, ending our pursuit.

I drove along the adjoining road, parallel to the canal, while Jim put out the call for back-up and gave the motorbike's location. We did all we could, but they were well gone and we couldn't catch up. We drove along, the adrenaline still rushing from the gun and the chase. Then what did we see only a car coming towards us with a number of young men in it – all of them familiar faces to us from the north inner city and their less than law-abiding behaviour. We pulled the car over to have a chat with them, and it turns out the car is not theirs. We had lost our armed would-be robber, but now we would retrieve a stolen car for our troubles.

Back at Fitzgibbon Street, the suspects were interviewed. The car was parked in the back yard of the station, which was entered through a locked gate. When cars are stolen for the purpose of joyriding, it is described as an 'unauthorised taking'. But this car had been stolen over a month earlier, therefore was categorised as a stolen motor vehicle rather than a less serious 'unauthorised taking'. The suspects were released pending completion of investigations. Jim and I went back out and continued policing the inner city. When our shift finished later on and we returned to Fitzgibbon Street, we discovered, to our shock, that the stolen car was no longer in the yard. It transpired that the gate had inadvertently been left open for a short period and in that time the car had brazenly been repossessed by the thieves.

Out we went again, and after scouring the streets and visiting places where we suspected the stolen car could have been taken, we caught sight of it. We placed it under surveillance and after a number of hours pounced as a person approached and entered it. We made another arrest and again took possession of the car, this time ensuring it would be stored out of reach of anyone who might want to steal it yet again. Finally, our shift ended. The armed man had been planning to rob the Credit Union, so we had prevented that from happening, and in the aftermath we ended up getting a conviction at the Central Criminal Court for an audacious car thief. It wasn't a bad day's work after all.

Our days out patrolling were always unpredictable, and we had many hair-raising incidents and close escapes. I particularly remember a day down on Sheriff Street, where we both got out of our unmarked car to respond to a situation. When we sat back into it, Jim turned to me and said, 'Where's the walkie-talkie?' It had been sitting on the dashboard, and now it was gone. I looked around at all the kids milling about the street and I knew we had a big problem here. There was no way we could return to base with our hands in the air and no walkie-talkie, so it had to be found. But how?

We went down to the detective unit at Store Street and put out feelers among our sources. A line of potential enquiry opened up that way, but we'd have to make a deal to get the device back. That wasn't an option either, but then the bit of information we got gave me an idea as to where it might be. Again working sources, I discovered there was a strong possibility the walkie-talkie was in a specific house. We got a search warrant, as discreetly as possible. Before heading to the house, we drove to Fitzgibbon Street, where Donal, my younger brother, was stationed. We corralled him into joining our endeavour and the three of us drove to the place. While myself and Jim went to the front door, my brother went around to the back of the house.

We knocked, the door was opened, and a large man blocked the entrance, making sure to delay us getting in, a common tactic. Meanwhile, my brother had scaled the back wall, and from the top of it what does he see, only our suspect, with a package, rapidly digging a hole in the garden with a carving knife to bury the package. My brother leapt from the wall and pounced on the man. Suffice to say, we got the walkie-talkie back.

Assignment to the CTF was for a fixed term, after which those lucky enough to have joined its ranks would have to return to the station where they had previously been based. However, for me and Jim Fox, our stint with the CTF ended when we both successfully applied to be appointed to detective duties. Jim headed for a specialist fraud unit within CDU, while I returned to Fitzgibbon Street, but this time as a detective. Once assigned to detective duties, I was required to carry a firearm. I had done basic firearms training while at the Training College in Templemore, but had not scored well. So I headed for the firing range and achieved the results I needed to be provided with the standard issue Smith and Wesson .38 revolver.

There was a particular duty that was specific to the Fitzgibbon detectives that required a firearm. In the 1980s there was a huge level of unemployment and the dole was the sole source of income for many households. One member of the detective unit at Fitzgibbon Street attended daily at North Cumberland Street unemployment exchange to protect the large amounts of cash stored on the premises, which was paid out to the dole recipients. This was back in the days when everyone used either cash or cheque books.

When you walked into what was known as the dole office, you had to go up the stairs to the second floor, where there was a long room with thirteen counters. The cash payments were handed out at the last two counters. To protect the building, you would walk the perimeter, outside and inside, staying on the move and watching everything. Throughout a tour of duty you would make occasional visits into the staff area behind the counters. My partner, Dominic Hutcheon, and I would decide between us which one of us would do dole office duty on days we were working. There was one day, shortly before I got married, when I needed to take a day's leave to do wedding-related shopping, so Dominic would cover the exchange duty. I went to town that day with my future wife and parked the car. As we walked to a shop, I saw the first edition of the evening newspapers which would go on sale at about midday. I was rooted to the spot by the headline: *Garda shot at Cumberland Street Exchange*. I can never forget the horror that ran through my veins when I saw those words. I forgot about the wedding shopping and went immediately to nearby Jervis Street Hospital, where I knew Dominic would have been taken.

As Dominic sat on a trolley, being attended to by a physician, he described the scene he had faced only a short time earlier at North Cumberland Street. The staff were behind the counters. Beside the first counter was a doorway that led to a kitchen area. Dominic was in the kitchen when he heard a commotion outside. He immediately stepped outside, whereupon the door shut and locked behind him, and found himself facing two armed robbers, who were standing at counters 12 and 13, threatening the staff. The raiders had a sawn-off shotgun and a handgun. Dominic drew his Smith & Wesson revolver and shouted, 'Guards! Put down your weapons!' The two armed men turned and looked at him, then the man with the shotgun opened fire at very close range, hitting Dominic in the face and leg.

Dominic was a skilled marksman and he now fired his gun six times, using all the bullets he had in the chamber. He hit the man who was firing at him, but the bullets issued to us were designed for minimal impact and this didn't fell him. The two raiders then rushed past the counters where Dominic stood injured and ran down the stairs and out of the building. The armed robbers jumped into a getaway car that was waiting for them outside and sped off. The gang must have panicked because they brought their injured accomplice out to a house in Kilbarrack, but later dumped him and drove off. He died where they had left him. The man's name was Thomas 'Buckets of Blood' O'Driscoll and I recall John Harbison, the Chief State Pathologist, conducting the post-mortem and noting that he possibly would not have died if he had been brought straight to hospital.

My wedding took place a week later, and I was delighted when Dominic and his wife were there to celebrate with us. He was later awarded a gold Scott Medal for his bravery that day. His marksmanship was incredibly skilful – to fire six bullets and all to hit the intended target and no one else, in such a small space, was an astounding piece of controlled firing. I don't think there were many others who could have done that.

Advancement to higher ranks in the Garda Síochána requires taking promotion exams. After serving a number of years in the detective unit, I sat the sergeants promotion exam and achieved the required standard to go forward for promotion. Like most applicants, I was not successful at the first try. However, I was looking for more variety in my work, so when an opportunity arose to do a course leading to quali-fication in scenes of crime-related functions, I jumped at it.

The course was fascinating. It covered all aspects of all types of crime scene and I gained a huge amount of knowledge from it. At the end, when we qualified, we were each given our own scene of crime (SOC) kit box. It was like a customised toolbox, containing fingerprint brushes, powders, index cards, tapes, evidence bags – basically everything you would need to examine a variety of crime scenes. As a qualified scenes of crime examiner, there were two particular cases that really stand out in my memory, where I had an opportunity to use my recently acquired additional skills. One involved some disturbing anonymous letters; the other was the murder of a woman in a flat on Gardiner Street.

During the scenes of crime course, we had studied the investigation of crimes associated with the sending of anonymous correspondence. This is surprisingly common, even to the present day. Later, I had my own personal anonymous correspondent who sent nasty letters until the day I retired. One of the characteristics of this type of crime, we had learned on the course, is that it is very rarely a once-off occurrence. It is normally part of a regular pattern of behaviour. We also learned about the electrostatic detection apparatus (ESDA) at the document section of the Garda Technical Bureau (GTB), which could analyse the paper on which the letter was written. The page was dusted with a powder that settled into the grooves of any indentations made on the page. The beauty of this was that if a person used the same notepad, you could pick up the words written on the page before the current page.

All of that knowledge would prove very useful on the day I was asked to go to a house near North Strand to deal with a family who were near breaking point. The parents brought me in and we sat down and they explained that they had been receiving anonymous letters from a person who appeared to be stalking their daughter. The letter writer was able to accurately describe the young girl and her daily movements and they made it clear that they were deriving sexual pleasure from watching her. The parents were absolutely distraught and felt they had to move away from the area for their daughter's safety. I had never encountered a case like this before, but my SOC training allowed me to reassure them that there would be more letters, and that sooner or later the writer would slip up and we would catch them.

I took one of the letters with me and, aside from the usual fingerprinting, had it analysed on the ESDA, but nothing turned up. It was a single page of writing with nothing else hidden underneath. This happened numerous times, the letters revealing nothing, and the parents had started the process of putting the house on the market. I asked them to resist the temptation of opening and touching any additional letters that arrived; they should let me know and I would collect them immediately. I gathered the unopened envelopes, sparing the parents from reading those horrible letters and ensuring they were untouched by anyone other than the letter writer. This went on for months, with the ESDA never able to garner any useful information. It was frustrating, but I asked the parents to be patient.

Finally, we got a result from one of the letters scrutinised by an expert in document examination at the GTB. At last! This time, the writer had used a notepad. When the powder settled into the pen indentations, you could see the hidden words from a previous letter. Our perseverance had paid off. I could only make out seven words: 'Catering Manager, Roches Stores', 'fly' and 'apple tart'. It wasn't much to go on, but it was a start.

I went over to Roches Stores, then a large department store on Henry Street, and asked to speak to the catering manager. He came out and I asked him if he had received a letter of complaint regarding a fly in an apple tart. His response was one of bemusement. No, he hadn't received any such letter and he clearly regarded this earnest young garda as being for the birds, talking about flies and apple tarts and making no sense at all. I had my lunch and then went back to the station. I wasn't there long when I was called to the phone. Apparently the catering manager wanted to speak to me. I picked up the receiver and a shocked voice at the other end said, 'All right, you have to tell me how you did that. How did you do this?' It was the catering manager and he was not laughing at me now. He told me that thirty minutes after I left, a man walked into reception and handed in an envelope addressed to him. When he read it – yes, it was a complaint about a fly in an apple tart. He was utterly gobsmacked by this turn of events.

I was pretty gobsmacked myself, but I went straight back to Roches Stores to collect the letter. Now I had a name and an address. But before advancing the investigation, I had to establish what breach of law, if any, had arisen. I recalled a case my father had investigated, involving anonymous letters suggesting that vegetables for sale in Dublin's fruit and vegetable market had been contaminated. It gave rise to a prosecution for breach of section 12 of the Criminal Law Act 1976 – making a false report intending to show an offence had been committed, giving rise to apprehension for the safety of persons or property.

In my case, the letters had a sexual theme and each was accompanied by a torn-out page from a sex education textbook, but nothing that could be classed as lewd or pornographic. I rang the office of the Director of Public Prosecutions (DPP) for advice, and explained the issue to a solicitor. With what crime exactly could I charge this letter writer? She asked me a question in return: Was I sure the writer was a man? I replied that given the description of self-pleasuring contained in the letters, it was certainly a man. She remarked that women were far more likely to send anonymous letters. 'It has to be a man this time,' I said. We discussed it further and agreed that the Post Office Act wouldn't grant me power of arrest and that there was no solid breach of law that we could identify. I put down the phone and stood there thinking it over. Then I realised that there was one avenue open to me: the only true power I had was to let the letter writer know that we knew about their behaviour and to ask them some questions.

I brought a colleague with me and we went to the house and knocked on the door. It was just a few doors down from the young girl's house. A man opened the door and I said that we wanted to have a conversation with him about some letters we believed he had written and I suggested quietly that he might wish to conduct that conversation down at the station, in private, away from his family home. He nodded, then opened the door wide and said, 'No, that's okay, come on in.'

In the sitting room, his wife joined us and we sat down. I described what we knew, although I didn't reveal everything, and I asked if he wished to talk about it. He denied all involvement. I reminded him that the letter came from this address and bore his name, so how could it not be him? He looked at me and said, 'Well, someone else here must have done it.' I looked at him in surprise and said, 'You're hardly nominating your wife as a suspect?' He looked at me steadily and simply said, 'Ask her.' I turned to his wife, who had been perfectly silent up to now, and she said, 'It was me.'

Obviously, my first question was: Why? She explained, very matter-of-factly, that the kids on the road had been kicking the ball against her front wall and it made her angry, and the letters were her retaliation. I remembered then that some of the letters mentioned ball-playing, but of course we hadn't known that was a clue to motive, that they told more than they seemed to tell. It was a bizarre way of thinking, and I was quite blindsided by her admission and explanation. Those letters had been deeply upsetting for her neighbours, directed against a young girl, and entirely unsavoury. But at the same time, I was very glad that we had our culprit – and that I could now go and tell the parents categorically that there was no threat to their daughter's physical wellbeing. When I did so, their relief was absolutely immense. They indicated that they did not wish for us to pursue the matter further. So that was where the case ended, for them and for me.

That was a very interesting experience because it showed me the huge importance and impact of our 'silent work' – the sort of work that doesn't show up in the crime statistics, that isn't measured or spoken of or rewarded. And yet it was crucial that this unusual case was handled thoroughly and delicately. Those parents were tormented by this campaign of abuse, believing their daughter was in danger of sexual assault or worse. I was so pleased that persistent police work had paid off and delivered a satisfactory outcome. The family were living a nightmare and had almost sold up and moved away, uprooting their whole life. The serious approach and the positive result was, I understood, the bedrock of good policing.

The murder case was a very different challenge but certainly another steep learning curve. On 14 October 1987 we received a report of a woman's body being found in a bedsit in Gardiner Place – one of those three-storey Georgian-style buildings converted into flats. The woman was identified as Margaret Meek, and the flat belonged to her husband, from whom she was separated. Margaret lived in Belfast, but she regularly travelled down by train to visit Ernest Meek. He had had to leave their family home in Belfast when the marriage broke down and he had relocated to Dublin, but Margaret still kept in touch and visited him. It appeared to be an open-and-shut case: the body was found in his flat and the crime scene told the story of a murder having taken place, but there was one crucial element missing – a weapon.

A specialist team from Garda HQ examined the scene, bagged up any evidence they could find and went on their way. When they left, I decided to go in and have a look myself. The bedsit was sparsely furnished and there wasn't much in the way of personal belongings beyond some clothes. It was musty and cold and didn't feel much like a home. I went into the bedroom area – it was a single bed and an old wardrobe empty save for a few metal and plastic hangers on the rail. I was just closing the door again when I spotted something on the floor of the wardrobe. It was a little piece of leather with a clip on it, about two inches in size, but I had no idea what it was. The trainer's voice from the SOC course floated through my mind – *No matter how insignificant something appears to be, if it's at the scene of a serious crime, examine it and take it.* It was a sentence that had really struck me at the time and had stayed with me. I picked up the little item and bagged it in an SOC envelope. In the kitchen I found a lightweight plastic bag hanging from a broom handle. It was filled with food waste. I tipped it all out on the counter and poked through it. Mixed in among the bits of rotting food I found a few pieces of a letter. I patched them together as best I could and bagged them up as well.

The open-and-shut nature of the case was even more assured when we got a call from the Royal Ulster Constabulary (RUC) in Belfast. It turned out that Ernest Meek had gone from the bedsit to Connolly train station, where he had boarded a train to Belfast. Once there he handed himself in to the RUC. I went with Tim Doyle, my detective sergeant, to collect him from the border, where the RUC officers handed him into our jurisdiction. Meek made a full statement, describing how he had stabbed Margaret to death in the bedsit, then left. He had thrown the knife out of the train window 'near a bridge with arches'. There were a couple of bridges that met that criteria, but our best guess was that he meant the Nine Arches bridge near Skerries.

A search team walked the line out at the bridge and the murder weapon was found. It was a knife stored in a sheath. That's when my unidentified bit of leather suddenly made sense – on examination it turned out to be a clip from the knife sheath. It was the only piece of evidence in a subsequent criminal trial that connected Meek directly to the crime scene. My old SOC trainer would have been very proud – and he was proved perfectly correct: if it's at a scene of serious crime, don't overlook or dismiss it. A key lesson for any detective to learn early on.

There was one other unforgettable moment arising from the Meek case. I was part of the search team that located the knife, and we let the state pathologist, John Harbison, know that we had found it. A pathologist who has come to certain conclusions during a post-mortem is always eager to hear that those conclusions have been proven correct. If they get the chance to see the weapon, it can help them to make sense of the evidence, in some cases, and can back up their opinion. So I wasn't surprised when Harbison asked me if he could examine the knife. His offices were part of the Trinity College Dublin complex, opposite Pearse Street Garda Station, and I decided to walk over there myself. He had asked me to bring the knife to a particular lecture hall, so I tracked that down and opened the door. Below me, the seats, filled with students, stretched down to the 'stage' at the front, where Harbison was standing. He saw me up in the gods, as it were, and called out my name, then cried out dramatically, '... and he has the murder weapon with him!' I got a big round of applause as I walked down the steps to the front. I was thinking to myself, well this is one lecture they'll all remember; no one will snooze through this one. Harbison, who was quite the character and loved a bit of drama, examined the knife there and then, making it part of his lesson. I wasn't going to forget that lecture either.

There are always little details from a murder case that stay with you. It's such a shocking, seismic event in the lives of the perpetrator and the victim and their family, but you usually find there are some minutiae that stay with you. In the case of Margaret Meek, I was struck by the fact that the couple had been chatting over a pot of tea and some biscuits – the most normal thing in the world – and it was after that he suddenly stabbed her to death. It appeared to have been a spur of the moment killing. I have also never forgotten what he said to the detective sergeant who interviewed him – 'I murdered her because I loved her.'

These cases were fascinating and I enjoyed being part of a team that was working to solve a crime, but I was starting to get itchy feet. In truth, I found the beat in Fitzgibbon too quiet. Yes, those interesting cases cropped up, but generally it was routine enough and I was no longer getting all I wanted from it. I remember a colleague there once saying, 'Well, what do you want?' And I said to them: 'I just want to be a busy policeman.' I went up for promotion again, definitely ready to move on now. Not having been successful at my first attempt, I was surprised when, in 1991, I was placed first on a list of about two hundred successful applicants for promotion to the rank of sergeant. On promotion, detectives at lower ranks must revert to uniform duties, and I would do this in a small station in County Kildare. I had to follow the career path, but I had a feeling Kildare might not be quite as busy as Fitzgibbon Street and Dublin's north inner city.

CHAPTER 3

MURDERS AND MARCHING ORDERS

Rathangan is a small town in north Kildare, and it was even smaller when I arrived in 1991, when its population was around 1,080. It's a pleasant spot, with the Slate River and the Grand Canal flowing through the town, the rolling landscape of the Curragh nearby and the grand sweep of the Bog of Allen. Driving down there for my first day on the job, it was forty miles by road, but it felt like I was stepping back in time after the tightly packed warren of streets of inner-city Dublin. This was a whole different vista and I wondered what sort of crime might be committed around here – it didn't seem possible to have thoughts of wrongdoing in a place like this.

That sense of a time warp was reinforced when I arrived at the station on Leinster Road. It was a three-storey building with timber sash windows that was built in the eighteenth century and had served as the RIC barracks for the area. It was then a two-man station. I would be the sergeant in charge, working alongside one member of garda rank. It would probably be a short posting while I waited for an opportunity to return to Dublin and I was going to take over from a sergeant who had been working there for decades. I knew that I would be a novelty at first, the unknown newcomer.

I pulled up outside the station and parked on the main road. I was back in uniform, of course, and also had the Garda Síochána's brand new style of anorak with GARDA across the back in large silver letters. As I pulled on my anorak and went around to the boot, I noticed some young lads sitting on the steps of a nearby building, watching me with curiosity. I knew I looked a real newbie in my uniform and crisp new coat and I could feel them staring and sizing me up. From the boot I took my large SOC kit box, all ready for whatever might come my way. I shut the boot and began walking towards the station when I heard one of the lads say, 'Ah Jaysus, he's a vet as well.' I suppressed a smile and thought that he'd be sorely disappointed if he thought I'd be delivering calves.

The town had a historical link with the Garda Síochána. Colonel Eamon 'Ned' Broy was a Rathangan native. Born in 1887, he had a colourful career in law enforcement, culminating in his decision to take the side of Michael Collins during the War of Independence. As a member of the Dublin

Metropolitan Police he famously snuck Collins into the file room in Great Brunswick Street Station (now Pearse Street). There, Collins pored over G-Division's records of Republican activity. Broy went on to become a Garda Commissioner from 1933 until 1938.

My time in Rathangan passed quickly and I enjoyed the place and the people and managed the different pace of life. The tiny two-man station was a hub for everything going on around the town. One of my weekly duties was to stamp the dole slip of every single person who claimed social welfare in the town. That was a garda function back then, along with other matters far removed from fighting crime, such as gathering agricultural statistics. To my relief, my SOC training proved absolutely invaluable and it meant that I was called to numerous crime scenes in the county. I was kept busy with burglaries, stolen vehicles, traffic accidents and the like, reducing the amount of time I spent in the station waiting for something to happen.

It was interesting that one of the issues that arose there was anonymous letters. Yet again, I was faced with complaints about an unknown letter writer, although in this case the person was focused on salacious gossip, sending allegations about cheating partners and the like. It turned out to be a woman, again confirming that this is something more likely to be done by women than by men, but what she was doing was not a criminal matter, so it went no further. It did make me think about that case when I was in Fitzgibbon Street, but also about another woman I had met; she suffered from bipolar disorder and letter-writing was one of the symptoms for her. She didn't write them anonymously, but she did fire off missives to politicians, the president, RTÉ presenters and others with a public profile. It struck me as a noteworthy overlap between mental health problems and the need to intrude into other people's lives in this way. I don't know the psychology behind such actions, but on a human level it's a nugget of insight into how people – and perhaps people who feel they have very little control – try to mould the world into a shape they can live with in some way.

While I was working on the murder of Margaret Meek back in Fitzgibbon Street, I had at the same time been studying for a BA in public administration. In the thesis I had to write for that qualification, I set out and explored ideas on how better to evaluate police work. In this I was led by the writings of Sir Robert Mark, Commissioner of the Metropolitan Police in London. In his autobiography, *In the Office of Constable*, he described the police as the most taken-for-granted public service. In my own writing on the subject, I concluded that the measurement of success for the Garda Síochána should be the level and quality of our service. Even at that relatively young age and early point in my career, I was thinking deeply about policy and how to effectively tackle crime and how to effectively evaluate the outcomes of that work. This was where my natural leaning was leading me, and I was hoping to be able to put some of these ideas into practice in my own career. I would get that chance very soon.

After a year in Rathangan, I was moved back into Dublin, this time to the busiest station of them all, Store Street. I had wanted busyness, and I was certainly going to get it here. I was still attached to the uniform section and soon after I was assigned to a community policing unit. This was C District, which included the north inner-city areas of Temple Street, Gardiner Street, Sheriff Street, Dominic Street and environs. From my first day there, it was plain that we had our work cut out for us because those communities had been ravaged by drug selling and addiction. Adding to the problem was the fact that historically there were poor relations between the guards and the inner-city community. I think those issues dated right back to the Lockout of 1913, and over the years the ill feeling had cemented into a belief that the gardaí didn't understand the problems and didn't care enough to find out. As a community policing officer, you first had to work to overcome that instinctive reaction.

Fresh out of Rathangan's pastoral market town location, turning up for work at Store Street was a markedly different experience. This was Dublin in the early 1990s, where heroin had taken hold over the previous decade. This was long before the Celtic Tiger years, a time when the buses were orange, the pubs were filled with smoke and there was dereliction and poverty all around the city. The original Store Street station, beside the Coroner's Court, was a very old building that always reminded me of *Hill Street Blues*. There had been no renovation work done and it was falling down in places. It was due to be demolished and replaced by a new building. Space was at a premium – we had a tiny space to work and the highest rate of crime in the whole country. There were so many prisoners coming through there every day, and huge numbers of gardaí and detectives, and if you did manage to get a bit of desk space you had to guard it with your life because if you turned your back on it, someone else would have shunted your stuff aside and taken your chair. It was managed chaos every single day. I absolutely loved working there.

The station gave out onto the junction of Busáras and Amiens Street, looking across to where the IFSC (the International Financial Services Centre) now stands. Back then, that area was just warehouses that backed onto Sheriff Street. To this day, it annoys me when I hear people insist they remember no-go areas in the north inner city at that time. That is simply not true. There were areas, and Sheriff Street was one of them, that were difficult to police, but we were in those areas in numbers and on a regular basis. We never stopped policing those areas, ever.

There was a huge rate of crime around those streets, mainly handbag snatching and theft from cars. These were the crimes of drug addicts, who needed to get ready cash to buy their next bit of gear. Dublin wasn't used to this sort of crime – it rolled in on the wave of drugs that crashed through the north inner city from the 1980s. In his 40 years in the force, my father never once made a drug arrest, and between 1981 and 1991, I had never made one either. Now here I was, in the midst of an epidemic that was tormenting and scourging these communities. The pace of it was staggering – in 1998, there would be around 5,600 drug-related arrests. It was a complete sea change that engulfed those communities suddenly and deeply. It was very distressing to witness.

Handbag snatching was a regular occurrence and thefts from cars were the bane of our lives. That went on all hours of the day and night. A big draw was the car stereo, which was the usual target – you broke the side window of the car, reached in and grabbed the stereo and anything else that looked like it might be worth a few bob, and you sold it off immediately for a few pounds, which you took straight to a dealer. It happened to parked cars and cars stopped at traffic lights. While I was working in Fitzgibbon Street, I remember hearing of heart-rending cases of burial shrouds being stolen from the cars of parents whose children were dying in Temple Street Hospital. That was the clearest indicator of how low a drug habit could drag a person. Alongside all that, the joyriding was constant too, with cars speeding around the city, tyres screeching, doing handbrake turns. It was dangerous for the young drivers as much as for the other drivers and pedestrians.

Working in those areas, trying to bed myself into the local community and support its people, was a joy, though. It was tough and challenging, but it was also highly rewarding. I understood that community policing had to be built on respect, so I gave it freely and worked hard to earn it. My approach was in that word 'support' – I saw my role as being to support the communities in their endeavours, to provide a listening ear to the problems and to the information about people causing those problems, and to create a relationship between our community unit and the people who lived there and wanted to see their area grow and thrive. It was a mutual collaboration towards a shared end – and there was so much work to be done.

While I was officially assigned to a community policing unit, there was a tendency for those recently promoted who had previously been assigned to detective units to be placed on temporary assignments assisting with major investigations. I was no exception. At Store Street I was also brought in on other cases, and serious crime, because of my background as a detective. One of those cases was an internal investigation regarding the Garda Representative Association (GRA).

The GRA had a difficult history. The association had weathered a string of coups and splits; for example, in the 1980s detectives tried to form their own, separate association, but it was disallowed by a court ruling. That only served to create even more dissatisfaction and later another split would result in the formation of the Garda Federation. In the latest iteration, members of the Central Executive Committee (CEC) of the GRA had presented themselves at Mountjoy Garda Station and made criminal allegations relating to misappropriation of association funds about their General Secretary and other members of the CEC. In 1987, the GRA elected John Ferry as their General Secretary and the CEC members making the criminal allegations had not supported him in that election. An investigation team was set up to examine these allegations and I was part of that team. I took statements under caution from the General Secretary and other senior members of the association. The team made a forensic examination of the association's financial and other records and we gathered all the available evidence. We would not get involved in the politics of the association but would conclude that there was no evidence to support the allegations of criminal wrongdoing made against John Ferry and his supporters on the CEC. An investigation file was submitted to the DPP but no prosecution was directed.

I was also drafted in on an unusual murder case. On 16 January 1994, Edward Doody was fatally wounded in the course of a domestic incident. His wife had grabbed a knife and stabbed him once in the chest. By fluke, really, the knife cut into an artery and he died where he fell. His wife did not deny that sequence of events. This seemed, on the face of it, a very straightforward conviction.

However, the proper investigation of a crime does not involve only an attempt to ensure conviction. The Supreme Court has established principles in relation to the gathering of evidence and has ruled that investigators are under a duty to seek out and preserve all evidence bearing on the guilt or innocence of an accused person. In this case, when I looked deeper into the Doodys' home life, it became clear that Edward Doody had been regularly violent towards his wife. It was relevant, too, that only one blow was delivered. There was no frenzy, no bloodlust – it spoke of something else.

My superintendent asked me to prepare a report on the case for the DPP and I set about doing as thorough a job as I could. I interviewed people who knew the family and could attest to the stress Mrs Doody was under. I spoke to the people who ran hostels where she had sought refuge and listened as they described what she was running away from. This was years before the words 'coercive control' would enter the lexicon, but I could see that this woman had been abused throughout her marriage. On the day of the murder, her husband had advanced towards her and she genuinely believed he was going to hurt her badly, perhaps even kill her, and in self-defence she'd grabbed the nearest weapon and lashed out at him.

As part of the investigation, I attended the post-mortem of Edward Doody, which was conducted by Chief State Pathologist John Harbison. As he was dissecting the brain,

Harbison suddenly became highly animated, exclaimed loudly and then grabbed a camera to take photographs. He had found something extremely rare in the dead man's brain – an intact aneurysm. He excitedly showed me what he had found and I could see that the aneurysm is a like a flaw or weak spot on a blown-up balloon and it keeps stretching until the point where the flaw explodes – and you have a brain bleed that likely kills you. It was rare to find an aneurysm in this condition. Harbison described how many different factors, such as stress or alcohol, could at any time have caused the aneurysm to erupt.

I leaned over and looked into this man's brain, at the aneurysm that was silently lying in wait to kill him one day. It suddenly made sense to me how these things happen – the fragility of us, the good or bad luck, the stress growing denser and denser, how people could be walking around with an unknown condition such as this and anger, stress or alcohol could make them blow. It was a reminder – and policing is full of them – of how our lives are so often shaped by the luck of the draw, by forces close to home but beyond our knowledge.

I wrote up the report, putting forward a very detailed picture of what had happened on the day and what had preceded it. In November, I was informed that the DPP had decided a prosecution was not warranted. The role of the victim in his own demise was understood, and his wife did not have to face criminal charges. To my knowledge, that was the first time a woman had not been prosecuted in such circumstances.

The other notable case I was seconded to was my first gangland murder. As the drug landscape shifted and changed, from heroin to cannabis and then cocaine, more and more people were attracted to what looked like easy money. This was where Ireland's gangland culture flourished, on the back streets of the inner city, where the canny sellers took in the money and didn't sample the product. I had no idea then how much that culture would become part of my work and career, but I was there at the start, when the crimes related to drugs continued to expand and become more and more challenging to police.

The Bridewell Garda Station hadn't had a murder case for many years, but around 1993 they had a number in quick succession. Detectives were drafted in from other stations to help with the workload, and I was one of them, brought across from Store Street. The first of those murders occurred on 3 April 1993 and the victim was a man called Michael Godfrey. He had been taken from his bedsit on North Circular Road, murdered somewhere, and his body was found on waste ground in Scribblestown, near Blanchardstown. The investigation had been ongoing for a number of weeks and we had identified one of the main suspects, PJ Judge, known as 'Psycho'. He was a dangerous man, often described as a psychopath, and it was believed he was involved.

We rounded up and arrested all the suspects, PJ Judge among them, as well as another man who was considered dangerous, Mark Dunne. We got a search warrant and searched Dunne's house, but nothing was found. Later that same day, I obtained another warrant to search his house again. This was unusual, but I had information from a source who alleged there was now a concealed weapon in the house. Back we went again, and this time we found ammunition in the house.

At the station, we prepared to interview the suspects. For the interview with Dunne, we took all of the unnecessary furniture out of the interview room so it couldn't be flung at us. We put the suspects in different rooms and a pair of officers questioned each one simultaneously. We had the day to question them, then they would have to be released. The interview with PJ Judge yielded nothing because he didn't utter one word for the duration of it. He was silent from first question to last, staring at us blankly. At the end of the day, he was released without charge, while the investigation continued.

It was different for Mark Dunne in the next interview room. He also chose to stay silent, but the ammunition found at his house ensured that he would be charged and brought next door to the Bridewell District Court, where he would be remanded to custody in Mountjoy Prison. That was done, and then of course someone had to bring Dunne over to the prison. It had been a long day and everyone was eager to finish their shift and clock out, so myself and Detective Garda John Carroll volunteered to deliver Dunne to his home for the foreseeable. We led him, handcuffed, from the station and as we went through the door and onto the path outside, there was PJ Judge, who had just regained his freedom. He was walking off down the road and I could see Dunne watching him, eyes narrowed.

We put Dunne in the back of a patrol car and drove from the Bridewell towards North Circular Road. Dunne had been silent for so long at this stage that we were both surprised to hear his voice – he suddenly piped up that he wanted to talk to us, he had things he needed to tell us. This was a big change from 'No comment', but we were obliged to bring him forthwith to Mountjoy Prison. We signed him in and then explained to the prison guards that the prisoner suddenly felt like talking. Inside the gates of Mountjoy are two waiting rooms and they let us use one as a makeshift confessional. Detective Carroll and I listened while he spoke about the murder of Michael Godfrey. It appeared to us that the coincidental sighting of PJ Judge had rattled Dunne and he believed Judge must have talked to us, to Dunne's detriment.

We finished up and handed Dunne back over to the prison guards, who led him away to his cell. As he went, we could hear him roaring to the ceiling high above, 'PJ Judge is a rat!' I remember thinking that was very unwise in Mountjoy – and of course we knew it wasn't true.

The focus of the investigation then moved to trying to find the murder weapon that had been used to kill Godfrey. We had information that there were firearms hidden in a particular area in Tallaght, and we searched it with a fine-tooth comb. We spent hours searching, but turned up nothing. We were packing up to go home when I decided that, given we had the team gathered, we might as well search the other place that we'd heard mentioned, a bit of waste ground out near Abbotstown. There were reports that some people had been seen there, maybe acting suspiciously. The information was vague, but I felt we might as well rule it out at any rate. I called in the Dog Unit to meet us there and off we went again.

At the site, I walked up an incline to get an overview of the place. While I was standing there, surveying the search area, my phone rang and it was the Dog Unit saying they were up on the main road and ready to join us. I walked back down to go and meet them and as I strode back towards the road, a piece of cloth on a tree branch caught my eye. I hesitated, looked at it, then hurried on to meet the dog handlers. Unknown to me, another sergeant, Andy O'Rourke, had seen me hesitate and it raised his curiosity. As I walked away, he walked over to the tree to take a closer look at whatever had caught my eye. He saw the cloth and felt it was worth exploring. He started digging at the ground beneath the branch and then, to the surprise and delight of everyone present, a shout went up – he had uncovered a buried firearm. It was a sweet moment for the search team after all the hours of finding nothing. We were pretty sure it was the weapon we were looking for, so we bagged it up and brought it back to the Bridewell.

After all that, we went out for a pint because it was my birthday. There was a further gift in the fact that forensics delivered the information that not only was it the Godfrey murder weapon, it had also been used in a shooting in St Joseph's Mansions in which a relation of the notorious drug dealer Derek Dunne had been wounded. I knew the Dunne family from my time at Fitzgibbon Street, but they were going to become a central part of my work in the near future.

Some time later, a member of the Garda Mapping Team attempted to visit the scene of the weapon find to prepare maps for court purposes, only to find that the site had been bulldozed in preparation for the building of the M50 motorway. We were lucky to have found the gun when we did, otherwise it would have disappeared for ever.

In December 2000, Mark Dunne went on trial at the Circuit Court for involvement in the murder of Michael Godfrey. It was a striking case because there were 99 witnesses to be called and attested. As a result, the court was jam-packed with people. As I looked on I marvelled at how unwieldy the system was in practice. Many of the 99 called to the stand were gardaí, each giving their little piece of the jigsaw puzzle of Godfrey's final hours and the aftermath of his death. It was inefficient, to say the least. I would think about this trial again when I got to see how courts in Europe work, where evidence is collated and witnesses are kept to a minimum. The other problem it gave rise to was that the ensuing bedlam was difficult to manage and the trial was adjourned on one occasion because the jury members accidentally saw Mark Dunne arriving in handcuffs, which was prejudicial to his case. He sacked his legal team in advance of the trial. In the end, he was acquitted; he was innocent of all charges the state had preferred against him. Meanwhile, in October 1997, in another gangland incident, PJ Judge was shot dead in the car park of the Royal Oak in Finglas.

Less than one year after his acquittal, Mark Dunne, accompanied by his nephew Glen Dunne, entered as burglars into the home of a woman, who Dunne raped at knife point. They claimed to have been hired by the women's estranged husband to carry out the attack. Dunne was convicted by a jury, following a twelve-day trial during which he again sacked his legal team and conducted his own defence. Mr Justice Daniel Herbert said Dunne had imposed 'the worst burden I have ever seen on any victim'. Dunne was given concurrent sentences of 14 years for rape and six years for each count of burglary and false imprisonment. His nephew Glen was stabbed to death in November 2001 by a former boyfriend of his partner.

By now, I had quite an amount of experience under my belt on a number of different fronts and I was again eager to move on and do something new. I submitted an application for the position of sergeant on a local Crime Task Force. I waited. One morning I came into work in Store Street and there were two envelopes there for me. I opened the first and the letter said that I was being transferred to a surveillance unit in the Garda National Bureau of Criminal Investigation (GNBCI). That was unexpected. The second letter told me I was being assigned to head up the Drug Unit in Store Street. It was a district unit that was now being expanded to become a divisional unit to cover the whole north inner city. I stood there with the two assignment letters in my hands, perplexed. I hadn't sought either position, and I had no particular interest in drugs policing or surveillance work. What should I do?

I sought the view of the inspector in charge of administration. I showed him the two letters and asked him what I should do. He didn't hesitate: 'It's very simple. Look at who sent them. Which is the higher authority?' An assistant commissioner had assigned me to the NBCI job, so that took precedence. To the inspector, it was clear, but I was hesitant. I had up to then avoided too closely following my father's footsteps by joining the GNBCI, which was previously known as CDU. I wanted to forge my own route, plus I wanted to stay local because I loved working in the north inner city. It was out of my hands, though. Part of being a garda is accepting where the organisation sends you, and that's what I had to do now.

I went straight over to NBCI to accept the position and register with them. I was shown where I would access the firearm I would be issued with in my new role and the fleet of vehicles that would be at my disposal. When that was done, I went over to Fitzgibbon Street station for a meeting, where I happened to bump into my old boss from that station, Detective Superintendent Jim Murphy. He told me I could expect notification of a move to the GNBCI, but I would not be going. I shrugged and told him it was already done. He looked at me and said, 'We'll see about that.' He left me standing there while he went straight into the office of Chief Superintendent Peter Fitzgerald. After a few minutes the door swung open again and Jim said to me, 'Right. You were never over there. Forget about it.' It turned out that it had been a coincidence that I was simultaneously identified to replace two sergeants who had been promoted to inspector, but now there was final agreement: I would stay in Store Street.

This was turning out to be one of the oddest days of my career. But yet again, I did as I was told and reported over to Store Street for duty as a sergeant in the divisional Drug Unit. I sat in my poky office thinking, *This is crazy, I don't want either of these jobs, what am I doing?* Little did I know in that moment that I had just embarked on the happiest and best days of my career.

PART 2

WINNING BACK THE COMMUNITY (1994–1998)

CHAPTER 4

A RAVAGED CITY

The North Central Division Drug Unit (NCDDU) office was a cramped space on the first floor of Store Street Garda Station. I started there on Monday 28 February 1994, sharing responsibility for the unit with Sergeant Willie Johnson. I had worked in all three districts in the north central division, so it was a familiar beat, but drugs policing was not familiar to me. I was going to have to learn how that worked as I went along.

Around me, the old Store Street building looked the same, and the streets also looked the same, but life for those living on those streets had got steadily worse. The unprecedented scourge of the 1980s had become the relentless 'normality' of the 1990s as heroin was traded openly at corners and injected in alleyways. The people of the north inner city were already hounded by poverty, unemployment, lack of opportunities and resources, and now they were being hounded by the 'quick fix' offered by drugs. Their sons and daughters were being sold an escape, but it was anything but a way out. They were dying every week, the churches filled with funerals of youngsters who never made it out of their twenties, some who never made it to their twenties, and before they died they lived out miserable, cold, brutal lives of addiction and illness.

I could see it everywhere I walked around the north inner city – from Gardiner Street to Sheriff Street, from Temple Street to Buckingham Street. I walked every inch of those streets, talking to anyone who would talk to me. Like many people, I knew the academic side of the drug problem, the facts and figures read from a safe distance. Later, the Rabbitte Report would set out the drugs problem in black and white over 80 pages, the gathered information of a ministerial task force set up to tackle the demand for drugs that was creating such a lucrative market for suppliers. The report included maps showing the main areas affected and the problem was starkly described in its colour-coded neatness: yellow for the lowest levels of drug addiction, increasing in scale through orange, green and blue. There was a huge blanket of yellow across south Dublin, with clots of orange and green in Clondalkin and Tallaght; there was a good stretch of yellow across north Dublin too, but jarring with that were the patches of green, orange and blue in the north inner city, Ballymun, Crumlin, Cabra and Finglas, denoting increasing numbers of addicts. The colour purple indicated the highest level of addiction and there was just one square of purple on the whole map – Mountjoy.

It gave a simple and very effective account of the drugs landscape in Dublin. It was a Dublin of contrasts, with a hidden side known only to those who had to live there, just a river away but a world apart. The report told one story, but working the Drug Unit put us into the reality of what those blocks of colour actually meant. And it was clear to me that the drug problem was just one part of the deeper problem. It was the areas affected by unemployment, in particular, that were on the front line. It was the communities in those areas that had been sidelined and ignored for years, their opportunities withering away, replaced by a stunted view that couldn't see past the end of the road. This was a bigger problem than drug-taking; it was about social disadvantage that touched every part of these people's lives from the moment they were born. They lived in communities that were terrorised by drug-related crime and heartbroken from drug-related illness, prostitution and grief. Life felt like a dead end for those people, and I could understand how that translated into drug use.

The whole situation was made even worse by the fact that the Garda Síochána and the communities did not see eye to eye on either the problem or the solutions. There was a deep seam of distrust towards the Gardaí and a strong sense that we were not doing our job, that we were failing them, that we didn't care about what happened on those streets. That disconnect made policing extremely difficult. To my mind, as I watched and listened and learned, it made sense that we had to work with the local people – after all, we had a common cause. They wanted the dealers out of their communities, they wanted to protect their youngsters, and we wanted to achieve the same things. And I could see that we weren't going to achieve anything without the community's help and their insider knowledge. They were the ones who knew exactly what was happening, and I felt it was our job to listen to them.

When I started on the Drug Unit, my Chief Superintendent Peter Fitzgerald gave me a written instruction to talk to ICON. That was an unusual instruction to receive, particularly as I had no idea what ICON stood for or what it was. It turned out to be the Inner City Organisations Network, a collection of community projects set up to campaign for the rights and needs of the inner-city communities. I attended my first ICON meeting, at Croke Park, with Chief Superintendent Peter Fitzgerald and Detective Superintendent Jim Murphy. It was led by ICON's chairperson, Fergus McCabe, who was obviously a gifted community leader and was forging positive relationships. I was impressed by the volunteers' commitment and vision, and struck by their description of the crisis gripping the inner city – 'a human and economic crisis', as Fergus said. I remember thinking: we can do business with these people.

The feeling was not entirely mutual at that time. The Gardaí came in for serious criticism, especially from Tony Gregory, TD for Dublin Central and a formidable defendant of his constituents. My first meeting with him did not go very well. We were at loggerheads; voices were raised and tempers heated. He was hugely frustrated by the lack of help and resources directed towards solving the problems of the inner city and, to him, the Gardaí were a very significant part of the problem. He had seen gardaí of various ranks come and go, but felt nothing solid had been achieved, and he wasn't shy about putting forward his opinion. I was just another face he had to deal with, until I moved along to another role in my organisation, another person who didn't live there and didn't really know what it was like, another well-intentioned garda with a shoestring of resources looking to scale a mountainous problem. Tony Gregory and other community representatives had seen all this before and they had contempt for the Gardaí, there was no denying that.

One of the worst affected places in the north inner city was St Joseph's Mansions, a flat complex that was notorious for drug selling and taking. It epitomised the nature of the problem facing these communities, and the shocking extent of it. When you went into the complex, it was a devastating sight. The bleak, grey utilitarian blocks were centred on an internal area that was no doubt planned as a communal green space but was now a wasteland of concrete, rubbish and debris. Stolen cars were spinning about, brakes screeching, and crashed and burnt-out cars littered the place. Normal human family life was slowly ebbing away as the tide of drugs washed in, bringing 24/7 crime, open dealing and injecting, discarded syringes where children should be playing, and a sense of complete despair. About half of the flats were boarded up, planks nailed over their smashed windows. It was a haven for crime and the families left living there were desperate to get out, petitioning the Corporation for social housing elsewhere.

Our priority was not to let the Mansions become a no-go area, to support the community who wanted the drug pushers put out, to let the dealers know they didn't have sole jurisdiction there. One of our tactics was to carry out raids to try to flush out sellers and drug stashes. I remember one particular raid, which was huge in scope, with around a hundred and fifty gardaí drafted in for a 6 a.m. blitz search. We set out from Fitzgibbon Street and charged into the flats, shouting warnings as we were about to enter each residence. When it comes to drug raids, it's all about speed because you need to catch the culprits with the drugs in their hands. You need to get in and get handcuffs on them, or they will swallow, stuff or flush the drugs out of reach.

The sound of garda boots thumping across the concrete reverberated off the walls of St Joseph's, the commotion of feet and shouts ripping through the early morning quiet. We immediately started putting in doors. With the right equipment, this is a quick and easy task – the battering ram knocks the door out of its locking mechanism and it swings back on its hinges, cracking against the wall with a bang. Then you try to get down the hallway and into the rooms as fast as possible, handcuffs at the ready. There was never any great sense of threat during those raids because heroin addicts are not violent – they're passive and can be slow-moving, depending how long has elapsed since their last hit. I was part of those raids and I knew the reasoning behind them, and I knew the communities supported them, but still, I'd find myself looking on at the chaos, at the uninvolved residents roused from their beds in this way, and there would be the niggling thought: perhaps there's another way.

I was on a mass search at one particular flat complex renowned for drug dealing. On that occasion, I heard something that resonated deeply. We carried out the lightning raid and we found three-quarters of the flats had a drug connection – a staggering number. As we rounded up suspects and stashes, I met an older man who'd lived there all his life and was watching the raid and what it was turning up. His face was weary. He said to me, 'No matter how bad it is, you can't abandon everyone else.' That really struck me, and I have never forgotten his words. He was right – you can't tar everyone with the same brush and shrug and walk away and abandon people. There were always people in those flats who wanted nothing to do with drugs and wanted a different way of life, and those people needed our protection and support. By preserving the place for them, we were preserving an alternative for all the others. We could leave a light on so that one day they might find their way home. The man's words crystallised that thought for me – there is another way, and we can find it if we win back the community.

This meant that relationships with the community had to be our top priority, and that in turn meant I had to recommend the right officers for recruiting to the team. The average garda at that time didn't see drugs as part of their brief or beat and weren't equipped to deal with them. There was one group of officers who had taken it on directly and became a sort of legend in doing so. The 'Mockeys', who worked out of Store Street, included future Commissioner Nóirín O'Sullivan among them. They were an undercover unit of eight officers and their name referred to the fact that they were 'mock junkies', posing as addicts so they could move among the buyers and sellers and catch them in the act of selling. It was unorthodox and successful, with a high arrest rate, and many of those officers were later appointed to the National Drug Unit. Their work seemed separate from 'normal' policing and most officers were somewhat fascinated by it, but it didn't form part of their beat. It was being taken care of by a specialist unit, so it didn't concern the rest of the force. When it came to my turn to build a team, I had to find people who instinctively understood that drugs policing was community-based and an essential bedrock of the entire purpose and vision of the Garda Síochána.

I was a 34-year-old sergeant then, but I had an unusual level of discretion and reported directly to Detective Superintendent Jim Murphy. I was afforded a significant input into identifying personnel for recruiting into the Drug Unit. Choosing officers for a drugs unit is very important to get right. You'll get lots of officers wanting to be part of it, but their reasons can vary widely and not all are suitable for it. I was looking for some specific qualities: an understanding of how to police drugs problems; an ability to engage with and talk to every person in the community; a level of empathy with the people they are both helping and arresting. I say 'a level of empathy' because I was always looking for gardaí who understood what community policing was, and what it was not. We were not social workers; that's a different job. What they had to understand was that a community garda has a relationship with the community for the purpose of policing, therefore they have empathy, but not too much of it. They are engaged and engaging, which means that people will talk to them.

There were two gardaí assigned as community officers to St Joseph's Mansions. They did a very good job and were in and out of my office all the time with information. That meant they clearly understood their role – to engage in order to find out, then to deliver information that could be useful. They were Seán McLaughlin and Larry Duggan and eventually I was able to bring them into the Drug Unit to work with us. They knew the job and how to do it – and, indeed, they went on to do excellent work in drug units in other counties, bringing that know-how with them.

The people I recommended for the Drug Unit were gardaí of true quality, likeminded, hard-working, tuned into the job and brilliant at doing it. They joined others including Seamus Boland, who were already in the unit before I joined its ranks. I was eager to keep him on because it was clear to me that he fit the profile exactly and would play an important role in developing the appropriate relationships with the local community that would enable us to tackle the wide range of drug-related issues that were devastating those inner-city communities. He did stay on, and he made a huge contribution to the unit and to the community before being promoted to sergeant and taking charge of the South Central Drug Unit working out of Pearse Street station.

I recommended the recruitment of Angela Willis and Paul Cleary, both of whom later became Assistant Commissioners, who were key and dedicated members of the team. We ended up a unit of fourteen officers – small, but as effective as we could be. It was a coincidence of highly capable people, who all went on to long and successful careers in the force, some far removed from the public eye. I had managed to gather about me one of the most highly motivated and immensely skilled units of officers that I ever had the privilege of working with – and we were ready and able to do our job.

In the spirit of forging positive community relationships, I spoke regularly at community events. I accepted every invitation to speak, be it at a discussion group or meeting or protest. There was a drug-related funeral every week in Seán McDermott Street church, which at times doubled up as a venue in the evenings for drug-related protest meetings, at which I would occasionally speak. For a garda, that was a baptism of fire – to ascend to the pulpit in that large, echoing church and speak out to the people of the community who were so filled with sorrow and rage. When I spoke at community meetings, I had to first allow the people there to vent their anger, I had to experience that, but once that was done, they would realise that I was willing to listen and to explain and to try to work together and then we could talk. And when we talked, I had to speak to them, not at them – first and foremost, I had to be respectful.

I always kept the old man's words at the forefront of my mind: 'You cannot abandon us because of those others.' His words encapsulated a critical necessity in policing these areas – if you wrote people or an area off, then the extremes could prevail, then you'd get no-go areas and hopelessness. If people feel abandoned, democracy fails. We had to instil confidence in these communities that we wouldn't abandon them, and that was why ongoing, honest, respectful communication was an essential part of our approach to drugs policing in the north inner city.

Over time, we shaped and honed that approach. This was a relatively new area of law enforcement, so we were learning and adapting in real time. The government and its agencies were aware that policies and strategies needed to be put in place, but the research and data weren't there to guide them. But there were moves to bridge this gap and they were working. In the north inner city, ICON had created a community-based movement called the Inter-Agency Drugs Project (IADP), which involved participation by locally based representatives of statutory services. I was nominated to chair its Supply Control Subcommittee and it was a welcome means of sharing our viewpoint and the voices of the people in the communities we were policing. Following the murder of Veronica Guerin, within an incredibly short period of three months, a task force of seven ministers of state, chaired by Pat Rabbitte, produced what is referred to as the Rabbitte Report, which, based on the perceived success of the IADP, recommended the creation of eleven local drugs task forces to integrate policy and practices in those areas identified as having a high prevalence of problem drug use.

The correct analysis of any problem leads to fitting and effective solutions, and this was my preoccupation at this time. I was becoming more and more convinced that the annual *Report on Crime*, published by the Commissioner, with its tables of statistics, was not the optimal way to evaluate policing. I was also aware that attempts to focus on drug buyers and addicts would not deliver results for the drugs problem. The use of the drugs was the central outcome – it was visible, terrible and gave rise to antisocial behaviour and crime – but spreading out from that was the whole web of interlinked problems and causes. You didn't get to those strands by focusing solely on the centre of the web.

I wanted to change the focus and the approach of our work, so that it matched what we had learned while working out in the communities and with ICON. The NCDDU was uniquely placed to understand where the pitfalls lay and what needed to change. The culmination of this came on Friday 10 November 1995, when I set out the priorities that the NCDDU had adopted to the subcommittee on drugs of the Dáil Select Committee on Legislation and Security at Leinster House. They were anxious to hear how the gardaí and community were working together to address drug-related problems in Dublin's north inner city. The meeting took place in the Dáil chamber and was attended by eight TDs and the IADP, and was chaired by John O'Donoghue TD, a future Minister for Justice. As a result of a particular view of former Garda Commissioner Paddy Culligan, who believed the Garda Síochána should not be the subject of scrutiny by the Oireachtas in the same way as other parts of the public service, no commissioner or garda representative had appeared in such a setting since the 1980s. I was the first in a number of years to be granted permission to appear. I was glad of the opportunity, seeing it as a good way to engage in impactful communication. In addition, for a person with a keen interest in Irish history, I found it an extraordinary and unforgettable experience to get to sit in and speak in the Dáil chamber.

During the meeting, I argued that we needed to focus on quality of arrest, rather than the traditional quantity of arrests. I believed that any means of evaluating performance should recognise the quality of any given arrest and any particular seizure of controlled drugs. Since 1947, the *Report on Crime* had provided a breakdown of incidence, detection rate and judicial outcome of cases for about 125 specific offence categories. By this reckoning, twenty arrests for cannabis use trumped one arrest of a heroin supplier who was a chief cause of the problem. This was the wrong way round – and the people in the community already knew that and were saying it, loudly. I set out our plan to target heroin because it contributed most to the crime problem, which wasn't the case for cannabis, for example. Our plan was to target heroin, and the heroin suppliers. The users were victims, in need of help and treatment. They weren't the ones we needed to focus our policing resources on.

This new approach would take us away from the long-embedded emphasis on numbers to evaluate our work – the number of arrests, the number of drug seizures. Instead, for us it would be all about making sure we caught the criminals who were considered significant in the drugs trade. The question then was: How do we take down these experienced criminals who are usually clever, resourceful and often never touch drugs themselves? They were business people, with a head for profit margins. And they were raking in the profits. It was estimated that, in 1993, £1 million was being spent *per week* on heroin. It was a huge, growing and rewarding market for those who could tap into it and evade detection. These suppliers knew the system, often used 'mules' to carry the goods and devoted their every waking minute to not getting caught. How could we, a small team of fourteen officers, build up the kind of evidence that would see them put behind bars?

One thing we heard again and again from the local people was their utter disgust when 'one of their own' was dealing drugs to their neighbours and local community. This was a source of huge anger – everyone had so much to deal with as it was, and then these lads were happy to make it all so much worse in order to make money off the backs of other people's misery. Young people's misery. This is why they saw the sellers as 'scumbags'. The other thing they hated was that these newly wealthy young men, who never worked a day in their lives and were usually drawing social welfare payments every week, were swanning about in nice cars, designer clothes, living in decent houses. It was galling to those affected by the brutality of the drug environment they created. The fact that dealing was worth it because it afforded this 'easy', wonderful-looking existence was pouring salt on the wound. It was this flashy lifestyle that was seducing their youngsters into dealing, into using, into committing crimes to fund their habit, into illness and into early coffins. And no one was doing anything about it.

This was where our Drug Unit could make a difference, I realised. It was the natural progression from our line of thinking – to go after the ill-gotten gains of the sellers and deprive them of it. That would take away incentive. There was recently enacted but not yet used legislation that I thought might help us in this. The Criminal Justice Act 1994 enacted money laundering legislation that allowed for the seizing of wealth after prosecution on indictment. However, this legislation was yet to be used by the Garda Síochána. There was no training given for its implementation and there was a generally held view that local gardaí couldn't use it, that it was only for the Fraud Squad. This was in the days before the establishment of the Criminal Assets Bureau (CAB), remember, so this was new territory. I consulted the Fraud

Squad about using the Act. They said they had been told not to upset the banks by enforcing the Act's provisions. That instruction seemed to have led to a certain inertia about using it. But I knew now that I could lawfully use it – as long as I was very careful. This would be our focus: chasing the assets.

Around this time, the local community around Store Street station led a march on a house in Buckingham Street. I talked to some people about this, and they explained that a person known to us as a major dealer was trading there and they wanted to get him out of the area. I reckoned they knew what they were talking about and decided to target that house. We mounted a surveillance operation and, sure enough, it soon became clear that this house was a conduit for a lot of heroin. It was owned by a local man called Michael 'Roly' Cronin, who had no visible means of income, but was enjoying a very good life with a house, a decent car, a mobile phone and exotic holidays. He was one of ten main sellers, identified by the local community, who were targeted by their local drug unit operation. The others included Tony Felloni and Derek Dunne, who, like Cronin, were responsible for a huge percentage of the heroin being brought into Dublin. We set our sights on them, among others, with a view to dismantling their enterprises. That was our end goal: keep going until we had dismantled the whole operation and it couldn't work any more – and to take out as many people in their network as necessary to achieve that.

Cronin had been arrested before, but like all other caught dealers, in court he presented the case that the heroin he was found with was for personal use. I began to compile a dossier on his wealth and assets, so that we could prove there was another motivation clearly at work – personal gain and lifestyle. My team were fantastic, they were out on the streets every day, doing the leg work, while I was typically in the office, surrounded by paperwork as I tracked the money. We got threatening calls from associates of Cronin, but we persisted.

My efforts paid off when I discovered that the unemployed Cronin had £50,000 in a bank account. It was the evidence we needed. But now we required a prosecution on indictment because the assets could only be frozen following such a prosecution. We needed a case against him and a direction from the DPP to prosecute on indictment. There was only one way to get that: we had to catch him in the act. The team stepped up their surveillance work and we finally got a break when he was caught, but with only 8 deals of heroin. It was a relatively small amount, not unreasonable for a user to have, so Cronin was probably not too concerned, but I talked to officials at the office of the DPP and showed that we had other evidence of supply and profit. The DPP decided to run with it. On 22 February 1995 I went to the High Court, where a senior counsel would make an application on behalf of the DPP, under the 1994 legislation, for a Restraint Order to freeze his assets.

That's when it all went wrong. The judge was almost

ready to get started, and I was in the adjoining consultation room, desperately trying to get additional information on the £50,000 that formed the crux of our case. My source was no longer contactable. Peter Charleton, SC, who would represent the DPP, and who is now a Supreme Court judge, entered the room. I briefed him about the evidence I could provide. He asked me to clarify how much money was in the account and then left the room briefly. While he was out of the room, I received a phone call. It was bad news. A significant amount of money may have been withdrawn, leaving an unknown balance. After all my pushing to have a prosecution on indictment and for a first application to freeze assets under the recently enacted money-laundering legislation, was I now going to have to request that the state pull the plug and abandon the application, leaving a very dissatisfied High Court judge, among others?

Peter Charleton, SC opened the door and beckoned to me; the judge was about to sit. My brain was racing, as was my heart. And then it came to me – the legislation speaks of 'realisable assets', not only money; so Cronin's property on Buckingham Street would be sufficient to support the application. I hurried into the court and took my place to give evidence. During that process, I referred to a bank account but was circumspect about the amount it held, simply saying that I believed it had at one time had a balance of £50,000. I placed emphasis on Cronin's property assets. Judge

McCracken listened, and then he awarded a Restraint Order on Cronin's assets. Disaster had been averted.

Some months later, Cronin's case came to trial before a judge and jury in the Criminal Court. We didn't succeed in getting a conviction for supply, but he did plead guilty to possession. He was handed down a three-year sentence – suspended. After all that work, he was free to go about his business again. As he walked out of court, a free man, he grinned at me and my Drug Unit colleagues who were there and said impishly, 'You're never gonna catch me again, lads!' Without a conviction for supply, the Restraint Order was lifted. We were back to square one. In sport they shout 'next ball' to encourage each other to draw a line under the last play and go again. Now we had to wait to play our next ball, to take the lessons from it and go again.

In spite of the frustration around losing Cronin like that, we were making headway in our efforts to stop the flow of drugs into and around the city, and the sellers were being harassed in their work as much as possible. We searched their houses, confiscated their stashes and interrupted their businesses in every way we could. But as hard as we fought back, the sellers kept making headway too. Their market was growing as more and more youngsters fell into the habit. The treatment centre at Pearse Street was seeing rises of 25 per cent per year in people seeking help. We were fighting a trend that seemed to be going only one way – up.

The communities were only too well aware that the problem was continuing to grow, and their frustration and resentment and anger grew alongside it. They felt left behind, that the government had forgotten about them and that no one outside the north inner city truly understood what their lives had become. They were living on a knife-edge all the time, with the muggings and the syringe robberies. There were whole families wiped out by heroin, where elderly parents buried a number of their children.

The community decided to take on a more active role in trying to contain and solve the problem. They felt they had to take this on themselves, that no one was going to help them, so they had to sort it out in their own way. The streets of Dublin's inner city became a scene of marches and vigilantism. Down by the flats on Seán McDermott Street and over at St Joseph's Mansions, the residents began holding vigils day and night, vetting anyone who wanted to enter the complexes. They rostered shifts to cover the entrances and exits every hour of the day and night, all week long. For the night shift, fires were lit and those on duty stood around them for warmth, watching closely and questioning anyone who arrived or left. It made me think of the origins of policing – the Watchmen. The use of nightwatchmen stretched from Roman times to eighteenth-century London, and now here it was again, around the fires outside the flats. We were happy to work with the residents, as long as they didn't break the law. They could watch and gather information and then pass it on to us – registration numbers, names, etc. – and provided they left the actual policing to us, that was a workable setup.

The problem was that as tensions continued to rise over the months of 1996, the idea of direct action took hold in a much more dangerous way. Out in West Tallaght, a group called Tallaght Against Drug Dealers took a militant approach, wearing balaclavas and carrying firearms, engaging in punishment beatings, burning out cars and carrying out evictions. Their view was that the only solution left was to evict, maim or kill drug dealers, and they professed themselves willing to carry out summary justice. The rhetoric became more and more inflammatory, until the vigilantism threatened to spill over into serious criminal behaviour. The danger was not just to the people themselves, both vigilantes and targets, but also to the work we were trying to do. The vigilantism could stretch our resources so thinly that the only ones who would end up benefiting would be the drug dealers, who could take over an empty pitch while we all fought each other on the sidelines. That had to be avoided. For now, the peace was still holding in the inner city, but it felt volatile and we knew it wouldn't take much of a spark to send the place up in flames.

The spark came on 21 August 1996. Garda patrol cars arrived at the Mountain View court flat complex in Summerhill and arrested three suspected dealers. The arrests were clapped and cheered on by residents. That night, a crowd gathered and petrol bombs were thrown at a car, purportedly belonging to a dealer, and there seemed a danger of the residents taking the law into their own hands. The gardaí returned to quell the situation, and a riot situation erupted, with residents later claiming the gardaí were intimidating and heavy-handed with their batons. It was a shocking outbreak of violence. It felt like that pressure cooker of tension and volatility had finally exploded, and who knew what it might unleash.

The Drug Unit wasn't part of the Garda response that night, but when I heard about it, I was very concerned about where it might lead. It was clear that things could have got really out of control, and that remained a possibility if there was retaliation of any kind. I headed into work early the next morning, visited the office, then went out to walk the streets, talk to people and get a better sense of what had happened. As I was walking between Summerhill and Fitzgibbon Street, I bumped into two men I knew to be part of the vigilante scene – Noel 'Duck Egg' Kirwan and George Royle. These two men were well known in the area for their involvement in the 'direct action' approach. They were open to talking about the previous night's events and agreed to help to try to calm things down. To that end, I helped ICON broker an immediate meeting between the Acting Chief Superintendent at Fitzgibbon Street, Michael O'Donovan, and a number of community leaders.

The visitors arrived at Fitzgibbon Street station and were brought to a room that had been set up for the meeting. It was the room where the officers paraded for duty and it had been set up with desks and chairs. When I saw it, I sighed inwardly in exasperation. I could see that it was not appropriate for these community leaders. The staging looked like a classroom, with a top table for the gardaí and then rows of desks and chairs for the local people. It gave an air of hierarchy, with the gardaí at the head of the table. Unfortunately, I was only a sergeant and could do nothing about it. As it happened, once the meeting got underway the community leaders didn't like what was said any more than they liked the setting in which it was being said, and they got up and walked out. The Acting Chief Super was disappointed and asked me to see if I could do anything to help.

There were rumblings of more trouble that night, and I had been told of petrol bombs being prepared, so I was very anxious to get people talking again. I arranged a second meeting, this time in Store Street, and I was delegated to conduct the meeting. When the invited people began to arrive that afternoon, it was clear attendance had grown since the Fitzgibbon Street meeting that morning. Now our number included a number of local politicians including Tony Gregory, Christy Burke and Joe Costello. I made sure the seating was equal and favoured no one, and we had a much more productive encounter.

It turned out that ICON had a public meeting scheduled for that evening that had been set up weeks earlier, but now we agreed that representatives from the Garda Síochána would attend as well. That night, we all gathered at Rutland Street School in Summerhill. ICON community meetings typically attracted a crowd of maybe one hundred interested people, but it was evident that tonight was not going to be typical. Hundreds of people had turned up to voice their opinions, interrogate the gardaí and demand change. There were perhaps four hundred people squashed into the school hall, with hundreds more outside, straining to hear the proceedings. Inside, the hall was packed, sweaty and smoky. The windows were nailed shut – because of the constant threat of break-ins – so the room soon heated up 'like a sauna', as one journalist commented. I arrived with the acting chief super and Michael Duggan, the local detective inspector. We made our way to the front of the room, where the speakers were standing, and there was a marked hostility in the air at the sight of us.

I was used to this type of setting, I knew all these people and I knew I had nothing to fear from them. Yes, they were angry and they would certainly vent that anger at us, and that was fair enough, but they wouldn't do any more than that. The acting chief was taken aback by the size of the crowd and the identities of some of those present. He was anxious and said quietly to me that we might need to make a quick exit. This was my daily world, so I was surprised by this reaction.

I remember moving away to avoid receiving an instruction to leave. I spotted Angie Bates in the crowd, a Store Street uniformed sergeant with a track record in the Drug Unit and respected by the community. We kept our distance to ensure that even if others decided to leave we could remain. Angie was similar to me, well used to the people here and well aware there was nothing to fear.

The Rutland School meeting turned out to be a memorable event in my career. I never saw myself as a public speaker, but I stood up in that heated, packed atmosphere and spoke directly to those people, reminding them that we would continue to work with them, and that we wanted to be accountable in our work for them. It was absolutely crucial that we were there that night. We didn't receive a warm welcome, but it was important that we took those hits and stayed standing because it did calm things down, as we'd hoped. The crowd were gracious enough to applaud my contribution, and I felt a sense of relief that the bridges hadn't been burned down to the ground. Despite his reservations, Michael O'Donovan spoke as well. As acting chief super he was not going to be well received, but his presence and willingness to participate would prove beneficial in the long term.

After the meeting a march about a thousand people strong left Rutland School and walked over to Liberty House, to St Joseph's Mansions, to St Mary's flats, ending at the Four

Corners, where Killarney Street, Seán McDermott Street and Buckingham Street meet. They held a peaceful vigil, then the community leaders asked everyone to go home and not to cause any trouble. The crowd did as they were asked.

A few of us, including the acting chief, went for a pint in Ryan's, beside Fitzgibbon Street station. We stayed a short while and talked about the evening, our hopes that it would mean there would be no rioting, in the near future at least. Michael O'Donovan thanked me for my work that day and then told me that RTÉ had requested a live interview at their outside broadcast (OB) unit the following morning. He asked me to do the interview and I agreed. Back at home that night, however, I began to think that the acting chief hadn't actually intended for me to do the interview, that I must have taken him up wrong. I had never given an interview of that nature before, on the national airwaves, but then I got a call from RTÉ, giving me the time and place, and I had to accept that it was true.

The next morning I again walked from Store Street to Summerhill, to meet with presenter Aileen O'Meara at the OB unit. Richard Crowley was in the RTÉ studio and was interviewing local people, a representative from Dublin Corporation and me. I listened as the locals described the horrors of living with drugs on the streets. Then Brendan Kenny from the Corporation described the situation at St Joseph's Mansions, how their efforts to refurbish the flats had been thwarted, how most of the flats were now boarded up, and he said it was 'a law and order problem'.

When my turn came, I spoke about the importance of cooperation between all the agencies, that the solutions could only come from collaboration. I reiterated my view that we could not let the drug dealers drive a wedge between the community and the gardaí. When asked if the flats were no-go areas, I told the listeners that the Garda Síochána did not consider any area to be a no-go area, while clearly there were areas that proved more challenging than others to police. I described my own walk through Summerhill that morning, and how I had passed a garda who was standing at the Mansions, on duty. 'He's there, we're always there.'

There was much coverage of the riot and the meeting, which had been attended by a number of journalists. There was a very interesting photo published in the newspapers, which showed Gerry 'The Monk' Hutch sitting in the audience, listening attentively. Christopher McKevitt, one of the journalists, asked Hutch what he thought of John O'Driscoll, the head of the local Drug Unit, and he said: 'He's not that popular.' There were also photos of me talking earnestly in front of a bank of microphones. I was very glad that we had a presence there that night, standing shoulder to shoulder with the community. The picture did, I feel, speak a thousand words.

I was very pleased when I received a letter from a retired chief superintendent to say he thought I had given an excellent interview. That did wonders for my confidence, because public speaking was never an easy task. But it soon became clear that there was concern further up the chain. There was a growing unease about the Drug Unit officers seeming to be so embedded in the community. Only weeks before, subversives had murdered Detective Garda Gerry McCabe while he was undertaking a cash escort in County Limerick. There was also clear evidence of an attempt by subversive elements in some locations to take control of anti-drug protest groups. Garda management were uncertain how to handle the vigilante scenario, while there was a cautious acknowledgement that subversive elements might not be a feature of the community approach in Dublin's north inner city. However, I was still convinced that our approach and attitude were correct.

The Cronin investigation was still ongoing and it took time, but we finally had a breakthrough in 1997 when we found a large quantity of heroin during a house search. It was large enough to prove supply beyond doubt. Cronin went back to the Central Criminal Court to go on trial. We gathered all our evidence of motive, to prove that Cronin's motive was in no way to feed a personal habit, but rather to accumulate wealth and fund a lavish lifestyle. We were able to show Circuit Court Judge Cyril Kelly evidence of holidays abroad and property wealth, and the judge was very receptive to this new angle. He assessed the evidence and gave Cronin a 10-year sentence. We had our prosecution on indictment.

Then we brought Cronin back to court regarding his original three-year suspended sentence, and the judge lifted the suspension and raised his sentence to 13 years.

It was a huge moment for the Store Street Drug Unit. It had taken dedicated, painstaking work, but we had shown that the legislation was there to take drug dealers out of action and deprive them of their drug wealth. It was important for a few reasons: the quality of the arrest and of the prisoner; the successful seizing of assets; and the community response to it, in that they felt truly heard and they could see proper results that benefited them. To my astonishment, when Tony Gregory was asked by RTÉ to comment on the conviction of Michael 'Roly' Cronin, he replied: 'Michael Cronin was very significant in that area, there is no doubt about that, significant first because he was supplying heroin, which, of course, causes most misery in disadvantaged areas, but, I think, it was a great result of a partnership which has developed over the last number of years between the Drug Unit at Store Street, led by John O'Driscoll and groups like ICON.' It was a long way from the loggerheads of old.

There would later be a coincidence in the fates of Tony Gregory and Michael Cronin. In January 2009, Tony Gregory died at the young age of 61. On 7 January, I attended his funeral at North William Street Church. Standing outside after the funeral mass, I was chatting with colleagues and ICON members about Tony's life in activism and his criticism of the Garda Síochána, and how he changed his mind in the face of our hard-won efforts to tackle the problems he so abhorred. We mentioned the Cronin sentence as a big part of that change. Later that evening, about 8.40, at Langrishe Place in Summerhill, Cronin was sitting in a car with two men. The man sitting in the back seat had 'turned Turk', unknown to his accomplices. Unseen by the two in the front seats, he raised his gun and shot Cronin and the other man in the back of their heads. Cronin died there in the car; his companion died later in hospital. It was the end of the road for the drug dealer, on the same day that Tony Gregory made his last journey through the streets of the north inner city.

The Cronin operation and outcome was successful policing, and it was how we wanted to police. The NCDDU was being hailed as a success in all quarters, but I knew that it was a success because our results were aligned with the community's stated needs. What was most important was that the success had flowed from consultation and good communication. So now we had a modus operandi, a solid team and ever stronger links with the community, which was all we needed to target the kingpins of the city's drug trade. We were ready to take on more.

CHAPTER 5

EMPTY POCKETS

They were three thousand strong and they carried banners and a coffin. Their chant echoed through the streets: 'Pusher, pusher, pusher, OUT, OUT, OUT!' The huge crowd wound its way from the north inner city, down O'Connell Street, over the River Liffey and on towards St Stephen's Green and the Department of Justice. It was 27 September 1996 and the inner-city communities were trying to raise awareness about the effect of drugs on their lives, demanding that the government prioritise and help them. The age profile of heroin users kept dropping, and now there were children as young as 13 becoming hooked and seeking treatment – and dying. We were doing all we could in the NCDDU, but there was still so much work to be done.

Assistant Commissioner Pat O'Toole sent a request for submissions from divisional officers on how to deal with the drugs scourge and how to improve life in the afflicted communities. As the request filtered down through the ranks, it ended up on my desk and I sat down to write my own submission. In it, I described the work of the Store Street unit and our approach. I wrote, too, about the whole question of evaluation, arguing for a move away from bald statistics to a deliberate focus on quality of arrest and seizure. I reiterated that the Garda Síochána was accountable to the people it served and emphasised the importance of taking every opportunity to talk to the community and to maximise every interaction. My ideas on how to carry out drugs policing were being continually honed through our work on the ground – and the results we were delivering from our sparsely resourced unit.

There can be moments in life when it feels like nothing will ever change, when everything feels unrelenting and immovable. For the inner-city communities, that certainly seemed to be the shared feeling – that they were caught in the vice grip of the drugs market, as consumers and casualties, and they couldn't see any way to break free. But that all changed in 1996 with the deeply shocking murders of Detective Garda Gerry McCabe and journalist Veronica Guerin; and with the setting up of the Criminal Assets Bureau (CAB), one of the most significant and impactful changes to occur during my 41 years on the force.

Before that happened, however, the NCDDU had to forge on with limited resources, working all the angles. Our Drug Unit was very busy, with more work to do than we could ever be expected to complete. We had to be focused; we had our targets, both the drug sellers and the drugs being sold. The team of top-class drug investigators in the NCDDU were achieving far beyond what could reasonably have been expected of them, but they did not have the time or experience necessary to take on the additional burden of the financial investigations we had identified as a means of tackling the suppliers. It made sense to separate out the strands and specialise, so while they gathered evidence during searches, I spent a lot of time behind my desk, following the money trails left behind by the key suppliers we were actively investigating. This was the first time drugs policing had been carried out in this way – identifying and chasing the assets – so we were in new territory and building our own pathway through it.

The inner-city community had confirmed for us who the major dealers were and we set up surveillance operations on them. We set up Operation Pizza to target the infamous Felloni family, based in the Dominick Street flats. Operation Family Tree targeted Derek Dunne and his family network, who worked out of Grenville Street. Operation Main Street focused on those who were openly selling drugs around the O'Connell Street area. Operation Cooperation investigated prolific drug sellers who did their business around the north inner city but didn't live there. We chose the codenames ourselves, bandying names about in the office until we found one that fit. They were fairly literal – Family Tree was so-named because that drug business centred on various branches of Derek Dunne's family. We chose Pizza because of the Italian connection of the name Felloni – although we were later told that Regina Felloni was highly insulted because she thought it was a reference to her 'spotty face'. That, of course, had never occurred to us.

Over the years between 1994 and 1998, those operation codenames became widely known and reported in the media. The residents of the inner city knew the codenames and who each operation was targeting. This proved very beneficial to us because it meant that they were aware of our work, that they knew we had listened to them and their concerns and that we were going after the very people they most wanted to prevent doing business on their streets: those who were causing the greatest damage. Those codenames told the local people that we were working with them to protect their communities.

While I was working on the Cronin and Dunne cases using the Criminal Justice Act 1994 – the money-laundering legislation – I was also tracking the assets of a man who had been a thorn in the side of law enforcement since my father's days as a detective, one of the most prolific criminals and repeat offenders the country had ever seen: Tony Felloni. His case would feature many 'firsts' as we finally figured out how to contain him and his cash-rich heroin operation.

The story of Tony Felloni's criminal career stretched right back to 1959, when a teenaged Felloni was convicted of stealing a scooter and bound over for 12 months. From then, he never did an honest day's work in his life, living off the proceeds of his criminal work, which ranged from assault and burglary to blackmail and larceny. He was very well known to my father and his colleagues, given his bewildering level of repeat offending. He received suspended sentences, concurrent sentences and some jail time, but nothing put him off his chosen career. He was adept at gaming the justice system, using legal aid, the appeals process and the bail laws to stay out of a prison cell and continue committing crimes with limited consequences. He was arrested by many gardaí over the decades, but charge and conviction would be followed by prison release and another spate of crime.

In 1965, when my father was promoted to inspector, he was sent to Donnybrook, his first time beyond the north inner city as a garda. While there he became involved in the case of 'Anthony Best', who rented rooms from two ladies on Victoria Road and then used their house as a base for storing stolen goods. He told them he was the brother of the footballer George Best, and the ladies believed him. As always with Felloni, his smooth good looks and stylish attire made him seem well-to-do and honest. He was a master con man. He was storing the booty from numerous burglaries in the house at Victoria Road, until my father and his colleagues paid him a visit, arrested and charged him – as Tony Felloni, of course.

Felloni had a long career in break-ins all around the country, the sort of smash-and-grab crimes that are high-adrenaline but not always high-return, but that changed in the 1980s when a brand new avenue opened up to him. In the early 1980s, Larry Dunne and his family brought heroin to Dublin and became the biggest dealers in the city, creating the first generation of addicts. They opened the floodgates as others began to realise the potential income that could be made from importing and selling drugs. One man who took notice was Tony Felloni, always with an ear to the ground for a money-making scheme. When Larry Dunne was arrested in 1986, many were hopeful that it would topple the heroin operation in the city, but things were already too far gone. After his sentencing, Larry Dunne said: 'If you think we're bad, wait till you see what's coming after us.' He was to be proved right, because what was coming after him was the likes of Tony Felloni. By the mid-1980s, Felloni had taken Larry Dunne's place as the biggest dealer in the north inner city.

There was a definite 'before and after' to Felloni's lengthy life in crime – before 1980, he had never received a drug conviction, even though he had over twenty convictions to his name. After 1980, he received only drug convictions. He had become a full-time drug trafficker, and he had never earned so much money. But like Larry Dunne before him, he was caught, and in 1986 he was sentenced to ten years in prison for supplying heroin. He emerged after seven years, in 1993, just in time to take part in the heroin epidemic of the 1990s. He went straight back to his old ways, dealing out of his parents' flat in 73 Lower Dominick Street, making life very difficult for his fellow residents. As his children grew up, they either became addicts themselves or joined the family business. His two key helpers were Luigi and Regina, who were deeply involved in his drug operation. My father had dealt with a young Tony Felloni; now I had to deal with an older, experienced and equally ruthless Felloni and his son and daughter.

Our Drug Unit were regular visitors to the Felloni home, conducting searches in the hunt for their drug stash. As with all of the houses we searched, the owners had no idea that we were also searching for evidence of the wealth accrued from the sale of drugs as I slowly built a picture of the money flow. I well remember a particular search at the flat on Lower Dominick Street, on 28 October 1995, when I entered with a number of my team. Tony was there, along with Regina, Luigi and Luigi's girlfriend, and his father. My priority was to get to Tony quickly and handcuff him, in case he had drugs on his person. We did this, not even giving him time to rise from his seat before we had the handcuffs on his wrists. But it turned out Regina could move quickly too. As we secured her father, she leapt up in a rage, grabbed the nearest blunt object – a glass ashtray – and fired it straight at my head. I ducked, and it shot over my head and landed on the floor. Before it had landed, the officers behind me had taken a firm hold of her. The Fellonis looked on as we searched, Tony's father shouting with his usual high indignation that there were no drugs to be found. The eagle-eyed Garda Angela Willis spotted some shaving brushes at the kitchen sink and wondered why they were being kept there. She examined them – and discovered that the handles could be unscrewed and opened and when she did so, she found packets of heroin hidden inside.

We arrested Tony Felloni and brought him back to Store Street with us. The heroin Angela had uncovered had a street value of £500–£1,000. Felloni was charged at the next sitting of the District Court. He was awarded bail, his mother brought in the money, and he walked out, free to do as he liked again. It was a blow to me and the team – this was the fourth time we had brought him before the courts on charges of supplying heroin, and the fourth time he had been bailed out and walked away. The bail laws were working against us. Of course, all the local community saw was a man who was arrested over and over and yet never actually paid for his crimes. Their resentment ran as deep as our frustration.

The bail laws had on occasion thwarted my father's efforts to imprison Felloni, and now I was facing the same predicament. But as it happened, 1996 turned out to be a watershed year in that regard as well. Not that I could have known that when I was in the High Court on 26 January, arguing to revoke bail for Tony Felloni in what would be unusual circumstances. I had obtained a warrant in the District Court for his arrest on the basis I believed he was about to abscond. My reason for requesting his bail be revoked was that I had reliable information from a source that he had plans in place to abscond to South Africa. The District Court judge revoked bail and granted me an arrest warrant on the basis that I believed Tony Felloni was about to abscond for the purpose of evading justice (Section 33(1), Criminal Procedure Act 1967). This was the only time in my career that this occurred – that a person out on bail who had not committed a crime, was subject to rearrest to prevent absconding. That was one of the 'firsts' in the Felloni case. I arrested Felloni and, naturally, he appealed, landing us all back in the High Court.

There was an earlier event, unknown to all of us at that time, that was now going to play a part in the proceedings. In one of Luigi's recent court appearances, he was seeking bail and a woman presented as his bail person. Tony Felloni was sitting at the back of the court, watching and listening. Garda Peter Oates, one of my team, was questioning the woman. She had a bank book to prove she had the means to provide the bail monies. Peter asked her various questions about the bank book, the money, and then he asked her the killer question: 'Who are you?' There were audible gasps in the courtroom. The woman looked deeply uncomfortable, then she quietly admitted that she was not who she had claimed to be – she was not the account-holder of the bank account. The defence solicitor of course stood up immediately and said, 'I had no knowledge of this.' We had no doubt this was true. As it turned out, the bank book belonged to a neighbour of this woman and the entries had been falsified – there was no money in the account. It was all a ruse to bail Luigi out of jail time. As soon as the woman confessed, we heard noises at the back of the court. Tony Felloni had jumped up from his seat and run out of the courtroom. He knew the game was up.

Now fast-forward to the High Court, where Felloni was appealing the revoking of his current bail, the one he has been denied because I swore he was a flight risk. I was cross-examined closely on the source of this information, but highlighted the need to protect the person's identity. Then I was asked: Does this person have a criminal record? I answered truthfully: Yes. I was pressed hard to say more, but once again declined, on the basis that there was a potential threat to life if I did so. I had to swear to my belief that Felloni posed a flight risk. I swore, knowing that I had good information that he was planning a runner to South Africa. Felloni then got up into the witness box to be questioned by the judge. In the course of questioning, the judge asked him about his son's arrest. Felloni stated that the first time he met the woman using the false identity was after Luigi's trial. With that, the judge halted the testimony. He raised his hand and said, 'You are lying.' He went on to point out that the woman had been arrested immediately after her admission of guilt, so Felloni must be lying about when he met her. On the basis that Felloni had lied to the High Court in sworn testimony, the judge refused to grant him bail and he remained in custody. And just like that, the Felloni bail problem was solved – and he largely brought it on himself.

Later that year, on 26 November 1996, a bail referendum was held to amend the constitutional provision regarding bail. The proposed amendment was to allow a court to refuse bail to any suspect if it was believed that they would commit a serious offence while out on bail. The turnout for the referendum was very low, about 29 per cent, but it passed. I'm sure my father would have approved.

When it came to criminals like Felloni, however, a prison sentence would not be enough. That was the wrong attitude. We had to locate and then confiscate the wealth he had built up from his activities. If he went to prison – a prospect that didn't bother him – and came out to a nice stack of money, we had failed; that's how I saw it. We wanted these criminals to serve time and come out to nothing. That would prove a powerful deterrent to others. To that end, I kept on tracing the money, through eight different banks and building societies in Dublin, and then on to accounts in Belfast and London. This was the first time a drug unit had investigated in this way, and this deeply. With pen, paper, calculator and persistence, I followed Felloni's money in every direction it led.

One of our concerns was that the assets might be in the children's names, and therefore out of our reach. The goal was to freeze *all* the assets, no matter how they were hidden – but to do that, we needed to catch all of them. We already had heroin stashes linked to Tony Felloni himself, and we suspected Regina and Luigi were selling too, but in order to invoke the legislation we needed a prosecution on indictment, which meant catching each of them in the act. We were helped in this when we discovered that a flat in a house on Hollybank Road in Drumcondra rented to a 'Rose Moloney' was in fact rented by Regina Felloni. We understood that she visited infrequently, but that it was potentially a storage base for the family's heroin dealing. The team set up a surveillance rota and prepared to watch and wait for the long haul, until Rose/Regina showed up.

The first day of the stake-out was on Holy Thursday, 2 April 1996. We had eyes on the house from outside, but I had secured a search warrant, so we were able to send two officers into the house. Seamus Boland and Darragh O'Toole entered the flat and began searching it methodically. They had only been in there a matter of minutes when the alert went up that Regina Felloni had just driven up the road. We were surprised by this unexpected bit of luck, but we were ready. Regina made her way to the flat, put her key in the door, turned it and stepped inside to be faced by the two Drug Unit officers. They handcuffed her and put her sitting on a chair and she looked on as they continued to search. She must have known how this was going to end when Seamie Boland began to climb up into the attic. Up there, he found two coffee jars stuffed with packets of heroin, a weighing scales and other drug paraphernalia. It was later assessed that the street value of the find was about £30,000. That amount would guarantee a prosecution on indictment.

I wasted no time in recommending to the DPP that a Restraint Order be applied for in respect of any and all assets, known and unknown, in the name of Tony, Luigi and Regina Felloni. On 5 April, barrister Shane Murphy made an application on behalf of the DPP before Mr Justice Carney of the High Court for the issue of a Restraint Order pursuant to the provisions of Section 24 of the Criminal Justice Act 1996. The High Court reviewed the evidence and granted the order. This was the first time in the history of the state that a criminal's assets had been frozen (other than the Cronin case, where the freezing order was rescinded). It was a testament to the NCDDU's approach and plain hard work.

On 20 June 1996, Tony Felloni was sentenced to 20 years in prison by the Dublin Circuit Court for the crime of the sale and supply of heroin with an estimated street value of £350,000. It was another first – the longest sentence in the history of the state handed down for drug trafficking. It was an incredible outcome for the Garda Síochána and our Drug Unit, and it cemented the view in the north inner city that the Garda Síochána were on the side of the community, were working with dedication to rid the city of heroin and were worth talking to and working with and helping. It was the culmination of so much work and effort, but it was worth it on every level. In addition, Luigi was sentenced to six years in prison and Regina to six years and nine months for their roles in the drug trafficking business. The Felloni operation had been collapsed – but that wasn't the end of it. The Court hearing regarding their assets would begin in 1997, and that was a whole other battle.

Six days after that unprecedented sentence for Felloni, journalist Veronica Guerin was shot dead in her car as she was stopped at traffic lights on the Naas road. Her killers were in the pay of John Gilligan, the head of a cannabis importation and dealing business of a very different order from the hands-on local street business of the Fellonis. It was estimated that this gang had shifted and sold on cannabis to the value of about £17 million in the previous four years. It was the sheer impunity of the killing that shocked the most. It spoke to the gang's view of the Garda Síochána and all the forces of the state, their sense of being untouchable and beyond the law. The entire country was united in shock and outrage and the long-time demands for resources to tackle the drug trade became an urgent clarion call. One of the key responses was the setting up of the CAB, which would greatly help in my efforts to claw back the drug wealth accumulated by Tony Felloni and by another NCDDU target, Derek Dunne.

We had set up Operation Family Tree to target the drug-selling activities of the Dunne family, headed by Derek Dunne (no relation to Larry Dunne). The plan was to dismantle the entire enterprise, person by person, deal by deal. The family were north inner-city folk, from Grenville Street, and that made it worse in the community's eyes – they had betrayed their own by making money from their misery. Worse again, not only was he dealing drugs, but Derek Dunne was doing so even though he'd been dealt a lucky hand in life. He had been a gifted footballer, playing in the League of Ireland, and nicknamed 'Maradona' for his prowess with a soccer ball. Even with all that, he still visited harm on his neighbours. There was a huge backlash towards Dunne for his abandonment of his community.

Even though we had the wholehearted support of the community, it was difficult to gather the evidence needed to get criminal charges against Derek Dunne. It was a cat-and-mouse game, and the mouse was pretty nimble. We got word that there was a house in Glenmalure Park where heroin was likely being concealed. The house belonged to Derek's brother, Seamus (James) Dunne. On 16 December 1994, we went to the house with a search warrant. Seamus Dunne was not there, but we conducted our search, also using trained sniffer dogs.

Eventually, we discovered bags of heroin concealed in the frame of the sliding door between the two downstairs rooms.

On that same day, 16 December, we also entered a house at Estuary Court, Swords. Garda Seamus Boland had obtained a warrant. We made our usual speedy entry and found two people inside, Christopher Byrne and Audrey McAllister. Byrne was found to have six batches of heroin, totalling 96 street deals, in a cigarette box and a further 200 street deals were found hidden behind a mirror in the bathroom. It was another successful outcome for Operation Family Tree and it produced positive media headlines and a commendation from the Minister for Justice, Nora Owen, for excellent police work.

Byrne and McAllister had been promised up to £500 a week to help distribute the heroin from a 'safe house', but received only about £170 a week. Both pleaded guilty to having heroin with a street value of between £5,000 and £7,000 for supply to others. In the Circuit Criminal Court, in February 1996, I told Judge Moriarty that Operation Family Tree was targeting a particular family and their associates. I told him some targets had brought the heroin into Ireland and others helped distribute it from safe places and that, up to that date, about 10 people had been arrested in our operation.

Judge Moriarty said he could not ignore the use of people like Byrne and McAllister to ensure the ongoing supply of heroin, which he identified as the greatest single cause of crime and untold misery for the addicts they helped to supply.

The Judge remarked that when they were wooed by the offer of £500 a week to help distribute the heroin, they knew what they were doing was wrong and, despite Byrne's relationship to major figures involved, they could have refused. Byrne was jailed for six years, with the final three years suspended, and McAllister for five years with the final 40 months suspended.

As for our other house search that day, Seamus Dunne went on the run, and was believed to be in Liverpool. So you can imagine our surprise when the man himself walked into Store Street late on New Year's Eve, ready to take the rap for the £18,000 worth of heroin that had been found in his house. He was putting his hands up to protect others.

Store Street was still decorated with its paltry Christmas decorations, a bit of tinsel, a fake tree dragged out of a store cupboard somewhere, none of it really lifting the atmosphere of the bedraggled old building. It would be demolished soon, but it was still the NCDDU's home at that time. It was so near to midnight that almost everyone had left, and there were no takers for interviewing a man who wanted to put his drug involvement on the record. But Family Tree was of great importance to the unit and no opportunity to achieve a prosecution could be missed. So Seamus Boland and myself arrested Seamus Dunne and brought him to an interview room to take his statement, in which he took responsibility for the stash of heroin. The charge sheets were prepared and he was formally charged. Once he was safely in a cell, myself and Seamie looked at the clock: fifteen minutes to midnight. It was just time enough to beg a lift to Ryan's pub, where we raised a pint at midnight and wondered what the New Year would bring.

So we were making good headway against other members of the Dunne clan, but Derek was still at large and we weren't sure when we'd catch a break. When it finally came, I didn't recognise it at first. I was at my desk, working flat out to complete an investigation file to a tight deadline when a member of the team told me that someone in UK Customs wanted to speak to me. I took the call and listened distractedly – half my mind still on the report – as he told me that he was pursuing a number of suspects and thought I could perhaps assist him. He reeled off some names I didn't recognise, and I was just thinking this pointless exercise was wasting precious time when he said a name that got my full attention: did I know a Derek Dunne? The lightbulb clicked on: if I could help him, he could help me in my efforts to target Dunne. This was my first taste of international collaboration, and it left me in no doubt as to the crucial importance of it to law enforcement investigations. It would become a much relied upon tool in my future work.

I was back and forth with HM Customs over the coming months, sharing information and keeping abreast of their solidly growing case against Dunne. He was a regular visitor to the UK, where he was buying the heroin that ended up on the streets of the north inner city. He had no idea that law enforcement in two jurisdictions were now taking a keen interest in him and his travel plans. The UK had a better case against him, for importation of Class A drugs, so it made sense for us to work together to secure his arrest when he was on a visit to England. We got word that he was soon heading off on another drug-buying trip and tipped off our friends in UK Customs. The plan was for us to confirm that Dunne was on the flight, and they would be waiting for him at the other end.

We wanted to be completely sure that he was on the plane, so myself and Seamie Boland went out to Dublin Airport in the hopes of spotting him and watching him embark. If we saw it with our own eyes, we could give one hundred per cent confirmation to the Customs waiting for him at his destination. This was 5 January 1996 and the airport wasn't too busy in the post-Christmas period. We watched people arriving at the gate for the departure to Manchester, but Dunne wasn't among them. They were calling the closing of the gate, and there was still no sign of him. I saw a member of Airport Police and went over to double-check with him the location of particular flight departures. I walked up to him and opened my mouth to speak, when who do I see, only that familiar face – Derek Dunne. He was speaking into his mobile, standing right behind the policeman I had approached. I asked the policeman some inane question, then turned and walked away.

We had an anxious wait for the next few minutes. We both felt he had noticed me, so would that spook him enough for him to not take the flight? But then we thought, sure, he wouldn't have any idea we were there for him. We crossed our fingers and waited. The flight was called. We watched. When most of the travellers had gone through the gate, Dunne suddenly walked towards it, and off he went, through passport control and on to boarding. We stayed in place, watched the gate close, then watched the aircraft rise into the sky. He was on his way. The relief was huge. I called the UK Customs and confirmed that Derek Dunne was definitely on his way to them. When the plane landed at Manchester, he was arrested on suspicion of exporting heroin from the UK to Ireland and remanded in custody, slated for trial that June.

When the trial began in June 1996, Seamie Boland and I were required to be present as witnesses. We flew over to attend at Liverpool Crown Court, but the trial was adjourned for a few days, so we returned to Dublin on Tuesday 25 June, because we both had a case to attend in Dublin District Court. We were due back in Liverpool the following Monday morning. The next day, Wednesday 26 June, still fresh from the success of seeing Tony Felloni sentenced to twenty years and hoping to see the same justice meted out to Derek Dunne, we drove to the court and did our duty there. As we drove away afterwards, I mentioned to Seamie that I had a music stereo unit in for repair at Pleasant Street, but wouldn't have time to collect it before we had to head back to Liverpool. Seamie said, 'Sure let's do it now and just get it done.' I drove over there, collected it, then we headed towards Store Street. On Aungier Street, I stopped at a red light and out of the car in front of us steps Brian Meehan. He was known to us as a significant player in the drugs trade. I didn't recognise the driver of the car, but Seamie did. It was Paul Ward, another person suspected of involvement in serious crime. We took the registration number and recorded the sighting for intelligence purposes.

On we went, and Seamie waited patiently again as I jumped out on O'Connell Street to run into Telecom Éireann to pay a bill. I came out, bill paid, got back into the car and looked over at Seamie. He appeared very shocked. He said, 'You won't believe what just happened – Veronica Guerin has been murdered.' There was a sense of pure disbelief as we listened to the news bulletins on the radio. As the coverage unfolded over the coming days, and the name of Brian Meehan began to be connected to the murder, we realised that potentially what we had seen on Aungier Street was members of the hit team making its getaway. The fact that we had seen them meant that, whatever alibi they had concocted, it would now have to include being on Aungier Street at 1.30 p.m. When the time came, we gave evidence in court of what we had seen that day.

Over the next two days, as we assessed any information we had in the Drug Unit in Store Street that could help the investigation into the death of Veronica Guerin, we focused on one particular individual. By Friday 28 June we were convinced that Charlie Bowden, a man who was little known in law enforcement circles, was a key figure. Late on Friday I contacted Dick Kelly, my chief superintendent, and sought to meet with him. He was busy, in charge of policing a Tina Turner concert at Croke Park. I met him at his home late that night and he made arrangements for Seamus Boland and myself to meet with the Security and Intelligence section the following day. Charles Bowden was subsequently prosecuted and found guilty of drugs and firearms offences and sentenced to six years in jail.

Bowden turned state witness in the prosecution of those charged with the murder of Veronica Guerin. Brian Meehan received a life sentence in 1999 for her murder, and is still the only person convicted of the murder. (In 2002, the Court of Criminal Appeal overturned Paul Ward's earlier conviction for the murder, but he was not released from custody as he was serving a 12-year jail sentence for his part in riots at Mountjoy Prison in 1997.)

Back in Liverpool on Monday morning, the trial got under way again, but it was short-lived. Derek Dunne's defence team argued that a fair trial was no longer possible, given the huge amount of publicity on the Guerin killing all weekend, which included references to the Dunne family and their drugs connection. The family in question was that of

Larry Dunne, no relation to Derek, but the judge felt that a trial at that time would be prejudicial. He ordered a retrial for that September.

It was at this point that the government introduced the Criminal Assets Bureau Act 1996 and the Proceeds of Crime Act 1996, which were pushed through quickly to provide the necessary tools to deal with the proceeds of crime. This was an innovative approach. In addition to a criminal process providing for the seizing and forfeiture of assets following a criminal conviction, the Civil Courts would play a role. In my work following the money, there was an onerous task of securing a criminal conviction to enable the process of seizing and forfeiture of assets. Now, however, CAB legislation brought in a civil burden of proof, whereby no conviction was necessary to initiate proceedings and the defendant had to prove their wealth was *not* accrued from criminal actions. It completely changed the parameters.

One of the most important decisions in the setting up of CAB was to make its head officer a senior member of the Garda Síochána. Commissioner Pat Byrne and Minister for Finance Ruairi Quinn were unequivocal about this. Others felt it should be headed by the Revenue Commissioners, but while it would be an independent statutory body, it was essential that it would be led by a senior garda officer. It is an independent statutory body, multi-agency and multi-disciplinary, linked to a number of government departments as well as the Garda Síochána. Another important decision was to ensure anonymity for non-Garda employees. There had been attacks on officials before – most notably Dr Jim Donovan, a forensic scientist, and Brian Purcell, an employee of the Department of Social Welfare, who would go on to serve as Secretary General in the Department of Justice (DOJ) – and this measure was designed to allow CAB staff to carry out their duties without fear of reprisals.

CAB is an excellent model and is designed to dismantle the financial structure of criminal gangs. It can prevent those displays of power that threaten to unseat law and order and social cohesion. When drug gangs reach that point of open displays of power, it is a dangerous tipping point. That was realised after the murder of Veronica Guerin, and CAB was part of the answer. Its two key senior positions, chief bureau officer and bureau legal officer, were initially filled by Detective Chief Superintendent Fachtna Murphy and Barry Galvin, respectively. They were both convinced that the best way to tackle criminal gangs was through their money, which was why the 'seize and freeze' powers of CAB were so welcome and so crucial. For me and the Store Street unit, the arrival of CAB was like a well-equipped cavalry coming over the hill. We had been standing guard over the fort alone, with very little ammunition, and now here were the reinforcements, armed to the teeth and eager to get to the front line. It was a game-changer.

I met with Fachtna Murphy and Barry Galvin just a few weeks after CAB was set up. They were extremely pleased to be handed the basket of cases based on our work in the NCDDU. In future meetings, we discussed our key targets and CAB felt the Derek Dunne case looked promising. They took it over and when CAB brought it to the High Court, the judge complimented the evidence provided. It was still insufficient for a criminal charge, but as CAB was engaged in a civil forfeiture of assets, the judge was able to order the freezing of Derek Dunne's assets. That was CAB's first court case – and one of the first Confiscation Orders made under the new proceeds of crime legislation. This was groundbreaking, providing proof of concept; despite the fact that Derek Dunne was not the subject of any criminal charge, the Court could consider his wealth to be the proceeds of criminal activity and start the process of depriving him of it.

We also discussed Operation Pizza and the lengthy money trail I was arduously following for the Felloni trial. It would come before the court in 1999, and I was working away all the while, preparing as much evidence as possible. CAB would take over the case and I would work with them. Frank Cassidy, who would later be appointed CAB's second chief legal officer, was appointed as receiver and he would ensure all Felloni assets would eventually transfer to the state's coffers. My own investigation had turned up evidence of bank accounts in Belfast and London, so now I requested permission to travel to London, with Seamie Boland, to talk to the City of London Police with a view to pooling our information. Permission was granted and we flew to London.

Back in those days, accommodation was available in some police stations for visiting members, and we availed of this by booking rooms, for stg£10 each, at Liverpool Street Police Station. Once our bags had been safely deposited there, we went to meet Jed Wilson, who was attached to Wood Street station in the City of London, a detective assigned to the Financial Investigation Unit, Special Crime Department. We set out our findings on the Fellonis, which would eventually lead to a freezing order being granted on their bank accounts in London and Liverpool. That wasn't our last port of call regarding bank accounts outside our jurisdiction; I would later meet with the RUC in Northern Ireland and secure an order from Belfast High Court to freeze Felloni accounts held in Belfast. That was the first case of accounts being frozen in Northern Ireland for a case being prosecuted in Ireland – another Felloni first.

Once our business had been conducted, Jed Wilson invited us to join him for a pint. It was Holy Thursday, 30 March 1997, and London was heaving with revellers. He brought us to a pub owned by a former Arsenal manager, Terry Neill's Sports Bar on Holborn Viaduct. When we arrived there, we were introduced to Terry Neill himself, a Belfast man, and his wife. We shared a pint and stories with an interesting group of serving and retired police officers, including the chief of the City of London Police. Into the pub then came a very well-dressed man, who had pulled up outside in a showy Bentley and proceeded to call for drinks for everyone in the bar. The side-of-mouth comments told us that he was 'a bit of a gangster' who now appeared – or wished to appear – to have gone legitimate. I watched with some amusement as he tried to pay for the pub-wide round of champagne with a credit card, and Terry Neill's wife very clearly told him it would be cash or nothing. He did as asked.

Another man joined us then, a journalist who clearly had a few drinks on board already. He was introduced to me and then made some disparaging remarks about 'the Irish'. A City of London police officer overheard and he said quietly to me: 'Do you want me to have a word with him? Ask him to apologise?' I said, 'No, it's okay, I'm going to talk to him myself.' I had something on my mind. In the headlines that day was a court case at the Old Bailey during which VCR tapes containing key evidence had gone missing. It was not yet known who had removed the tapes from the courtroom and it was a big breaking story. This journalist had told the group in the pub that he had been at the Old Bailey that day. I engaged him in conversation, batted away his clumsy attempts at an apology for his comments and said casually, 'I'd say you know who took those tapes today? The journalists must have an idea about it?' He confided that he did know. I called over one of the City of London officers and said to him, 'This fella wants to tell you something.' They talked in low tones together, then the policeman turned and hurried from the pub. I understand the VCR tapes were recovered soon after.

In the end, Derek Dunne did not get much time to enjoy his ill-gotten gains. He was acquitted, on the basis of insufficient evidence, by the retrial jury at Liverpool Crown Court in September 1996 and subsequently moved to Amsterdam with his girlfriend, Rachel Mitchell, the daughter of gang boss George 'The Penguin' Mitchell, at the time suspected to be the richest criminal in Ireland. In June 2000, Dunne was gunned down outside his apartment and left for dead on the street. He seemed to have crossed the wrong people. Another man shot with him was believed to be an associate of John Gilligan and was wanted for questioning about the murder of Veronica Guerin. The drug crime circles can be small ones.

The Felloni trial dragged on for two years, with appeals and constitutional challenges as the family attempted to preserve their wealth. However, it didn't work and by June 1999, the assets of the Fellonis, amounting to more than £400,000, had been confiscated. That might not have been all of it, but it was a huge sum of money, and Tony Felloni was entirely deprived of it because it came off the back of addiction and violence and misery and death. It was our final 'first' in the case – Tony, Regina and Luigi were the first criminal gang to come out of prison to no money, wiped accounts, empty pockets. It made their whole enterprise pointless. It's easy enough to endure jail if you know a pot of money is waiting for you at the end of it, but if there's nothing? That's a very different prospect.

Tony Felloni was released from Mountjoy Prison in 2011 and the gardaí never heard of him again. He didn't re-emerge onto the street dealing, as he had in 1993/4. He came out to a transformed drugs scene, one based on greater violence but with complex hierarchical business structures, with effective bail laws, and the resources-rich Criminal Assets Bureau working with international partners to chase down the drugs, the bosses and the dealers. I couldn't help thinking of my father, and how pleased he would have been to see the incorrigible Tony Felloni finally put out of business for good.

In April 2024, Tony Felloni died after suffering a heart attack. At his funeral in north inner-city Dublin, as the coffin was taken from the church, the 'Love Theme' from *The Godfather* was played.

CHAPTER 6

THE NATURE OF SUCCESS

The Store Street Drug Unit was delivering results and garnering headlines. There continued to be raised eyebrows in some quarters about the ability of one particular drug unit to create such a positive response when, looking at it from the perspective of the annual crime report, they were not adding any spectacular additional numbers to the crime statistics. The concept of quality over quantity had not yet been grasped by everyone. The reality was that our unit was engaging in best practice, but that hadn't yet been articulated at that point, so none of us knew that's what it was. The NCDDU knew the relevant law, worked within it, and was respected by prosecution and defence lawyers for that.

We had adopted a number of what we considered to be key elements of successful drug policing. We had assembled a team appropriate to the task in hand and had gathered a significant level of relevant criminal intelligence that was not squandered on easily achieved drug seizures and associated arrests, which, while improving crime detection-related statistics, would not have any meaningful impact on the drug-related issues within the communities we served. Intelligence gathered would be fully analysed and utilised to inform investigations focused on targets that if apprehended would have a real impact on illicit drug-related issues in Dublin's north inner city and further afield. We also adopted other key elements of successful drug policing, including, accessibility/visibility on the ground; listening to the community; and communicating continually and effectively. It also greatly helped that we were receiving full support for our approach from the senior Garda management team in the division. It was a model that brought results and rewards.

The Felloni trial kept rumbling on, but we were operating on a number of different fronts at all times. Another of those targeting operations that became a household name was Operation Cooperation, which focused on a number of different suspects who were selling heroin in the north inner city but living elsewhere. One of those suspects was Michael Heeney, from Duleek in County Meath and known to everyone in Dublin's inner city as 'Country Mick'. He was a coalman by trade, but he seemed to be making far more money than any of his competitors and it wasn't from time spent throwing coal bags over his shoulder, that much we could see. The people of the inner city were telling us that Heeney was a dealer, so we followed up on that and began to watch him.

By April 1997, we were sure he was moving drugs and selling them, and we were ready to catch him in the act. A checkpoint was set up on the Ashbourne Road, where we knew he would be travelling, and the members of the Drug Unit manning the checkpoint put on their old uniforms, to pose as 'normal' gardaí. If Heeney saw any Drug Unit officers, he would quickly dispose of any drugs in his possession. So we had to lull him into a false sense of security, to make him believe this was a 'normal' road stop. He came along the road as expected, with his wife in the car beside him, and was stopped. A search of the car turned up small bags of heroin. That was enough. The two were arrested and the car impounded. When the vehicle was fully searched, we found more heroin, the total haul coming to a street sale value of £7,000. He was charged with possession for supply.

We didn't stop there. The investigation into the drugs business of Country Mick continued, so that we could present as much evidence as possible when the case came to trial and put him out of business entirely and for good. In September, the local Drug Unit in Navan, County Meath, searched his premises and turned up £30,000 in cash. A few weeks later, the Store Street unit conducted a search at his home in Duleek. We brought in the drug sniffer dogs and they kept pulling towards a particular tree in the garden. The officers investigated, and Heeney's unorthodox gardening methods came to light: a large quantity of heroin, with a street value of £100,000, was hidden in the tree. It was going to be a case of you reap what you sow for Mick Heeney. We also found cash to the value of £9,500. It was damning evidence.

The case came to trial in July 1998. Garda Paul Cleary told the court that Heeney was a significant dealer, shifting half a kilogram of heroin each month onto the streets of the inner city. The evidence was incontrovertible and Judge Cyril Kelly sentenced Heeney to 12 years in prison. It was a huge result for our unit, and it was felt on the streets. Tony Gregory congratulated us and noted that since 1984, when legislation was put in place providing for it, 'not one dealer has got a life sentence'. Seamie Lamb of ICON also congratulated us and said that for the Gardaí, finding out who supplied the local dealers was always difficult, but that we had listened to the community, who had identified Heeney for us. That was exactly the message we wanted to get across, and the Heeney case was very important in that regard.

Another key target in Operation Cooperation was Fergus Duffy, a 28-year-old London-based man originally from Tullamore, with an address at Gracepark Heights,

Drumcondra. The community had made us aware of him too and he was under surveillance. We worked with the GNBCI on it and in February 1997, I led a search team that included Angela Willis, Seamus Boland, Seán McLaughlin and Larry Duggan. Our destination was a bedsit at Phoenix Court on Infirmary Road, beside the Phoenix Park and within shouting distance of Garda HQ. As always, surprise and speed were of the essence. We burst through the door and sprinted through the rooms, finding an astonished Fergus Duffy standing in the bedroom. Beside him on the floor was a holdall filled with heroin. There was no trouble handcuffing and arresting him. When people are caught red-handed, as he was, the majority are very easy to deal with in that moment because they are resigned to their fate and therefore calm. That's how Duffy was – he knew the jig was up, that it was an entirely incriminating scene, so there was no point fighting us or shouting about innocence. No point at all.

Our search uncovered more quantities of heroin, weighing scales, drug-cutting equipment and small plastic bags to hold the final fixes that would have been distributed around the streets. While we were searching, there was a knock on the door and we all went still. One of the team went over and opened it, to reveal a very unfortunate customer who had chosen the wrong moment to come asking Duffy for heroin to sell and use. He was arrested too. They were both transferred to Store Street. When the heroin was assessed, the success of the operation became clear: it was almost two kilograms, 50 per cent pure, with a street value of £520,000. This was a major haul for us, but we knew from intelligence gathered during Operation Cooperation that Duffy wasn't the importer – he was the distributor. There were others behind him who were bringing the heroin into the country and we wanted to catch them.

Again, we had to be quick. That evening, around five o'clock, the search team swooped on the house in Gracepark Heights that was listed as Duffy's home address. A UK-registered car was parked in the driveway and it was seized. We found three suspects inside the house: John Walmsley, Eithne Coyne Sr and Eithne Coyne Jr, both from County Offaly but living in the UK. We also found travel documents and other items of interest. The three were arrested and later, along with Duffy, were charged with offences that included importation and possession for supply of heroin.

It just so happened that that night, 6 February, there was a meeting of the Dublin Citywide Drugs Campaign in Liberty Hall. As the attendees were walking to the venue, the evening newspapers were hitting the streets with their headlines shouting about a significant drugs bust. When they arrived, there were smiles all round – it set the tone perfectly for the meeting's discussion. We were so pleased to have charged Fergus Duffy and the Coyne mother and daughter, and they were seeing policing in action, which instilled confidence because it showed that we listened and heard. The headlines reflected this. The *Evening Herald*'s bold headline announced: 'BUSTED! People Power smashes £8m Dublin inner city drug ring.' This would help to ensure continued support for the rule of law and the Garda Síochána and help to alleviate concern about the escalation of vigilantism.

Fergus Duffy came before the court on 4 June 1997 and he pleaded guilty to possession of heroin for supply and to unlawful possession of a sawn-off shotgun at Gracepark Heights on the same date. He was sentenced to ten years in prison. The judge called Duffy 'a modern day horror' for his role in delivering heroin to the streets of the inner city. On 7 October, his three accomplices had their day in court. Eithne Coyne Sr pleaded guilty to the importation, via Dublin Ferryport, of the heroin found in the holdall and received a sentence of six years. Her daughter received a four-year suspended sentence and John Walmsley received a three-year suspended sentence, both having also pleaded guilty. It was another drug outfit put out of business. The court was told that the accused made statements claiming the drug run was organised by Eithne Coyne Sr's younger brother, Frank Connolly, known as 'Mr Big', who was from Tullamore, but had a pub and nightclub as well as a used car business in London.

As we had in the Heeney case, we were happy to use creative methods, when needed, to carry out a surveillance or search operation. We employed a slightly unusual plan as part of Operation Main Street, which tackled drug selling and use on O'Connell Street. This was drawing adverse publicity and impacting tourism and local business, so there was pressure on us to make inroads into those activities. One place of interest was a nightclub on Parnell Street called Subterania. We had been making efforts to gain access and make purchases, but the bouncers on the door were tough and wily and they weren't going to let any suspected garda across the threshold. A reinforced metal door with multiple locks had been installed. If we did manage to get in, they were adept at sending the alert and delaying us, and by the time we got inside all trace of drugs had vanished. It needed an alternative approach.

I arranged for a number of younger gardaí at Store Street to be assigned to the Drug Unit on a temporary basis. They looked youthful and trendy, they even had earrings and tattoos, so I felt they could blend in and look less like gardaí than the rest of us. They observed drug-selling and drug-taking inside the club and we knew then for sure that this was a key premises to take down. We chose the night of 8 March 1998 to make a lightning raid on the club. Our own Drug Unit staff and members from local detective units all gathered in the parade room at Store Street for debriefing. The plan was for everyone to pile into two Garda vans, pull up outside the club and run in as quickly as possible. Then our young gardaí, who would be inside already, would be able to point to the sellers and we would round them up as fast as possible. I had been pondering where the plan could go wrong, and it was obvious that the biggest potential for failure lay in the speed of access. If all the lads in the vans were impeded or slowed up for any length of time, we wouldn't catch the sellers with the drugs. So what to do?

While they were all in the parade room listening to the plan, I was getting myself ready. Then I walked down and pushed open the door. All the heads in the room turned to look at the door, and there I stood, in full uniform, every inch the garda. I was accompanied by a member of a neighbouring drug unit in Pearse Street, now headed by the recently promoted Sergeant Seamus Boland. I had called Sergeant Boland and asked for someone who could do a good impression of a drunk and they had held an audition and sent me this lad. I wasn't sure if it counted as praise or criticism, but I just hoped he was up to the job. My colleagues smiled in surprise to see me in uniform – which was a very rare sight these days – but I explained that I would create a diversion to help them get into the club quickly.

At 11.30 p.m. I set out to walk across to Parnell Street. The Pearse Street actor went ahead of me to get into position. As I came walking down the street outside Subterania, just an innocent copper on a normal evening beat, the young lad staggered into my path. I was impressed – he acted his heart out and looked very convincingly sozzled. I encountered him, stopped to have a word, then he got aggressive. We tussled back and forth, me shouting at him to desist, him trying to knock the hat off my head. The bouncers on the door looked over at this kerfuffle and naturally took an interest.

Then the plan hit a snag. As the 'drunk' resisted and tussled with me, a patrol car from an outside district happened to pass by and spotted us. They pulled over, took out their batons and approached us. They were very surprised to hear my reaction, telling them to get the hell away, but to my great relief they caught the hint and didn't cause any injury to the member with the Oscar-worthy acting skills. They moved on and left me to it.

The bouncers were still watching with great interest as I struggled manfully to subdue the aggressive young man. Slowly, they moved away from the door, transfixed by the scene, and walked towards us to watch and offer help. They were away from the door now and it was unguarded. Bingo! The two vans roared down the road and screeched to a halt and out the officers poured from the back. To the surprise of the doormen, they did not come to my assistance but instead bailed into the club before the bouncers could register what was happening. The team were in and down those stairs before anyone could give any kind of signal. The undercover gardaí were waiting for them and sprang into action, identifying the sellers with the drugs on their persons.

There was one more unexpected twist. Eamon Henry, a sergeant, who was a former detective, was standing outside the club, in uniform, guarding the door. A taxi pulled up and a man got out and clocked the garda standing there. He asked him what was going on in the club. This sergeant had done his homework before the sting operation, studying all the photos we had gathered of our key suspects. He recognised this man and immediately arrested him on suspicion of possessing drugs. We arrested 30 suspects that night, and of those, the man from the taxi turned out to be carrying the most drugs on him. Those inside had been selling in the club, so their stocks were depleted, but he was a fresh arrival and had his full supply in his possession.

It was a very satisfying and successful end to the night and the operation took a number of local sellers off the scene for a while. We were able to charge six people with possession of drugs with intent to supply. And the nightclub owners would find that renewing their licence would be a tricky business when their premises was proven to be a place where drugs were being sold.

That was a high-profile success story for the newspapers and it once again showed the community that we were serious about ridding the streets of drugs. Another case that was just as high-profile and important in this regard related to a drug trafficker called Thomas 'The Boxer' Mullins. His name had been given to us by the community and we followed up on it. He lived a lavish lifestyle with a seemingly never-ending supply of cash to draw on – although he had no obvious means of accruing that wealth. In a brave move, Tony Gregory had used his Dáil privilege to name 'The Boxer' publicly, such was the extent of his impact on the north inner city.

We worked in tandem with the Garda National Drug Unit and the UK police on this operation because Mullins had an address in London and regularly travelled back and forth. Mullins was only a young man, 26 years of age, but was already steeped in drug culture and crime. The two forces worked in concert and eventually Mullins was arrested in England. He was brought before Snaresbrook Crown Court in East London in January 1998, where he was found guilty of involvement in a stg£750,000 heroin smuggling operation. He was jailed for 18 years (reduced to 15 years on appeal) – another source of relief and celebration for the people of the north inner city.

Our conviction list was growing and was very impressive by this stage: Felloni, 20 years; Heeney, 12 years; Duffy, 10 years; Mullins, 15 years; and many others who received sentences of over five years. This was a total shift from the years before the NCDDU targeted suppliers in this way. Back then, as John O'Donoghue TD, who would later be Minister for Justice, Equality and Law Reform, highlighted in 1996, a two-year sentence would have been typical, and even then it might well have been suspended. The approach we had taken of tracking the assets and putting substantial evidence before the courts was paying off. We were putting the key people out of business, which disrupted the supply and made it more difficult for them to make money. This was exactly what we wanted to achieve – and it was, crucially, what the community wanted us to achieve. They regarded us as successful because our idea of success was now aligned with their idea of success.

When I signed up to do a master's degree in drug and alcohol policy at Trinity College Dublin in June 1998, I discussed with my tutor, Professor Shane Butler, what the topic of my thesis should be and suggested various subjects. He said, 'There's only one thesis topic for you – why the Store Street Drug Unit is so successful.' It was a great opportunity to review and understand the mechanics of our work, so I agreed to do it.

Before I could write the thesis, however, there were some interesting trips that helped to broaden my thinking further. The Garda Síochána became involved in the Oisin Programme, an EU-funded exchange programme for staff in Member States to visit each other's drug units and pool knowledge. It was aimed at staff at sergeant and managerial level who could implement good practice gleaned from their placements. Officers from the EU arrived into Store Street to shadow us and see the drugs problem in the context of Dublin City, and then it was our turn to go and observe another country. We were sent to Denmark and in September 1998 myself, Seamus Boland, who was now in charge of the South Central Drug Unit, working out of Pearse Street station, and Gearóid Begley, who headed a drug unit in Tallaght district, travelled to Copenhagen to shadow our Danish counterparts there, with the requirement to write a full report on our return.

It was a fascinating two weeks. Three colleagues from Copenhagen had some time earlier worked with us in Dublin. On an off day, we'd taken them to a GAA fixture in Thurles in which Dublin was playing. Bertie Ahern, the then Taoiseach, was in attendance. We spoke to his driver and arranged for our three visitors to pose with the Taoiseach for a photograph. On our arrival in their office in Copenhagen we could see this photograph in pride of place on the wall.

We learned that heroin was the main problem in both countries, but the average age of a heroin abuser in Copenhagen was 36 years; in Dublin it was 25 years. Those age profiles struck me immediately. Our heroin problem was new when I joined Fitzgibbon in 1984. At that time, we had a lot of youngsters aged 14–16 who were involved in street-level crime such as larceny, handbag snatching and joyriding; and they first encountered heroin in prison. If you ask inner-city heroin users, they will very often tell you they had their first hit behind bars. It was the worst place for these kids to be when they were already heading down the wrong path. Then they'd be released and we'd meet them years later and they'd be heroin addicts. That's what I saw in the Dublin age profile

– the youngsters who got caught in the trap early and now here they were, ten years later, still using.

My opinion had always been that we should target the suppliers and profiteers and offer treatment and support to users. I was impressed to see that Denmark had 150 treatment centres nationwide. This was in stark contrast to Dublin's almost total lack of resources. In Denmark, addicts could find a bed, a support network and methadone treatment to help them to rehabilitate. The inner-city communities in Dublin had few resources at that time. We also observed that the drug issues often occurred among the population of illegal immigrants, but that was unknown to us because Dublin in the 1980s and early 1990s was a place of emigration, not immigration, so that simply didn't apply.

We were interested to see that when the Danish officers stopped a person, their first question was: What's your ID number? Every single interaction started with that question. Once the person gave their number, the officer had complete access to all their records at the touch of a button. It was the sort of instant data we could only dream of back then. They were also suffering overcrowded prisons, which in Ireland could result in early release for some that so often led to reoffending. They had a different and unusual approach: when the prisons were full, the courts handed out a prison sentence with a future start date, when that person could be accommodated. When an officer took an ID number and checked it, they immediately knew if the person before them had a prison sentence pending. They were also handing out fines continually. If they did a search of a house or premises, they gave receipts for any items seized and the receipt doubled as a fine. It was an interesting idea.

One of the biggest differences, though, was the number of police stations in operation. To our amazement, there were only seven police stations in Copenhagen. To their amazement, there were 43 stations in Dublin, split into districts and divisions. Both forces had about the same number of employees, but in Dublin they were spread out and compartmentalised, whereas in Copenhagen they were concentrated in larger numbers in fewer stations. We could see the benefits clearly – resources were centralised, officers built up an excellent network of colleagues, information was shared quickly and effectively. I remember thinking that the Garda Síochána could certainly learn from that model.

By far the most extraordinary aspect of our trip was our visit to Freetown Christiana. This was a town based on cannabis use, founded by like-minded people who loved to smoke cannabis and wanted to do so freely. They took over Christiana and it became self-autonomous, with about 1,000 inhabitants. They governed themselves and the police and government weren't welcome there. We were astonished that the state had allowed its establishment and ongoing existence. The three of us went out to see it and as we walked through its streets, we could see the alarm go up and feel all the eyes on us. Obviously they had quickly decided we looked like law enforcement and they wanted to be sure of our whereabouts and intentions. We were used to those looks from the streets of Dublin, of course, when the very set of us made those who were up to no good keep a close eye on us as we moved about. It was that same feeling from the people here as they watched Seamie, Gearóid and I walking about – wary, tense, ready to take action if necessary.

On paper, Christiana might sound like a liberal utopia, but the reality proved very different. Those in favour felt that concentrating drug selling and use in one area would limit its foothold in general society, and that it might prevent users from progressing to harder drugs. But the criminal element soon realised that this was a blank slate they could exploit, a place where they could hide in plain sight. The peace-loving, joint-smoking residents who just wanted to live as they wished became surrounded by other elements, who wanted to cash in on the drugs trade there by whatever means necessary. Over the past twenty years there have been gang territory fights and shootings, including of police officers. The Danish government is still finding a way to work with the people of Christiana to bring it within the country's laws, to an extent. It presents an ongoing challenge to police and keep safe.

That experience always comes to mind when people suggest that legalising drugs might be the best option for Irish society. After years of working in the Drug Unit and community policing and then working against organised crime and drugs gangs in my later career, I've come to the conclusion that legalisation is not the answer. Christiana and, indeed, Amsterdam tell cautionary tales, which make clear the dangers and pitfalls of that approach. From a user's perspective, these drugs are simply too addictive. It would be irresponsible to make them freely available and expect everyone to manage their use. In terms of health management and burden on the HSE, legalisation would not work. If you think of the extent of our drug problem with law enforcement in place, it could be multiple times worse without that safety net. I'm thinking of some areas of Vancouver or San Francisco, where, in 2022, 647 people died from unintentional drug overdose, and where thousands of addicts roam the streets, people who are as much lost to themselves as they are to society. It is good policy on every level to seek to manage the worst excesses and outcomes of such addictive and mentally corroding substances.

It was, I think, the Nixon administration that introduced that unfortunate phase 'the war on drugs'. People say, well, we've lost the war on drugs, so we should decriminalise. But the war is not on drugs – it's on the *consequences* of drugs. Those consequences are many, far-reaching and affect all strata in society. It was evident in Christiana – when drugs are freely sold and used, when there is a liberal attitude, that's a siren call to crime gangs and they arrive in their droves. Where there are drugs and drug-takers, there is money. Where there is money, there is crime. The problem with legalising drugs is that it would increase the crime problem. It would start with the drugs, but it wouldn't stop there; the gangs would – and do – keep going and carry out other illegal activities. No amount of money is ever enough. Money fuels their behaviour and, when they've made enough, their sense of impunity and entitlement. I recall when the judge was sentencing Fergus Duffy, he said: 'Heroin does untold damage to this city and this country and ninety per cent of the crime I have to deal with arises out of your evil trade.' He wasn't wrong. It creates crime.

I do, however, see merit in policies relating to decriminalisation of drug possession, in particular circumstances, addressing health issues experienced by users, but only where those policies operate alongside and in harmony with drug-related law enforcement strategies targeting those who sell drugs for financial gain.

We are seeing this now in Dubai. The UAE is viewed by criminals as having a useful attitude towards crime, and people like some in the Kinahan OCG have moved their base there. Dubai has no extradition arrangements with Ireland, so that's a bonus for them. It is the case that state permission is required to do anything, but it is also the case that money talks and backhanders and bribes and percentage cuts can get things done. But I think any state should do all it can to disrupt and discourage organised crime because it presents a very serious problem. It leads to corruption and in that way it becomes a threat to the state and to democracy. In my later career I dealt with the Kinahan and Hutch organised crime gangs and these are definitely not people you want gaining a foothold and bending society to their will.

I always think of this when I hear of those huge shipments intercepted off the coast of Ireland, with their cargoes of narcotics bound for Ireland, the UK and Europe. The sums involved are mind-boggling. In September 2023, the MV *Matthew* was boarded by the Irish Army Ranger Wing and they found two tonnes of cocaine on board, with an estimated street value of €157 million. That really is a staggering amount of money, and it means a staggering amount of people are buying the drugs. When people say things like, 'It's just a bit at the weekend, it's recreational, it's not much, I just spend a hundred quid a month,' it amazes me how easily they lie to themselves.

The economics of the drug trade are stark and irrefutable. If you are in a nightclub in Drogheda, or Limerick, or Dublin, or Galway, or Cork and you hand over a few twenties for cocaine, say, that money goes back to the Irish dealer. It is whizzed through money-counting machines with all the other notes gathered from all the drug buyers like you, then it is vacuum-packed into bundles and smuggled out of the country and into the hands of money launderers, who specialise in 'cleaning' money for a fee – a fee known in some cases to have funded acts of terrorism. We have intercepted enough of those vacuum-packed bundles of cash about to be removed from the country to speak with certainty. Your casual spend becomes part of a huge and constant flow of money out of the country, leaving no possibility for it to be taxed or put towards any good or useful public services. It leaves you and it leaves the country and it ends up in the bank account of a criminal, who quite likely never touches the stuff himself and who enjoys a lifestyle you can hardly imagine. That parallel economy hoovers up this mind-boggling amount of cash continuously, leaving all of us without it. And when you then read about murders, human sex trafficking, gang wars, all the nefarious elements of narco-terrorism, those have all been bought with those twenties you chose to hand over in the nightclub. You can't kid yourself otherwise.

In 1998 I was informed that I had been successful in my application for promotion to the rank of inspector, and that marked the imminent end of my Store Street tenure. I was placed on a list to fill future vacancies and I didn't know what would be coming next. Until then, I continued with my work with the Drug Unit and I also worked on the thesis for the MSc in Trinity. It was perfect timing – the Drug Unit had made an impact and I was coming out the other side of it, so it was very useful to review and take stock. The statistics, while not my preferred method of evaluation, did tell an interesting story: in North Central district, 70 per cent of all drug arrests were of suppliers, compared to 30 per cent in other regions and divisions. This was how Operations Pizza, Family Tree and Cooperation became household names – because we were catching the right people, and we were putting them away for long stretches of time. And when they'd served their time, they emerged to bank accounts with a string of zeroes in the bottom line.

The thesis posed the question: Why was the Store Street unit so successful? If you simply look at the crime statistics, which is the usual method for evaluating police performance, the answer is that we reversed the trends that hadn't been delivering results. Nationally, the key drug crime statistics were as follows: 80 per cent of charges related to cannabis and 20 per cent to Class A drugs; 80 per cent of those charged were users and 20 per cent of those charged were suppliers. At Store Street, we reversed those statistics. Our targeting priorities meant that 80 per cent of our charges related to Class A drugs and 80 per cent of those charged were suppliers. That massive turnaround spoke directly to the local people on the ground. They could see the effect of these new priorities. Until now, the government and the Gardaí had been delivering those 80/20 statistics that were useless from the perspective of the communities afflicted. It looked like success on paper, but on the ground it felt like abject failure. When Store Street reversed it, that changed the whole narrative. The community felt seen and heard, and they slowly built up a sense of faith in us. When the vigilantism fell away, I knew then that they believed we were doing our job. We had earned their trust.

As part of my research for writing the thesis, I read a famous report by Lord Scarman (published 1981) that concluded that there are two main issues in the police–community relationship: consultation and accountability. Without knowledge of the report back when I began working the NCDDU, I had instinctively sought out both. I knew community policing from the inside; I endeavoured to be always close to the communities I worked in; and I gained a good understanding of them. I knew that the relationship between us had to be based on respect. At Store Street, we made consultation with the community our primary framework. We walked the streets every day and talked to everyone. We listened. The people of the north inner city felt consulted, and they were most certainly part of the process of gathering information and insights. Alongside that, I had always made myself accountable to them through all the many meetings I attended every single week. I never turned down an invitation and I engaged fully at each one. That was why, in the end, local politicians like Tony Gregory, Christy Burke and Joe Costello were able to change their minds and praise the work of the Drug Unit. Until that time, that really was unheard of.

In 1999/2000, when I was writing my thesis, I was looking back on the past three years or so. Now I can look back over the 41 years of my career. I find it extraordinary that my time in Store Street gained as high a profile as my time as assistant commissioner, when I was working on the big-ticket, major-publicity Kinahan organised crime gang. The Store Street unit received high praise and international awards. In fact, you can draw a line directly from the cramped office of old Store Street to my spacious office at Harcourt Square years later and how I operated as assistant commissioner. Its importance in my career cannot be overstated. Store Street was where I learned how to properly deliver a policing service to the public, how to trust my instinct, how to understand that statistics do not tell the whole story and that the whole story is worth digging out. It formed my ideas on evaluating police work, on the quality of police work and on the nature of success.

I measure success over my career by the people I helped. It's of no real use to make a difference to the crime statistics – you have to make a difference to the problem. At Store Street, that is exactly what the Drug Unit achieved. We listened in order to understand the problem, then we worked out the best solutions to solve it. It was collaborative, it was thoughtful, it was responsive, it was effective. We excelled in dogged determination. And our greatest success, by far, was in trans-forming our relationship with the community. Our approach and methods produced a sea change in attitudes. That is the success I value the most in my attempt to be a successful and dedicated public servant. My reward was seeing the public reaction to what we were doing and knowing that it mattered. I was concerned, however, without there being proper understanding of how we went about our business in the Drug Unit at that time, our approach was not likely to continue into the future. The success did continue for a while after I left the unit, until more like-minded people also left and there was then a totally new team with a different approach to drugs policing.

Looking back from this vantage point, I can now say that the most affecting experience of my career was the privilege of working with and living with the people of the north inner city. It was a privilege to see life from their perspective and gain a shared sense of purpose with them. As a garda, you enter into people's lives in a way others don't and can't – it's a unique relationship and experience. You get to see how people live and operate behind closed doors. On the beat, one minute you could be interacting with a wealthy resident in North Great George's Street or the CEO of a business; the next engagement could be with an unemployed drug addict in the squalor of a bedsit. You get to see how every 'half' lives and you walk into scenarios that other people will never see – houses, flats, drug dens, mansions, prisons – you get to know all the worlds. The north inner city community were incredible people and it was a pure joy and privilege to work with them. That period was the best time in my whole career, and leaving was a bittersweet parting.

PART 3

POLICING A CHANGING IRELAND
(1999–2004)

CHAPTER 7

NEW ROLES, MAJOR CHALLENGES

An interesting opportunity arose just a few weeks after I transferred to the Bridewell. As part of the Good Friday Agreement and the peace process in Northern Ireland, a number of officers from the RUC and the Garda Síochána were selected to undertake a Joint Leadership Development Program in the USA. This was the first joint Garda and RUC training initiative and it was delivered at the headquarters of the FBI in Quantico, Virginia, and included field visits to Washington and New York. The theme was Developing Community Confidence and we were treated to a panel of fascinating speakers.

In January 2000, about forty people chosen to participate in the initiative, half from the Garda Síochána, including myself, and the other half from the RUC, travelled to the US. The visit included a meeting with Janet Remo, US attorney general, and, for me and a few others, an early morning run with Louis Freeh, the director of the FBI. I also had an opportunity to meet and discuss policing issues with Bill Bratton and Raymond Kelly, both of whom had been NYPD commissioner.

One memorable field visit was with the FBI to a parking garage in the basement of the North Tower of the twin towers. It was here that nearly seven years earlier, on 26 February 1993, a van bomb detonated, intended, the FBI told us, to cause the North Tower to fall, taking the South Tower with it and causing hundreds if not thousands of deaths. In fact, six people were killed, including a pregnant woman, and many were injured. Prophetically, the FBI spoke to us of the danger of a repeat incident, but they anticipated that if it happened, it would again be at the base of the building.

The Bridewell turned out to be a short posting – I spent only about 18 months there – but in that time I experienced one of the most deeply affecting cases of my career. On 1 April 1999 we got word that a child had been knocked down in O'Devaney Gardens, a flat complex in Dublin 7, close to the Phoenix Park. I went straight to the scene, arriving after an ambulance had removed the small, lifeless body of six-year-old Carla Fitzgerald and had taken her to Temple Street Hospital. I spoke to the gardaí who had been first at the scene. They had established that Carla lived with her family in a ground-floor flat and she was playing right outside their window. Her parents wouldn't let her go any further, to ensure her safety, so she was kneeling on the ground just outside the window, playing with marbles. A delivery truck had arrived and reversed onto the path. The driver had not seen little Carla on the ground and had unwittingly reversed right over her. She had no chance of surviving the accident.

I went to Temple Street Hospital and nervously waited for Carla's parents to arrive. I spoke to the matron, who said: 'It is very important that the parents view their deceased daughter; they will regret it later if they don't.' I didn't question her wisdom, I was simply grateful for this woman lending me her experience and expertise. It was a very emotional experience to see Carla's parents' grief as they came to terms with her death. I stood by them, silent, allowing them to get through those first waves of pure, horrendous shock. My heart went out to them, but I knew I had to stay firm, for them. I had no doubt that the matron had been exactly right, and that it had benefited those two broken people to have that time with their daughter.

Today, O'Devaney Gardens is no more. The flats were demolished to make way for a modern, sustainable housing project with all the amenities a family could want. I remember hearing a long-time resident being interviewed and they remarked how wonderful it was to have a garden at last, after all these years. I thought only of Carla Fitzgerald. I had always been struck by the thought that if she'd had a bit of garden to play in, she'd still be alive. Those flats had been built in the 1950s, in a part of Dublin that was not considered prosperous. Perhaps that was why they had squeezed the residents into a gardenless place that had no playgrounds or areas for children to play. I felt it made her death even more terrible that the place where she was born, over which she had no control, was part of the reason for her being killed at just six years of age.

Accompanying family members as they identify their deceased relation and attending at the subsequent post-mortem examination are far from pleasant experiences, but I viewed it as a privilege to be there. You have the chance to bear witness to this person's life and death and to ensure everything is done correctly. The way to approach a post-mortem is to put yourself aside and focus totally on the person. I was always happy to put myself forward and ensure that the deceased was treated in the proper manner in their death, that we did right by them. The same applies when we are called to scenes of sudden death, be they of young people or the elderly. If your approach and tone and demeanour are right, you can have a positive impact during that awful time in the aftermath of a death. I see this as part of our 'silent work'. The first member at the scene has a responsibility to the victim, but also to the living who are trying to come to terms with the death.

No different from the world of medicine, where doctors and nurses have to deal every day with the dying and those they leave behind, as a member of the Garda Síochána you have to have the capacity to deal with such traumatic incidents. I have been annoyed at times when I have seen members seek compensation after involvement in such an experience.

After four decades on the force, I can say that the most challenging experience as a garda is not the dead bodies you witness – either at crime scenes or in the pathologist's lab – it is dealing with the bereft living. It requires all your reserves of decorum and self-restraint to deal with the distressed relatives of the deceased, to see that human face of fear, distress, grief and shock. I am not haunted by the many victims and dead bodies I witnessed while doing my job; they do not keep me awake at night. If I am ever disturbed by memories, it is the memories of those left behind, those who were bent double by the pain of loss, those who cried with broken hearts, the tears coming from the very depths of them. But when those memories arise, alongside comes the calming knowledge that in those moments, myself and my colleagues did right by those people. We did not let them down. That is what every garda should be able to say at the end – that it was a privilege, and that they made a small difference when it mattered most.

The route to detective inspector lies via a spell as an inspector in uniform, so the logical and expected next step for me after the Bridewell was a posting somewhere in the north city as DI. That's not what happened. There were managerial changes in the North Central Division and I knew I didn't feature in the plans for the detective units there. I was given two options: go out to Tallaght as a detective inspector; or head into uncharted territory by joining a bureau that didn't exist yet. The Garda National Immigration Bureau (GNIB) was about to be established, so I could find a home there, if I wished. I thought it over and very quickly concluded that I didn't want the commute all the way out to Tallaght every day, so I chose the new bureau. I had no idea what the work would entail, but I was transferred there in May 2000 and into what would turn out to be the longest posting of my career.

Martin Donnellan had just been promoted to Chief Superintendent and he now became the first head of GNIB. Superintendent Mick Finn, who was one of the first to be assigned to a drugs unit as a sergeant, was appointed to the new bureau too, and I went in as one of its first two inspectors; Pat Clavin was the other. The team also included Sergeant Gerry Goff and two other sergeants, Angela Willis and Michael Cryan, both of whom I knew and trusted from working with them in Store Street. We were there on the very first day when the bureau became operational. None of us had been involved in setting up a bureau from scratch before, so it was a baptism of fire.

Our place of business was in Harcourt Square, where we took over a section of the Special Detective Unit called the Aliens Office. It was in this office that foreign nationals from outside the European Economic Area (EEA), then known as aliens and later as non-nationals, who intended to remain in the country longer than 90 days were required to register and be issued with a certificate of registration. Those who intended to reside in the Dublin area came to Harcourt Square; outside Dublin the registration office was the local Garda district headquarters.

For many years the Aliens Office at Harcourt Square included three counters for those presenting for registration in the Dublin area, more than enough to handle their cases. In the mid-1990s a total of about 12,500 foreign nationals were placed on the register. In 1999, however, that number suddenly rose to 17,000, then by another 10,000 the following year, and by an additional 30,000 in 2001. In 2005 the number reached over 135,000. By the time GNIB was established, there were long queues for registration at Harcourt Square, stretching all the way around the block to Camden Street.

But there was by then another queue that Ireland had never before encountered: foreign nationals who wished to make an application for refugee status. They queued at the office of the newly established Office of the Refugee Applications Commissioner (ORAC), at Lower Mount Street, now known as the International Protection Office (IPO). In

1992, there were 39 such applications; by 1995 that number had risen to over 400; by 1998 the number was approaching 5,000; and by the time the GNIB was established in 2000, it was well over 10,000 for that year alone.

It made me think of those snaking lines of people outside the American Embassy back in my Texaco days, all queuing to leave the country. This was a complete reversal: from being a land solely of emigration, Ireland had suddenly become a land of immigration. When my father joined the Garda Síochána in 1939, Ireland's population was slightly under three million; over forty years later, in 1981, as I was joining the organisation and he was leaving, the population had risen by less than half a million. During my 41 years of service it would increase by 1.7 million, to 5.2 million. In fact, included in those who were now adding to the population were some of those I had seen queuing at the US Embassy in the 1970s, who, along with their families, had returned to Ireland looking for a share of Ireland's booming economy.

As we were entering a new millennium, Ireland was progressing from being a country of emigration to one that was a desirable destination for immigrants. Our changed economic fortunes offered the prospect of employment not only to many more Irish nationals but also to people from other countries that were not matching our improving economic and social circumstances. However, our changed migration patterns had taken the state by surprise and it was scrambling to catch up.

The GNIB was part of that response, established to tackle an ever-growing number of law enforcement issues relating to immigration-related processes. As might be expected, we quickly outgrew Harcourt Square and the office moved to a new home on Burgh Quay, which we shared with the Immigration Division of the Department of Justice, later renamed as the Irish Naturalisation and Immigration Service and later again as Immigration Service Delivery. In the new building we had 13 counters dedicated to the registration process, and even so we saw the same long queues from early in the morning.

The speed and level of this change cannot be overstated. Ireland is an island nation, with family lines casting back hundreds of years, anchoring them to the land. It was a place to visit but not to live for those not born here. All through the twentieth century, Ireland struggled to gain independence, then struggled to gain an economic footing, struggled to forge a new identity as a republic – and through all this struggle, no one looked on us as a land of fantastic opportunity. Between the Church and the weather, we would have laughed dolefully at such an idea. But then came EEC/EU membership, and the change began, moving us towards a capitalist society of inward investment and ever-expanding exports. The country began to thrive. The economic success and the benefits of EU membership combined to turn Ireland into an attractive prospect, and naturally other people wished to come and live here and enjoy those same benefits.

For the brand-new GNIB team, this presented a huge learning curve in every single way. We had to learn about immigration and the role and best practice of an immigration bureau as well as a whole new lexicon of words we either had never heard of or hadn't ever had reason to use before, such as human trafficking, people smugglers, deportation and transfer orders, illegal immigrants and asylum-seekers. There was a whole world of people movement that Ireland had never encountered, and an underworld to go along with it, and we had to learn all of its parameters and pitfalls as quickly as possible. We also had to become fluent in the legislation governing immigration matters and the powers we had as gardaí. Since shortly before my father had joined the Garda Síochána, there had been one particular piece of immigration-related legislation that members were required to be familiar with: the Aliens Act of 1935. Now, within a short few years, a plethora of new legislation was enacted, including Immigration Acts of 1999, 2003 and 2004, the Refugee Act 1996 and the Illegal Immigrants (Trafficking) Act 2000.

And even then we found that the wording of legislation could be ambivalent – again, because it was not an area of expertise for Ireland. It was only in 1999, for example, that the legislation was updated to remove the word 'alien' and change it to 'non-national', which has since become 'foreign national'. It was an across-the-board learning curve as we designed and operated the bureau, and our work fed into other agencies.

We did have a legal basis to provide a foundation for the new bureau's work. The role of the Garda Síochána in immigration matters was set out clearly by the Supreme Court when it stated that it was in the interest of the common good of a state that it have control of entry of foreign nationals, their departure, their activities while in the state, and the duration of their stay. GNIB faced significant challenges in each of these areas. Immigration control at Dublin Airport was a much simpler task in the mid-1990s, when there were only about 3.5 million passenger movements in a year and very few attempts at illegal entry. By 2000, the airport had over 12 million passenger movements and attempts to enter the state illegally were commonplace, with ever-growing numbers being refused entry. While the majority of applications for asylum were made inland at ORAC, a considerable number were also made to immigration officers at Dublin Airport and other approved ports of entry to the state.

Ireland has fifteen approved entry points, including seaports, where persons who are not nationals of the common travel area (CTA) are required to land. This also applies to cruise ships, which must enter at a legal port first, before moving elsewhere. When the decision is taken not to allow a person to enter or to remain in the country, there are two options available: the first, refusing leave to land;

the second, issuing a deportation order. Refusal of leave to land is relatively straightforward because it is usually an immediate decision and the person doesn't get further than immigration controls at an approved port, including Dublin Airport. It can be based on a technicality, such as an expired visa or an out-of-date or missing passport. When that happens, an immigration officer can refuse leave to land and order the person to return to their port of departure on the next available flight.

One problem we tended to encounter in those cases was when the next available flight was some time away. If, for example, a person had arrived from Brazil, there might be only one flight per week, so they had to wait a week to go back. We had no detention facilities at the airport, so those waiting to return often had to wait out their time in Mountjoy or another prison. This was very far from ideal – I recall the Brazilian ambassador raising his concerns about this arrangement, and I agreed with him – but the state had not provided alternative suitable accommodation. The only other possibility was the single 'aliens' room' in Fitzgibbon station, which was located beside the station's two ordinary detention cells, but was different in that it had an ordinary door and an always-made-up bed. Throughout my father's career and mine in Dublin's C District, this one room was sufficient to deal with the very occasional person refused leave to land at Dublin Airport. But now, what normally happened was that we rang around the stations one by one, only to be told 'no room', until eventually we had to use Mountjoy or Dóchas. It was frustrating because the numbers being refused leave to land were no longer a handful per year but rather, in 2004 alone, nearly three thousand at Dublin Airport. Fortunately, that has changed since my time, with the opening of a new garda station at the airport in 2022, which has immigration-related detention facilities.

Once in the state, non-Irish nationals must carry certain documents and produce them if asked by a garda. Asylum-seekers get a temporary residence card and must also carry and produce it, if asked. The Gardaí have the power of arrest of any person suspected to be in Ireland without permission. Attempts to remain here by people who entered illegally or who remained illegally resulted in a proliferation of bogus travel documents, bogus work permits, bogus colleges and bogus marriages. False documents were a daily occurrence at Dublin Airport and other approved ports of entry, as we identified people travelling with forged papers and passports. They were often of an impressively high quality – and of course they needed to be to get through a state border. Once in-state, though, the quality of document-checking lessens and poorer-quality documents are frequently accepted without detection. We once found twenty bogus passports that arrived by post to Kiltimagh in County Mayo. They weren't of a quality that could get a person through the airport checks, but they would probably have been sufficient for opening a bank account. We also found fifty bogus birth certs issued in Nigeria – these were genuine documents and officially stamped, but left blank for information to be added. There was a constant flow of this type of criminality that we were trying to stem every day.

That said, it was also understandable. When a country becomes a desired destination for migrants, those living elsewhere in less desirable circumstances, particularly where employment prospects are poor or absent, will arrive in numbers. For some, like fellow residents of the EU, it will be uncomplicated – they are entitled to live and work here. For others who can take a legal route, it may involve obtaining a visa and work permit or an undertaking to study here. However, for others their only hope is to get into Ireland by some unlawful manner and live and perhaps work here as an illegal immigrant. Others may enter lawfully, perhaps as a tourist, but remain longer than permitted, and they join the ranks of those unlawfully resident in the state. Irish people should have no difficulty in understanding the phenomenon of illegal migration. How many young Irish nationals travelled to the USA, stating an intention to enjoy a holiday when in fact they had already planned to take up employment and to illegally remain resident in the country? We aren't in a position to judge others for their choices.

Preventing illegal immigration begins and is most effective if done at the frontiers of a state – its air and sea ports. Members of the Garda Síochána who perform immigration control duties at ports of entry to the state must first be appointed as immigration officers by the Minister for Justice. While there is an immigration-related interaction with every person arriving in the state at an approved port of entry, there is no routinely planned interaction with people as they leave the jurisdiction. When GNIB was established it was the responsibility of local Garda management to provide personnel to undertake immigration controls at a port that was within their district. In 2001, GNIB took over responsibility for immigration controls at Dublin Airport. The airport was expanding, with additional immigration facilities being regularly added to cater for the huge increase in passenger numbers.

The relatively small land border with Northern Ireland was also part of our remit. In the early days of GNIB, we observed that illegal immigrants were making their way in growing numbers into Ireland by crossing the land border with Northern Ireland. A unit was established by local Garda management and based in Dundalk. They were very efficient in detecting irregular movements of migrants across the border, but we encountered a problem when refusing leave to land at the border as there was no UK Border Agency presence there to receive those refused leave to land. At that time, the UK immigration authorities had no more than three officers in Northern Ireland and they were based in Belfast. The senior UK official with responsibility for Northern Ireland, who was based in Scotland, worked very closely with us in addressing any immigration matters that arose.

Over one particular bank holiday weekend, I became particularly frustrated by our inability to return to Northern Ireland any foreign national who was refused leave to land at the border. I took out the relevant legislation and noted that a person refused leave to land could be returned to the jurisdiction from where they had travelled and not necessarily at the point they entered Ireland. So over the weekend we drove those refused leave to land at the border to Dublin Airport and put them on planes destined for UK airports that would have a UK Border Agency presence. It caused a bit of a stir in airports such as Manchester and Liverpool, but the UK immigration authorities ensured the new plan worked.

In 1980, about forty people were refused permission to enter the state when they arrived at a port; that number rose only slightly to just over fifty in 1990. By 1997 the number had increased dramatically to nearly eight hundred, but in that year a new phenomenon arose – about fifty of the people refused made application for asylum. By the end of 2000, the first year in which GNIB was in existence, 2,777 people were refused leave to land, but 1,573 of those made an application for asylum and were consequently permitted to enter to pursue their applications.

You can apply for international protection in Ireland for two reasons. First, if you have a 'well-founded fear of being persecuted for reasons of race, religion, nationality, membership of a particular social group or political opinion', and you cannot seek the protection of your own country. This is called refugee status. The second reason is that you cannot return to your country because you are at risk of serious harm, but you do not qualify as a refugee. This is called subsidiary protection status. The international protection or asylum system is clearly essential to ensure Ireland provides protection for those who have fled desperate circumstances. But that system is also vulnerable to abuse by those who seek to enter the country but would not be granted permission were they to provide an honest account of their circum-stances, including their true nationality and most recent place of residence.

There can be many pull factors for migrants, but one is any weakness in a country's immigration controls. Such weakness is often referred to as having a 'honey pot' effect. News of poor immigration controls, or none at all, at a particular port will quickly become common knowledge among potential migrants, filling flights or sailings to that place. An asylum application process that fails to establish the true identity or circumstances of an applicant, or fails to detect stolen or bogus documents, or poorly implements a removal process, all have potential to fill the honey pot.

When GNIB was established in 2000, one particular weak point in our controls was at Rosslare Port, where in that year alone almost two thousand foreign nationals were refused leave to land. The state has to respond quickly to any weakness. In the case of Rosslare, GNIB engaged with the French immigration authorities and arranged that personnel attached to GNIB would be at particular French ports in advance of passengers boarding vessels destined for Ireland and provide advice as to which travellers would be granted leave to land on arrival in Ireland. This cooperation proved effective and for many years the numbers attempting to illegally enter Ireland through Rosslare Port were reduced to single digits.

Among the common deceptions discovered in the asylum process was 'nationality swapping'; an asylum-seeker would claim to be from a country of which they were not a national to boost their chances of success. Another common ruse was foreign nationals arriving on board a flight and destroying their travel document en route, often flushing it down the toilet. Upon presenting at immigration control, that person would make application for asylum, stating they had no travel document and were uncertain which flight had brought them to the country. When entered into the asylum process, they might then engage in nationality swapping. In some cases, applicants had lived in another European country for a period and had left before they were removed. The other regular deception we encountered was an adult applicant claiming to be an unaccompanied minor, ensuring entry to the state and a referral to Tusla, the Child and Family Agency. Having been provided with accommodation suitable for unaccompanied minors, the adult would leave soon after and illegally take up employment, which was the true purpose of their travel to Ireland. This scenario resulted in distorted statistics regarding the number of unaccompanied minors who had arrived but could not be accounted for.

Ireland's newly vibrant economy and the Irish-born child rule in legislation – that a child born in Ireland immediately became an Irish citizen – made it an extremely attractive destination for people from Nigeria. It got to the point where we were receiving 50 per cent of all Nigerian nationals who sought asylum in Europe. Other EU countries were receiving no more than 5 per cent, so the figures were completely disproportionate. When GNIB was established, the number of heavily pregnant women arriving at Dublin Airport was alarming. Frequently, immigration officers would have to seek medical assistance due to concern about the state of health of a heavily pregnant women and her unborn child. On one occasion we were informed that all available ambulances on the north side of Dublin were deployed to Dublin Airport due to the number of calls made to provide assistance to pregnant women who had just arrived in the country.

The fact that a person born in Ireland was immediately entitled to be an Irish citizen increased the likelihood that the child's parents would also be granted permission to remain in the state. This served as a major incentive for pregnant women seeking a better life for their child and themselves. Between the beginning of 1999 and the end of 2003, some 10,335 non-EEA nationals secured residency in the state on the sole basis that they had an Irish-born child. A total of 2,400, roughly 25 per cent, of these parents never claimed asylum.

One heavily pregnant woman arrived in the country, made her way into Dublin's city centre and ended up in the Rotunda, where she gave birth and then tragically died. She was far too advanced in her pregnancy for flying – that was a measure of her desperation. When we examined CCTV footage following her death she could be seen calling to the offices of GNIB and ORAC after hours, potentially to make a claim for asylum, but the offices were closed.

In 2004, the government decided to hold a referendum to address the Irish-born child issue. The twenty-seventh amendment of the Constitution Act was passed by way of referendum in June 2004. Turnout was high at 60 per cent and the amendment was passed by a majority of about 80 per cent. Consequently, as of 1 January 2005, a person born in the island of Ireland is not entitled to be an Irish citizen unless that person's parents have been resident in the island for a total of three years during the four years preceding that person's birth.

When a person arrives into Ireland seeking asylum, they must present themselves at the point of entry and state their case. They are brought to the International Protection Office, their details are recorded, they hand over their travel documents and then they must wait to be called for a more in-depth interview at a later date. After interview, background search and consideration of all the facts, the IPO then decides on the application for asylum. If it is accepted, the person enters into the immigration process at Burgh Quay. If it is refused, a deportation order is issued and the person is given a timeframe within which they must leave the state. They are now in the deportation process. This was one of the key reasons for the creation of GNIB – to process non-genuine asylum-seekers.

Human trafficking was first experienced in Ireland at this time, too, associated with illegal immigration, while people-smuggling was becoming a regular feature of the immigration process. The need to remove from the state those who were refused leave to land and others who were refused permission to remain and made subject of a deportation or transfer order was now a regular feature of the immigration process. Much of our work went on without people noticing it or commenting on it, but the most high-profile aspect of GNIB was undoubtedly the removals from the state.

A deportation order is a legal order to leave the state. The Minister for Justice can legally issue an Irish deportation order against anyone who is not an EEA national and is in Ireland without lawful permission. Back then, the process was unwieldy because the Minister for Justice had to personally sign every deportation order. In 2000, the minister was John O'Donoghue, a Kerryman, and we often had to send a car down to the back of beyond in Kerry to secure his signature on the document. The minister was always available and eager to sign, but thankfully the process changed a few years later to allow a senior official in the Department of Justice to sign the order. Once the order had been issued and signed, that gave us the power of arrest. We then had to arrange for the person to leave Ireland. The most common countries of origin for asylum-seekers at that time were Nigeria, South Africa and China.

The manner in which GNIB was structured was similar to other bureaus. It had an administration hub to deal with pay and personnel issues and correspondence received, and an intelligence analysis section, but it also had what was called the Arrangements Office. It bore similarities to the busiest of travel agencies. It was here that all deportation orders received from the repatriation section in the DOJ were stored. Their receipt triggered the making of travel arrangements for those who refused to comply with a request from the Minister for Justice to leave the state, their application to stay having been considered and refused. Each person being removed from Ireland having failed to comply with a deportation order was accompanied, or escorted, by members of the Garda Síochána, usually those attached to GNIB. Flight tickets for those being removed and those who would accompany them were obtained by staff in this office. A large whiteboard displayed the travel plans for each day, revealing travel on a wide scale across the globe, from China to Brazil, Nigeria and South Africa and many countries along the way. Shorter journeys to European countries, often involving the execution of Transfer Orders – the return of asylum applicants to the first EU country visited on their way to Ireland – were also included.

The Arrangements Office had another onerous task: attending the High Court for the all-too-frequent legal challenges to a decision of the minister to remove a foreign national from the state or to the manner in which the Garda Síochána was implementing that decision. There was a very high attrition rate due to the outcome of court proceedings and a need to ensure that any decision of the court was reflected in how future attempts at removal would be fulfilled. The Department of Justice regularly notified GNIB of its intention to charter an aircraft to remove foreign nationals to their country of origin as the number of deportation orders for nationals of particular countries grew in number. In August 2001, Minister for Justice John O'Donoghue travelled to Nigeria to sign an agreement making it easier for Ireland to deport Nigerian nationals subject to a deportation order back to Nigeria. The government had earlier entered into a similar arrangement with Romania and Poland, which were then yet to join the EU.

Over the course of my 12 years at GNIB, it was our job to deal with the law enforcement element of immigration. It was a hugely important part of the process because it ensured that citizens of the country felt protected and could trust that those arriving had been checked and welcomed – or else checked and refused entry and returned to their country of origin. It was a balancing of the scale – once we were seen to be dealing with those not deemed authentic or lawful, then people could see there was a measure of protection there and could trust the process.

For the mass deportation flights, the Department of Justice would hire a commercial jet and hope to fill it with anywhere between forty and a hundred people who had been refused leave to stay. A garda escort would travel with them. They were usually very calm flights, but there were incidents of violence over the years, and we had to handcuff some deportees for everyone's safety, but that was rare enough. I do remember one person who had hidden a blade on his person, which he swiped at one of the GNIB team, gashing his face and scarring him. But that was highly unusual.

At GNIB, the lower your rank, the more you got to travel – the opposite of what happens in most companies. I did go on one deportation assignment because I wanted to understand the experience and process first-hand. It was a single individual, who was being deported to Estonia. I went along on the flight with two fellow staff members. We always used a team of three for individual removals to ensure there were always two of us with the deportee at all times. That avoided a one-on-one scenario if someone had to go to the loo, for example, and it also avoided a man and woman being alone together. So the three of us sat with the gentleman and escorted him off the plane in Estonia and handed him over to the authorities. There was no return flight that evening, so we stayed the night in Tallinn and met with some local officers to discuss immigration matters.

The mass deportation flights rarely proceeded as planned. We would gather up to a hundred people, but if the flight took off with 80 per cent of those on board, that was a good outcome. Inevitably, appeals would be lodged with the High Court, the solicitors would be busy with the paperwork, and many of our deportees would not be on the flight. The hire price of the plane didn't change, of course, so it proved a costly exercise. This situation was greatly improved by the establishment of Frontex, the European Border and Coast Guard Agency. Frontex supports EU Member States and Schengen-associated countries in managing the EU's external borders and in the fight against cross-border crime. Ireland is not part of the Schengen Area, but in 2007 arrangements were made that allow Ireland to participate in the agency. For a number of years I was Ireland's representative at Frontex management board meetings.

The coordination of removal operations provided by Frontex was particularly helpful. One country would take a lead role in a removal operation. In 2009, for example, Ireland was the lead country for three charter operations involving participation by other EEA countries. In February, GNIB escorted 31 Nigerian nationals back to Nigeria, in an operation that involved participation by the UK, Switzerland and Germany. Two months later, we returned 25 Nigerian nationals, in an operation involving participation by UK, Spain, France, Sweden and Poland. Later in that year, in October, we escorted 44 Nigerian nationals home, in an operation in which Slovenia, Hungary and Norway participated. Chartered aircraft were used an additional five times that year in operations led by other countries to remove foreign nationals who were the subject of a deportation order. In one of the operations led by the UK, another 30 Nigerian nationals were removed to their country of origin.

While I saw deportations and mass deportation flights as an essential part of our work, the public and political view did not always tally with that. Migration is a complex issue that needs to be handled humanely, fairly and with great sensitivity. While the majority of people resident in Ireland welcome foreign nationals who arrive as immigrants, they expect the state to have appropriate controls in place to ensure only those who have a lawful right to enter Ireland can enter and remain. The deportation and removal processes are an essential part of the immigration process system. Ensuring an effective removal process is in place greatly helps in providing a balanced immigration strategy that will maintain the support of the majority of people. It was a balancing of the scale – once we were seen to be dealing with those not deemed authentic or lawful, people could see there was a measure of protection there and could trust the process. I would always emphasise prioritising the enforcement of deportation orders issued to people who had engaged in criminal activity while in Ireland and had received court convictions. That helped ensure we received public support for the manner in which we undertook immigration control-related functions.

The public view could be volatile, though. There was, on the one hand, a sense of relief that the immigration process was working to remove any threats. On the other hand, there was criticism and concern regarding the mass deport-ations. There was one particular deportation charter flight to Nigeria that was hyped up by the media and generated lots of negative feedback and a deluge of complaints to the Garda Press Office. RTÉ requested an interview and the assistant commissioner asked me to do it. I agreed. I spoke to Pat Kenny on his morning radio show and explained that the flights were not as depicted in the media. It wasn't a military operation of any kind – it was a perfectly normal charter plane that had probably just brought people home from Lanzarote, and was now hired for one of our flights. I emphasised that the wellbeing of the deportees was a priority, that there was a room at the airport where we brought them before boarding, where they were checked over by a nurse, a doctor and an independent monitor. There were no cells, no handcuffs (except for a few rare occasions) and they had all the food and medical aid they required.

I was reminded again of the wisdom of Lord Scarman, who advocated that as long as your information has a sound basis and you have nothing to hide, you can speak plainly and honestly and people will believe and trust what you are saying. What I was saying was true and accurate and I could stand over it. And evidently the people listening could hear that and believed me because within half an hour of that interview being broadcast, the Garda Press Office rang and informed me that the incessant phone calls had completely stopped. The truth had calmed the situation and reassured people that Ireland was not remiss in its responsibilities towards failed asylum-seekers.

In September 2014, the Minister for Justice and Equality announced a major programme to civilianise the immigration function at Immigration Control at ports, starting with Dublin Airport, where that function had until then been carried out by the GNIB. The plan was that immigration controls would be undertaken by Department of Justice personnel, thus releasing Gardaí for core policing duties. The minister said this initiative made sense 'both from an efficiency and economic perspective' and outlined details of a further major reform of the delivery of immigration services, which would see the transfer of the registration function for non-EEA nationals from the Garda Síochána, who up to then had statutory responsibility for this function, to the Irish Naturalisation and Immigration Service, since renamed Immigration Service Delivery. These initiatives have only been partially implemented, and with a questionable level of success. The civilian staff were not provided with investigative functions and cannot make arrests or investigate breaches of the criminal law discovered in the immigration function; this role remains with the Garda Síochána. However, the success of the two initiatives is possibly in need of review to establish if they are effective in preserving the integrity of the state's immigration processes. When GNIB undertook the task, we provided data on the number of persons refused leave to land, while the DOJ provided data on enforcement of deportation and transit orders. Now, the DOJ provides both, sometimes, it would appear, conflating the numbers, making it difficult to establish exactly how many deportation orders are being enforced. Before I left the position of head of bureau at GNIB, I submitted a comprehensive document outlining my view of how the immigration process should operate into the future, which was shared with the Department of Justice.

The Covid pandemic impacted significantly on the removal process, rendering it difficult to enforce deportation orders. Of course, the arrival process was also interrupted as there was a significant reduction in international travel.

However, I have wondered why later, at some remove from the pandemic, it appeared the removal process had slowed significantly, particularly with regard to the use of chartered aircraft. I listened with some surprise in April 2024 as the government announced the chartering of flights for mass deportation as if it was a new idea. If you live long enough, you really do see how everything is cyclical, and things just keep rolling around and around again, history repeating on and on, the lessons never really learned.

CHAPTER 8

A TRAGEDY IN WEXFORD

I n September 2001, when I had been at GNIB for sixteen months, we were sent additional personnel to help with the ever-growing workload. We received nearly 30 additional personnel, which was very welcome and shows just how busy the bureau had become. Among those new colleagues was Peter Cullen, my old friend from Texaco, who joined us as a garda. There was also Seán Cullen (no relation) – we had gone to secondary school together and then met on the day of the medical exam at Garda HQ, but had rarely bumped into each other since then. Seán joined us as a sergeant. The two of them subsequently joined our Document and Intelligence Unit, initially headed by Seán and later by Peter, following his promotion to sergeant, and Seán's to inspector. This unit proved to be a huge asset to the Bureau. And there was John Foudy, who had been in my class in the Training College at Templemore. He would take charge of an investigation unit at Dublin Airport.

On September 11 and 12 2001, I was attending meetings at the Europol headquarters in The Hague. After a morning meeting on the first day, the devastating news of the attack on the World Trade Center in New York broke. I immediately recalled my visit to the North Tower in 1999 and the discussion with FBI officers about the possibility of a repeat terrorist attack following the attack of 1983. It was a shocking event and naturally there were questions surrounding the 19 Al-Qaeda terrorists and how they had slipped through the net of checks designed to catch those who might pose a threat to national security. In the USA, the Transportation Security Administration was established to strengthen security at airports and on aeroplanes. There was a ripple effect as airport and flight safety was reassessed in countries around the world and new measures introduced. This applied at Dublin Airport as well, where the security procedure changed and passengers had to comply with new requirements, such as removing their shoes and carrying only small amounts of liquids.

Not long after the 9/11 attacks, I was scheduled to attend a meeting of the International Fraud Prevention Conference (IFPC) in Bermuda. Along with document experts from the Garda Technical Bureau I would deliver a presentation at the conference. They travelled via London, but I chose to travel via New York so that I could pay my respects to the 9/11 site at Ground Zero. I walked from Times Square down to the site. The newspapers in the stands I passed featured headlines about poisoning from the dust clouds that had engulfed Manhattan and the threat of more terrorist attacks. There was a palpable sense of fear and anxiety and I have to say I could feel it myself – I went on foot partly because I really didn't like the idea of getting on the subway. When I reached the site itself, it was still raw – papers blowing in the wind, photo boards with images of the missing, total disarray. It was deeply affecting and I felt a sense of connection to those 441 first responders and police officers who had lost their lives trying to help their fellow citizens.

The IFPC was a gathering of experts from around the world to discuss matters relating to immigration fraud. There was so much work to be done in this regard and the pooling of information and resources was incredibly helpful. One of the difficulties we had, however, was that Irish legislation did not keep pace with the fast rate of change – the criminals were always working hard to be a few steps ahead and we had to keep up. When I joined the force, the Aliens legislation was just a couple of pages in the *Garda Síochána Guide*, which contained all criminal law and yet could fit into a single-volume book. From the 1980s, the updates and new additions came thick and fast – there were EU Directives and laws and new legislation for new problems, such as drug-related crimes. They gave up publishing updates to the *Guide*; had they not, today it would run to a number of volumes. Of course, all legislation is now easily accessible on a desktop or laptop computer, a facility not available back in the day. At GNIB, we developed our own comprehensive course on immigration policing and legislation as our staff had a huge amount of legislation to understand and learn in order to do their jobs effectively.

There was an odd contrast between the constant updating and additions and, at the same time, the glacial pace of necessary amendments. Soon after I took up a role in GNIB I spoke to a senior official in the Department of Justice about a defect I had encountered while attempting to implement provisions of the Illegal Immigrants (Trafficking) Act 2000. In 1999, the Palermo Convention provided a definition of both human trafficking and people smuggling, however this was not reflected in the Act of 2000. The Act created an offence of 'trafficking', which was in effect smuggling, but required that a prosecution would provide proof of financial gain to secure a conviction. The Justice official acknowledged that the Palermo Convention had not been considered when the legislation was drafted. People smuggling refers to assisting people who wish to be assisted by arranging their passage to a particular country. There is no further relationship between the smuggler and their 'client' after this. Trafficking means the movement of people, including within a state, by another person or persons who seek to exploit the victim for gain. The most common types of trafficking are for sexual exploitation, labour exploitation or the harvesting and selling of body parts.

Eventually, in 2008 the Criminal Justice (Human Trafficking) Act was enacted, greatly improving our capacity to tackle human trafficking. However, over the years, I was like a broken record, repeating on a loop that the legislation had to be amended to properly provide for people smuggling. When I visited the Department of Justice in 2022, one of my last visits before retiring, one member of staff called out cheerfully, 'Good news, John, you have your offence of smuggling!' This was the Criminal Justice (People Smuggling) Act 2021, which was passed 21 years after the Palermo Convention, and 20 years after I first highlighted the need for both human trafficking and people smuggling to be provided for in a way that reflects the requirements of the Convention of 1999.

We now have copious legislation with regard to immigration and all its facets, but there is one thing the legislation cannot really help with, and that is figuring out who is a genuine claimant and who is not. That requires information, research, persistence, an open mind and a bit of gut instinct as well. This was one of the most challenging aspects of my work in GNIB, when a person claimed to be a victim of trafficking and we had to establish if that was correct. The case of Win Lin was one such challenge, and it became, I believe, the longest-running High Court habeus corpus application in the history of the state.

The man in question, Win Lin, was a Chinese national who had been arrested during a drug search of a premises in Dublin that had been turned into a cannabis grow house. He was charged with various drugs offences under the Misuse of Drugs Act 1977, as amended. He pleaded guilty to one offence and was in custody, awaiting trial on the others. He claimed that his detention was unlawful and that he ought not to be prosecuted as he was a victim of human trafficking.

The Administrative Immigration Arrangements for the Protection of Human Trafficking from 2008 conferred certain benefits on foreign nationals when there were reasonable grounds for suspecting they were victims of human trafficking. However, onus was placed on a person of superintendent rank or higher, in GNIB, to make an assessment as to whether the person was in fact a victim of human trafficking. The drug offences in respect of which Win Lin was charged were serious and potentially carried a long prison sentence if he was convicted. However, if he was a victim of human trafficking, this was also a serious offence – a culprit could potentially receive a life sentence. I considered all the facts of the case and concluded Win Lin was not such a victim. He then sought an inquiry by the High Court into the legality of his detention under Article 40.4 of the Constitution, otherwise referred to as a habeus corpus application.

The case was heard in the High Court and I spent nearly eight hours in the witness box, giving evidence. The proceedings were adjourned a number of times due to the extent of examination of the circumstances of the detention, which was why it ended up running on for so long. The judge was extremely thorough, concerned about the man's welfare and anxious to arrive at the truth. The defence strenuously criticised our assessment of the accused's status as a victim and I was cross-examined at great length and in great detail. But my reasoning was clear and fair: there was no evidence to support his claim that he had been trafficked. On the contrary, we discovered that he was surfing the internet regularly while working in the grow house and that he was able to come and go from the house freely. Most damning of all, we found a photo on his phone of him on Capel Street Bridge on St Patrick's Day, one arm around a garda and a big smile on his face as he enjoyed the day's celebrations. It was clear that if he had wished to sound the alarm and alert others to his predicament, he had ample opportunity to do so.

The case finally concluded when the judge accepted my assessment and agreed that the man was not a victim of trafficking. I was gratified that the judge made special mention of the fact that the GNIB investigation had been thorough and professional. The case illustrated the onerous responsibility on the Garda Síochána to make decisions, often split-second decisions with regard to arrests or pulling a trigger, which is a stark contrast to the length of time it can take a court to reach a decision. We don't have the luxury of time and comprehensive information, which is exactly why every aspect of policing needs the right people with the appropriate training and knowledge. This is very much the case in immigration, when lives and liberty are at stake and the issues involved have such far-reaching consequences.

During my time at GNIB, the worst case I had to deal with was a tragic incident that occurred in County Wexford. None of us had the requisite training and knowledge and we had to equip ourselves with information very quickly to be able to investigate the case properly. It is one of the cases that remains with me very vividly to this day because of the circumstances and the loss of innocent lives. It was an unprecedented event in the country, and in my career, when it occurred, and presented a difficult and complicated investigation.

On 8 December 2001, I got a call to say that the guards in Wexford had contacted GNIB regarding a number of people found dead in a freight container. When I heard it, my first thought was of an incident in Dover, in the UK, eighteen months earlier, when 58 people were found dead in a Dutch-registered truck that had travelled from Zeebrugge. There were only two survivors. This was the first incident of this kind for GNIB and our big concern was whether it was a once-off, or would prove to be part of a pattern. A team of detectives from GNIB and from the GNBCI were despatched immediately to Wexford to assess the situation. It was essential that we were able to call on the GNBCI for assistance because we were so newly formed and were only developing our investigative capacity. It was going to be a huge learning experience for us, and we would need their expertise in preparing the book of evidence.

We set up base in Wexford Garda Station, although my team would end up spending most of their time at Wexford General Hospital. We required an operation codename, so I instructed a member of the team to organise that. Back in my Store Street days, we came up with the codenames ourselves, but by now that had all changed and there was an office up in HQ, part of Security and Intelligence, that gave out the codenames for all operations in the country. The idea was to have a list of neutral words, which were handed out one by one as each request came in. When my staff member got back to me with our codename, we had been issued with the word Suitcase. That was entirely inappropriate for this particular case and I told him so in no uncertain terms. He went back to HQ and requested a new name. It became Operation Kindred.

Our initial investigation soon established the circumstances. A container of furniture had been brought to Graffignana, near Milan, in Italy. The container had departed on a truck at 5 p.m. on 30 November 2001 and was brought to Busto Arsizo, 35km north of Milan. It was loaded onto a train that departed at 9.30 p.m. on 1 December, headed for Cologne, where it arrived about nine o'clock the following day. From there, it travelled by road to Brussels and then on to Ghent and then to Zeebrugge, where it arrived at 12.30 p.m. on 4 December. It was loaded onto a ship and set sail for Waterford Port. It was one of over fifty containers, all of which were unloaded at Wexford at about 1 a.m. on 7 December, and it remained on a truck overnight.

On 8 December, the consignment was collected and driven to Drinagh Business Park in Wexford, arriving shortly after 9 a.m. It was only about fifteen minutes later that the site manager unsealed the container to unpack it. To his horror, he discovered 13 unresponsive people inside the container, tucked into gaps between the furniture. He immediately alerted the local gardaí, who took over the search of the container. They discovered that eight of the people were dead, and five were alive but close to death. All thirteen were taken to Wexford General – eight to the mortuary, and five to the hospital wards to be cared for and hopefully resuscitated. They were in poor physical condition and there was no way we could interview them to glean information about what had happened. That would have to wait, and in the meantime, we had to piece together the puzzle ourselves.

First, we took the fingerprints of the 13 people and circulated them at an international level, in the hope of identifying them. Then we concentrated on a technical examination of the contents of the truck. There were no passports or ID documents to tell us the nationalities of the people, but we did find lots of pieces of paper with what looked like telephone numbers written on them. It wasn't too much to go on, so I decided to make contact with police in Dover, to see if we could learn from their dreadful experience of the previous year. When I reached one of the investigators, I explained what we were facing in Wexford and he was extremely helpful. He told me to look for chemicals in the container as a possible cause of death and also to check for information sewn into the lining of clothing. Those shortcuts he provided turned out to be invaluable.

We searched the people's clothing and we did find papers sewn into the lining, scribbled with yet more phone numbers. That gave us 164 phone numbers in total. We then realised that efforts had been made to disguise the numbers and we had to carry out mathematical calculations to decipher them correctly. We were naturally very curious to find out why the phone numbers had been obscured in this way. We fed the numbers through to Europol, and the EU-wide database soon confirmed that the numbers corresponded to phones held by known members of OCGs that engaged in large-scale human smuggling. That proved this was a tragic case of smuggling or trafficking gone terribly wrong.

The other telling piece of paper in the container was the headed stationery of a furniture company in the UK. It suggested that the people in the container, and those who sealed them into it, had likely believed that the ship was UK-bound and had no idea that it was destined for Ireland.

That would have skewed their calculations on how long the people would be inside the container. As the investigation progressed, this was confirmed. The smugglers, and those being smuggled, believed the container was bound for the port of Dover, a journey by sea from Zeebrugge of about four hours. The journey to Wexford, on Ireland's east coast, took 54 hours. In all, the people in the container spent a period of 101 hours and 15 minutes sealed inside the container, with absolutely no means of escape. For us, this opened up yet more lines of inquiry and legality: where did the people enter the container? In which territory did they die? How would we prosecute the criminal acts involved and in which jurisdictions? It was a labyrinth of questions and potential answers, all with different outcomes for our investigation.

As the case had ramifications stretching beyond Ireland, we kept our European partners briefed on the investigation. Pro-Eurojust, the forerunner of Eurojust (the EU Agency for Criminal Justice Cooperation), had been established in March 2001. This multi-agency body, comprising national prosecutors, magistrates from all Member States, promotes cooperation on cross-border serious crime. Ireland's first National Member, known as our Correspondent, was Michael Mooney of the DPP's office, and we gave him regular comprehensive briefings. When we established that the eight dead people were Turkish nationals, that information was passed along to Pro-Eurojust, along with our other findings. The outcome was an agreement that the suspects be prosecuted in Belgium, which was the port of origin. All the other relevant jurisdictions would therefore make any evidence uncovered available to the Belgian authorities. This was the first case of the newly established Pro-Eurojust where a consensus decision of this nature was taken.

At the mortuary at Wexford General Hospital, preparations were made for Dr John Harbison, the state pathologist, to carry out the eight post-mortem examinations. I ensured that detailed notes of all the identifying marks on the bodies, such as tattoos, moles, scars, etc. were made. This would assist correct identification and help ensure that relatives would only be shown the body that most closely matched their description of their loved one.

The post-mortem examinations began on 10 December and were carried out quickly. I remember standing in the mortuary with those eight bodies laid out, and it was the most dead bodies I had ever seen in one place. Dr Harbison concluded that the cause of death for all eight was anoxia, or oxygen depletion, due to confinement in a sealed container. His opinion was that those who had perished had died two to three days before 8 December. We asked a marine engineer and ventilation expert to examine the container and its cargo, to ascertain the amount of air that would have been circulating in the container and available to the people concealed inside. He expressed the opinion that the peak fatality period was between 24 and 36 hours after the container was sealed. That suggested that the deaths possibly occurred between eight and 20 hours after the ship departed Zeebrugge. He also described how those who were hidden higher up in the container, nearer the roof, would have survived longer.

It pained me to think of the manner of death of those people. A death in a sealed container is a truly nightmarish scenario. The heat builds up inexorably, the air becomes denser and denser and hotter and hotter, until people start to strip off their clothes to try to cool down. Bodies and survivors are usually found in their underwear or naked. The heat is severe. Then, as the oxygen levels start to drop, there is the utter desperation of trying to breathe. The breathing becomes shallower, you are gasping for air. All the while, you are in total darkness – apart from phone lights, while the charge lasts. There is no air and there is no way out. It's a terrible death. The fact that there were children in that container who had experienced this made it all the worse. It was a distressing scene.

While the post-mortem examinations were being carried out, I received a call from UK immigration. They had been contacted by a person who was expecting a family member to arrive illegally at Dover. I was given the contact details and I rang him. Our conversation made me fairly sure he was connected to the Wexford finding. I made immediate arrangements to have him flown to Ireland, very helpfully facilitated by Ryanair. He arrived with his father and we brought them to the mortuary, where they made a positive identification. As we located relatives, we flew them in and accommodated them discreetly, keeping them well away from the media. They did not speak any English, so we very carefully sourced interpreters who we were sure were not in any way associated with smugglers.

This was all happening in the run-up to Christmas, which provided a stark contrast to the heavy sense of loss and sadness surrounding the investigation. There was a GNIB Christmas party in Dublin, but I had a relative of a victim arriving in Wexford the following morning. I didn't tell the team. I thought, let them have their time off and I'll leave early and take care of it. I returned to Dublin that evening but skipped the party and made my way down to Wexford General very early the next morning. To my surprise, Mick Finn, my Super, was already there before me. He knew this man was arriving, and he knew I'd be there, but it was a mark of respect for him to be present. I was impressed by that gesture. The man we met had travelled over from Turkey. I could tell he was the sort of man who had never left his parish in his whole life – he reminded me of old neighbours of my relations down in West Cork who lived and died in the one locality. This was the first journey he had undertaken in his life, and it had brought him to the mortuary in Wexford, where he identified his relation. It was a very, very sad sight and my heart went out to him.

The Turkish people who died in the container were: Saniye Guler (29) and her children, Imam (nine) and Berkan (three), from Elbistan, in southwest Turkey; Hasan Kalendergil and his children, Zeliha (10) and Kalendar (12), from Pazarcik; Yuksel Ucaroglu of Antep, southeast Turkey; and Mustafa Demir of Aksaray.

All five survivors who were treated at Wexford General regained consciousness and their health improved. When the doctors cleared them for interview, we took statements from all of them. They were able to fill in all the remaining gaps in the story. They had all stayed at a hotel in Brussels, then were brought by taxi to a truck stop at Groot-Bijgaarden, 10km north of Brussels. There they met their smugglers – they had seen their faces clearly and were able to provide descriptions. The men cut the seal on a particular container that was loaded on the back of a parked truck and helped the 13 to climb inside. This was at 4 a.m. on 4 December. The 13 were reassured that their journey to the UK would take 'only three hours'. They described the hours passing, being buffeted by stormy waters in gale force winds, the fear and the panic starting to rise. Some were vomiting, some were fainting. It became more and more difficult to breathe and some of them passed out. It was an unending terror, trapped in the container, no airholes, no way out.

While we gathered all the evidence we could in Wexford, our European counterparts were tracking the smugglers.

The crew of the ship that transported the container, a mix of Russian, Ukrainian and Dutch nationals, were interviewed and the Belgian police were satisfied that they had no knowledge of the people in the container. These were not the targets. The Belgian police focused on the suspected smugglers and about ten days after the opening of the container in Wexford, the first suspects were arrested. A number of premises were searched. The Belgian police compiled a photo album of suspects and we showed these to the survivors, mixed in with photos of non-suspects, to see if they could identify anyone. They were able to do so and the evidence mounted.

In February 2003, the criminal trial of eight defendants commenced in Bruges. They were charged with manslaughter, being members of a criminal gang, human trafficking and involuntary assault. The prosecution argued that the eight defendants were part of an Albanian-led trafficking gang that had been responsible for smuggling hundreds of people from eastern Europe to the UK. The fifty hours inside the container endured by the dead and the survivors were set out in detail before the court. The smugglers had given them some cheese and eighteen bottles of water as their total provisions for the journey across the sea. The container had been placed close to the ship's engine, generating torturous levels of heat inside. There were four vents in the roof, but they weren't enough to provide sufficient oxygen for survival. Our marine engineer expert gave evidence, as did a number of gardaí. It was interesting to observe how the Belgian court operated – the minimum number of in-person witnesses possible, which made the proceedings much more efficient than we were used to in the Irish judicial system.

At the conclusion of the trial, a London-based Turkish national and six Belgium-based Kosovars and Moroccans were each convicted to between two and ten years in prison for their roles in the smuggling operation. The longest sentence was given, in absentia, to a Serbian man called Bekim Zogaj. This man, who was not in court and had not been located in order to be arrested, then spent the next ten years on the run, evading his sentence for what had happened to the 13 people in the container in Wexford. An Interpol arrest warrant was issued for him.

It turned out that Zogaj, who could speak 11 languages, took the name Aniello Vinciguerra and travelled to Australia in 2014, where he quickly hooked up with a group of Albanian men who moved around the country cracking ATMs and stealing their contents. They were estimated to have stolen about half a million dollars in this way before being apprehended. Zogaj vociferously protested his innocence at his trial, but he was sentenced to 15 years by the Australian court. When that sentence has been served, he may well be extradited to serve out his Interpol arrest warrant for the smuggling operation that killed eight people.

It was a harrowing case, but it was very satisfying to see those involved get time behind bars for their role in the smuggling. We couldn't save the lives of those who died in that container, but we could honour their lives, and the survivors, by pursuing the smugglers and seeing justice done. That was one of the most difficult cases I dealt with at GNIB, and it was certainly a challenge given that it was our first experience of this sort of tragedy. I am very glad and relieved to say that it did not form part of a pattern, as we had at first feared, and we never again faced that sort of situation at Irish ports during my time at GNIB.

There is one final instalment in this story. Some years later, in September 2005, I was in my office at GNIB headquarters on Burgh Quay when one of my staff came to tell me that there were two men in the building sorting out some issues regarding their immigration status, and the staff had recognised them as being two of the survivors from Wexford. I asked for them to be brought directly to my office. Two young men in their twenties, glowing with good health, stepped into my office. It was such a pleasure to see them looking so well and settling into their new home. I shook their hands and told them how delighted I was to see them looking well and happy. I told them about my first sighting of them – lying in hospital beds, close to death, having endured that hellish journey. We spoke about that time, and their lives since then. I was able to perform one final gesture of help for them, by ensuring they left GNIB with the documentation they required regarding their immigration status. It was at least a partially happy ending to a very sad tale.

CHAPTER 9

THE UNFORGETTABLE CASE
OF TWO SISTERS

While working at GNIB, I applied for another promotion, this time to superintendent. In December 2002, at my second time of asking, I was informed that I had been placed first on a list, with twenty-three other successful candidates, for promotion to that rank. This was soon followed by the news that from January 2003, I would be serving as district officer at Swinford, County Mayo. I can't say I was exactly delighted to have to move so far from home. I had known a rural posting was likely, but I hadn't expected to be 135 miles away from my young family. I was a regular traveller to Westport and I knew and loved Mayo well, but it was still a big wrench in personal terms. Nonetheless, it was what I had signed up for, so I got on with it.

At that time, in 2002, the county was divided into five Garda districts, one of which was headquartered in Swinford. There were five garda stations in the Swinford district: Ballyhaunis, Kiltimagh, Charlestown, Kilkelly and Foxford. Swinford is a former market town, a 20-minute drive from Mayo's county town, Castlebar. As superintendent I would be the district officer, based in the district headquarters in Swinford. I had been a long time policing in the city and perhaps had forgotten the nature of rural policing. After the fast-paced drug wars of Store Street and then the fast-changing world faced by GNIB, Swinford was somewhat of a culture shock. I had been used to travelling to meetings in Brussels, The Hague, Lyon, London, but now I was driving down fuchsia-lined back roads where I was held up by sheep being moved between fields, not by lads with sawn-off shotguns or syringes. I had been at the forefront of a rapidly changing Ireland for the past 16 years, dealing directly with drugs and immigration issues, but now in Swinford I stepped back into the other Ireland, where old traditions still held firm and the guards were called upon, but not usually for anything too serious. It was a very different world, and while I might have missed the hectic pace of the city, it was also nice to see that the quieter, slower Ireland was still there.

Back up in Dublin, my former colleagues were entertained at the idea of me in an 'easy' country station. Swinford had its own courthouse where the District Court sat and there was a hearing there one day regarding a theft from a farm. Some likely lads had made off with eight ducks and some hens, their criminal mastermind plan being to sell them to get some quick cash to buy drink. The postman dropped in the post to the garda station one morning and there was a large envelope addressed to me. I opened it and inside was a copy of a newspaper article with the heading: 'Swinford man stole eight ducks from farmer.' A Dublin-based detective superintendent who had sent it to me attached a note reading, 'John, what efforts are you making to curb the dramatic upsurge in serious crime?'

I could just picture them in Store Street and the offices of GNIB, enjoying a laugh over the major crimes I was now investigating. It was a far cry from drug raids and deportation orders and days in court with Tony Felloni, that was for sure. It reminded me of my time in Rathangan – the types of crimes we encountered and the manner in which we investigated and policed them. But very unexpectedly, that all changed in August, when our small corner of Mayo suddenly came under the national spotlight because of an unusual death that sparked headlines.

On Bank Holiday Monday, 5 August, I was driving back to Swinford from Dublin, leaving my family behind once again. It was a beautiful evening and being alone in the car meant I could indulge in the music I liked to listen to, so *Home* by the Dixie Chicks was keeping rhythm with the road as I drove. At about the halfway mark between Dublin and Mayo, I clicked to the radio to catch the latest news bulletin. The first item was breaking news: an elderly woman had been found dead in a house near Ballyhaunis, suspected to have been dead in the house for a number of weeks, and the gardaí were examining the circumstances surrounding her death. The news reader said that the woman's body had been removed to Mayo General Hospital for a post-mortem.

I hadn't received a phone call to notify me of the death, so I presumed that meant the townland where it occurred fell into another district, I guessed Claremorris. But I made straight for the station once I reached Swinford, and I was surprised to find a number of guards from Ballyhaunis station were there already. It appeared the death had occurred within my jurisdiction after all. They briefed me on what was known so far: at about 11 a.m. on 5 August, a man called Michael, also known as Sonny, had called an ambulance to the bungalow he shared with his two sisters. All three were in their sixties and seventies. Michael had discovered his sister Agnes's dead body in her bedroom. What worried me even more was that his other sister, Mary Ellen, had been taken to hospital – was this a case of physical abuse?

I was still processing the information and catching up on events when a garda called me aside and told me that Jim Fahy, the RTÉ News western correspondent, had been on to the station already, asking questions, particularly asking if there would now be a criminal investigation, given that it was an offence to conceal a dead body. I was still on the back foot regarding clear information at this point, but that question made me feel uneasy – there was something very peculiar about this case and it seemed others knew it before I did. Naturally, I wanted to see the scene for myself, but the gardaí who attended at the house had quickly concluded that there was no foul play, so the body had been removed to the hospital. I wouldn't be able to see Agnes's deathbed scene in full, which was unfortunate, but I could still go to the house to glean as much information as possible.

I drove out to Aghamore and started by speaking to relatives who lived close by. They told me that they had not seen the sisters for a long time. They did call to the house to see Sonny, but the sisters remained out of sight in their room. One relative told me that his last sighting of Mary Ellen was about ten years before, although sometimes he'd talk to her from outside the house when she was in the kitchen. He had seen Agnes about three years before, when a relative was being waked. Agnes had insisted no one else be present in the house when she visited. That was the last time he saw her. So we were looking at the lives of two deeply reclusive women, who lived in their own tiny world within the four walls of their bungalow.

I went over to the bungalow. The house itself was fine and normal, but the 'girls' bedroom', as Sonny called it, where the two women had remained hidden from the world, was an appalling sight. I had wondered about the smell of a corpse over the course of a few weeks – how did no one realise? But now I realised that it must have been easily masked by all the competing odours in that room. There was mouldy food, dirty dishes, urine – it was distressing to see how Agnes and Mary Ellen had been living. Years of debris and dirt caked every surface. I hadn't seen anything like it before – and I haven't since, for that matter.

Over the course of that day, I built up a more detailed picture of what had happened in the house. Even though all three siblings lived there, they did not live together, in that Sonny rarely saw his sisters. He left food for them outside their door, but they stayed out of sight and didn't speak to him often. On this morning, Sonny had got up about 10 a.m. and was walking towards the kitchen when he heard noises from the bathroom. The previous night he had spoken to Mary Ellen through the bathroom door, and she had asked him to boil some water and leave it in a jug outside the door. He had done this. Now, the noises from the bathroom caught his attention and he noticed the jug of water was still there, still full but now stone cold. He cautiously peered into the bathroom and saw Mary Ellen sitting on the floor. It had been so long since he had seen her, he was surprised by how grey her hair was. One look at her told him she was unwell, and he hurried to get Agnes to help her.

Sonny went to the bedroom and opened the door. He had not entered this room for twenty years, but this was an emergency, so he stepped inside. He could see a shape in the bed and called Agnes's name, but there was only a deep silence. When he stepped closer, he realised that what he was looking at was at a body so skinny it looked like a skeleton, with clothes hanging from its bones. In shock, he left the room and called the local doctor's surgery, telling them that he thought Agnes might be dead and that Mary Ellen was very unwell.

At 11.30 the GP arrived and went into the bathroom. He could see that Mary Ellen had injuries on her legs and bruising on her forehead. He went over to the girls' bedroom and saw Agnes, who was lying on her back on the right-hand side of the bed, leaving the space on the left where Mary Ellen slept. To his horror, the GP saw that Agnes was in a decomposed, skeletal state. Due to her condition, he could not get Mary Ellen to tell him anything about her own injuries, or how and when Agnes had died. He called an ambulance and Ballyhaunis Garda Station. When the gardaí arrived, the GP officially pronounced Agnes's death at 11.46 a.m. Mary Ellen was brought to Mayo General and Agnes to the hospital mortuary. That was the first time the sisters had been separated in many years.

It was frustrating that the scene had been cleared so quickly, but all present, GP and gardaí, were sure that there was no evidence of trauma or foul play. It was a natural death, albeit the body was kept in the room in the most unnatural circumstances. My own gut instinct was that this was likely a human tragedy, underpinned by mental health issues, and I knew we had a duty to protect the siblings as well as to find the truth of what had happened in the house. There were plenty of questions that needed to be answered, but I knew that it was necessary to take firm control of the investigation to avoid unwelcome media intrusion or speculation.

I got into the station bright and early the next morning, ready to get to work. I met with the investigating team and set out our priorities for them. First, we would establish the cause of Agnes's death and the date and time of her death. Second, we would establish the cause of Mary Ellen's injuries. Third, we would establish if the sisters had chosen to stay in the house or had been prevented from leaving, and prevented from calling a doctor to help them. I was acutely aware that if Mary Ellen's very poor state of health was the result of criminal actions, that would place heavy suspicion on the circumstances around the death of Agnes. While the gardaí at the scene and the GP had assessed there was no foul play involved, we had to uncover all the available evidence to prove or disprove that belief. Hunches weren't going to be good enough.

My next step was to call in more help. I was lucky that a divisional search team had recently been set up in the Mayo division, to ensure the availability of well-trained and experienced personnel with regard to gathering and preserving evidence. This team had advanced training in crime scene examination and could find any shred of evidence left at a scene. So I now asked them to join our investigation and perform a painstaking search of the bungalow and, in particular, of the layers upon layers of debris in the bedroom where Agnes had lived and died. I felt certain that the answers – or at least most of them – lay inside the bungalow, beneath the years of stuff and mess that had accumulated. It just needed a centimetre-by-centimetre search to unearth them.

The team assigned to the investigation spoke to every potential witness who knew the siblings and we began to understand something of their extraordinary lives. It turned out that all three of them had left Mayo in the 1950s and gone to the UK in search of work. About ten years later, Agnes returned home to care for their elderly parents in the family home. Michael followed in 1965, and then Mary Ellen in 1968. Mary Ellen had worked as a nurse and had lived a normal life in the UK. Their mother died in 1974 and their father in 1978, and the three continued to live in the house they had inherited.

In 1999, a doctor had to call to the house when Sonny was confined to bed with illness. Mary Ellen came into his bedroom to tidy it for the doctor's arrival. This seems to have been the last time they met face to face before the morning in the bathroom. Sonny ended up spending three days in hospital at that time, and another few days the following year, in 2000. When he arrived home from that stay, Agnes stood at the doorway to the living room and asked him if he was feeling well. That was the last time he ever saw Agnes alive. From what we could gather, Mary Ellen hadn't left the house since around 1993 and Agnes since 1999. Every day, Sonny left to do his farm chores, locking the back door behind him. When he returned, he shouted out a warning, so the sisters could retreat to their room. While he was gone, they prepared a meal in a pan and left it for him to cook. He would cook it and leave two plates of it outside the kitchen door. As he ate, the plates would be collected quietly and brought to the bedroom. He never laid eyes on his sisters during these inter-actions. It must have been like living with two ghosts.

Meanwhile, the assistant state pathologist, Dr Margaret Bolster, was conducting a post-mortem examination on Agnes's remains at her lab in Cork. As the body had been removed and it was not possible to conduct an examination at the scene, it was agreed that it could be brought to Cork for assessment. I received two welcome pieces of news. The first was that Dr Bolster had not found any evidence of skeletal trauma. She warned me that determining an exact date of death would be difficult, but in her estimation Agnes had lain dead in her bed for months, not weeks, as was originally presumed. The second piece of good news came from Mayo General, where the consulting surgeon was able to confirm that Mary Ellen's injuries were not caused by an assault, but rather were the result of untreated ulcers and falls.

While we were slowly piecing together an accurate picture of this very sad state of affairs, the media was eager to get any snippet of information about the family. There was morbid speculation about the length of time Agnes had been dead, with tabloid newspapers pushing the line that her death had been concealed so that her siblings could keep collecting her state pension. It added stress to grief and I was concerned about the effect on Michael and Mary Ellen if they heard this tumult of rumours and guesses. I think people – and those in the media – sometimes forget that the Garda Síochána has a duty of care to the family members in cases like this. We are trying to establish the facts of the matter, but we are also trying to limit allegations and gossip and speculation that could cause distress and could, ultimately, affect a trial. It's a difficult balancing act at the best of times, and with a story like this, which many people saw as sensational, it was even more of a challenge. But we owed it to Agnes, Mary Ellen and Michael not to jump to rash conclusions. There was enough grief there for them, other relations, neighbours and friends already without it being added to by wild speculation.

The search team were sifting through the contents of the bedroom shared by Agnes and Mary Ellen. One of the key finds was a huge number of notes scribbled on bits of paper and on those perforated sections of cardboard boxes that hold things like teabags and tissues. The sisters had pressed through and torn off the perforated sections, then used them to write diary-like notes. Agnes had written notes to particular saints on their feast days, telling them of the poor health of herself and her sister. As more and more notes were recovered and read, it became clear that the sisters had been declining in health for some time, but were fixed on one common goal: not to be separated from each other. There were some heart-breaking notes that spoke to their state of mind. One read: *Pray for us not to be separated from each other, not even to have to go to hospital.* Another read: *We don't want to be separated not even to my going to hospital, please ask that for us.* And another: *Don't bring Sonny back here until he is well, we are not able to look after him and no doctor can call here.*

There was another note that Sergeant Breslin was keen to show me. Agnes had corresponded with some religious organisations. There were notes from the Holy Rosary Convent in Cavan town, obviously replying to notes received from this room. On 9 January 2003 one such read: *Dear Miss Lyons, thank you for the gift of €10 for ourselves. Very kind of you. You have my sympathy on Una Lyon's death. May the light of heaven shine on her. May you and all who miss Una be comforted.* Another letter from the same convent read: *Dear Miss Lyons €50, 8 masses for the happy repose of the soul of Una Lyons. May she rest in peace.* It was possible the nuns in the convent knew of, or had even met, Agnes and Mary Ellen, and might also be able to shed light on the identity and death of Una Lyons.

Resources were scarce, with only one detective assigned to the Swinford district. However, I was a former detective and I was anxious to get answers as soon as possible. So I took on a detective role myself and drove to Cavan a day or two later and went to the Holy Rosary Convent to visit the Missionary Sisters of Our Lady. I had an appointment to talk to Sister Dympna. I explained the story to her and said that I hoped she might have some knowledge of the sisters, perhaps even their correspondence, which might contain valuable information for the investigation. With regret, she told me that she was unable to help because they did not keep correspondence. Once a response was issued and the request recorded, the original letter was destroyed. I was about to leave when she suggested it might be worth asking Sister Alacoque, who was in charge of correspondence. I sat in the waiting room, wondering if this was all a waste of time.

Sister Alacoque, an elderly nun, came to speak to me and to my astonishment she confessed that she had broken protocol with the letter received from Miss Lyons. The convent had a list of requests received from Miss Agnes Lyons dating back to 1951. The original letters were all destroyed, but a note was kept on each request. However, one letter was kept. It read: *Dear Sisters, Please pray for the soul of Una Lyons R.I.P, died last 2002. I am sending €50 to have Masses for her*

soul. *Thanking you, Sincerely, Grieving. (€10 for yourselves).*
Sister Alacoque told me that something about it made her
uneasy: 'I sensed something unusual about the letter.' It was
the way the person signed as 'Grieving', without signing their
name – for some reason, that struck the nun and she decided
to keep that particular letter. This was the letter she replied
to on 9 January 2003, which we had found in the bedroom.
I gave silent thanks for people like Sister Alacoque who act
on their gut, their sense of unease. I imagine a huge number
of gardaí have done the same over the years, grateful to the
person who followed their gut feeling and ended up being
able to shed light on an aspect of a case.

I thanked Sister Alacoque for her help and, before leaving,
asked her if she had any knowledge of who Una Lyons might
be. She said she didn't personally know the Lyonses, so she
couldn't say, but then she looked at me and gently said: 'Of
course, Superintendent, you are aware that the name Agnes
in the Irish language is Una.' Oh. I managed to compose
myself enough to reply, 'That's very interesting ...' without
admitting that the superintendent in fact had no idea that
Una was Agnes. I left the convent and was deep in thought
the whole way back to Swinford, going over all that we had
learned. I would have to await the scientific conclusion of the
pathologist, but this evidence pointed to Agnes having died
sometime in 2002 and that it was Mary Ellen who, left alone
in the bedroom, was requesting a mass be said for her. The

fear of separation had led the two women to an otherworld where death had no dominion, as the poet says. It was very difficult to understand, but easy to pity.

On return to Swinford, I received an update on the search of the bedroom at Aghamore. A note of considerable significance had been discovered and was shocking in its simplicity: *Agnes R.I.P. 13 Sep. 2002.* When Sergeant Breslin of the search team showed it to me, we looked at one another as the terrible realisation dawned – if the note was accurate, it was possible Agnes had been dead for many months before Sonny found her. Looking around that cramped room filled with detritus and dirt, where the two women had sequestered themselves, it really didn't bear thinking about.

We were still waiting for the post-mortem tests to tell us where, when and how, but by now we were fully satisfied that Agnes had died of natural causes. There was no call for a criminal investigation. I had been waiting patiently for the doctors to tell me that Mary Ellen was fit to be interviewed and that finally came in October 2003. I met Mary Ellen, with a female garda present as well to reassure her. My first impression was how well she looked after the ordeal she had lived through. I asked my questions sensitively and with care, and she answered politely in a quiet but deliberate manner. She described how Agnes became more and more reclusive as the years passed. Her health kept declining, to the point where she became unable to eat. She wanted me to know that their brother was good to them and had never treated them roughly in all their lives. Michael did not know what went on in that room, and he did not know Agnes was sick.

When I tried to find out about Agnes's death, Mary Ellen ran out of words – she had no memory of Agnes dying, no memory of any letters or notes to or from the convent. Her brain seemed to shut out that part when death put a gulf between them she couldn't cross. Before I ended our meeting, I asked Mary Ellen to provide a sample of her handwriting, which she did. When she left, we compared it to the note that read: *Agnes R.I.P. 13 Sep. 2002.* It matched.

It took until January 2004 for the full post-mortem report to be completed. Samples from the body had been sent to various expert labs in the UK and France for further analysis. The final opinion was that it was 'quite possible that she was dead for almost a year'. It tallied with the trail of evidence we had followed.

On foot of the report, the county coroner, John O'Dwyer, scheduled an inquest to be held on Monday, 16 February 2004 at Westport Courthouse. We knew this would attract media attention, so it had to be handled carefully. I prepared a comprehensive report for the inquest. It wasn't a typical inquest report. I knew we needed maximum accountability to end the speculation. So instead of the usual short file of facts, I wrote up a very detailed file to show unequivocally that this case didn't involve fraud and it didn't involve criminality of any kind, that it was, rather, a very tragic case and the family required support and privacy.

On the day of the inquest, the courthouse was, as we feared, teeming with media. I was very concerned about Mary Ellen, who was required to be present, so I organised for her to be brought to the courthouse separately, and to enter the building out of public view. She then remained in an adjacent room until she had to give evidence. I was called first to give my evidence, and I set out clearly the facts of the case and described the circumstances in which the sisters lived, and how those strange circumstances were freely chosen by them. I noted that Agnes was in poor health for a long time and had died in bed of natural causes. I described the room the sisters lived in – unheated, damp, squalid, a breeding ground for illness. I left no room for doubt.

When Mary Ellen was called, a silence descended on the courtroom. I was still in the witness box and I watched as she quietly entered the court. She walked forward and took a seat right behind her brother, Michael. I watched him turn around to look at her – he had not seen her since that awful morning when he had found her in the bathroom and then found Agnes' body. I could see that he spoke some words to her, but I was too far away to hear them. Mary Ellen simply had to confirm that her statement was correct – the court asked the bare minimum of her. After a life of seclusion, everyone was aware that this would be a hugely anxious experience for her and she was treated with great kindness.

In conclusion of the case, the coroner said: 'Agnes's death has caused sorrow, grief, speculation, media intrusion, accusations, bewilderment and profound sadness. May we look on this death with compassionate rather than judgemental hearts; may she rest in peace.' Afterwards, the coroner served my report on the media, to ensure the full story was out there and there could be no queries or question marks. It was over, and there it ended.

The investigation and the story of the Lyons sisters has stayed with me ever since. It was not a case you could forget. As with the post-mortem examinations I have attended, I felt it was a privilege to bear witness to their lives and Agnes's death and to ensure the truth won out and they were not punished further. It was an unfathomable way to live, but I suppose the women's fears and anxieties had grown larger together and engulfed them, until the point that being apart seemed like the worst thing in the world. That thought, that threat, became worse than the reality of the room they were living in. Their anxiety had created this tiny safe space, their bedroom, and they couldn't leave it. They were clinging on to each other like life rafts, desperately tried to evade whatever storm they could see raging around them. To this day, when I press out the perforated cardboard section of a teabag box, my mind is transported to that room. I think of those two women, who lived one life away and then came home to ignore life altogether. I think of those hundreds of scribbled notes on the bits of cardboard and, in particular, of the one written by Agnes that said simply: *I cannot be separated from my sister.*

PART 4

PATROLLING THE BORDERS
(2004-2015)

CHAPTER 10

AN UNEXPECTED TASK: DISASTER RESPONSE

I n 2004, there was talk among the senior ranks of the Gardaí about imminent retirements and promotions. There are always whispers of gossip and speculation around reshuffles, and the word being whispered about me was that I would be moved from Mayo back to Dublin, and into the Garda National Drugs Unit. There would be a vacancy in the superintendent spot there soon and the guesswork was that I'd be moved there. I was thinking that was likely myself. So it came as a surprise when I was informed that the detective chief superintendent and one of his detective superintendents were being transferred out of the GNIB, and I was being returned there. Like any policeman, I did not express surprise or question the order, I simply packed up my desk at

Swinford, enjoyed a farewell party with my colleagues there and returned into the fold of GNIB, the old familiar.

There are always two superintendents in GNIB: one based in HQ at Burgh Quay, one at Dublin Airport. I was lucky to be assigned the airport beat, which meant I had an office at HQ but spent a lot of my time out at our office in the airport. This made the job more enjoyable for me because I loved working at the airport. I had grown up in the shadow of it, living in nearby Santry, accustomed to the drone of engines overhead, so it felt part of the landscape of my life. I have always loved travelling as well, and for me, going out to the airport and being part of that world in transit was one of the joys of embarking on a journey. It was enjoyable to be part of the behind-the-scenes crew who run the airport 24/7, all year round. It is a world in itself, constantly busy, always unpredictable, and I thrived in that environment.

When you become a garda, they can only teach you so much in Templemore. No mentor could ever prepare you for every scene you will encounter in the course of your career. In fact, so much of what you come to know and understand can only be learned on the job, because it is a job that delivers the unexpected on a fairly regular basis. For some, that's an attraction, for others it's a challenge. We do our level best to step up to every new task. That year, 2004, just months after getting back to work on immigration matters, I would be asked to take on one of the most challenging roles of my career – and there was nothing that could have prepared me for it.

That December, I was hoping for a Christmas miracle in the form of a quiet spell when I could spend time with my family. It had so often been the case that the pace quickened at the end of the year, and I'd find myself spending Christmas Eve or Christmas Day or New Year's Eve down at the station or the office. Christmas Day was very cold, with the temperature staying around 0 degrees. It was good, crisp, cold walking weather, where you could see your breath whitening the air. The kind of weather that makes the fire in the grate even more enjoyable when you get home. I wasn't called into work on Christmas Day and there was no phone call on St Stephen's Day either. A miracle indeed.

It was 26 December 2004. The news on the radio mentioned an earthquake in Asia. As the day went on, the news that was filtering through became more urgent and more terrible. That evening, I watched the TV news reports with a sense of shock at the magnitude of what had just occurred: a 9.1 undersea earthquake that struck off the northern tip of Sumatra at 7.59 a.m. local time had triggered a mass of tidal waves that raced headlong at the coastline of Asia. Over the next seven hours, the waves struck relentlessly, some of them 30 feet high as they reared in towards land. The reports at first guessed at thousands dead, but that figure kept on climbing – they were talking about tens of thousands of people having perished in one of the largest natural disasters in history. The scale of it was staggering. I watched from the comfort of my fireside and couldn't even begin to imagine what it had been like for those people, and what they were facing now. The sheer level of loss and damage was just too much to take in. The word 'tsunami' would not even have been known to many in Ireland at that time, but it became all too familiar after that day.

When I returned to work at GNIB the next day, the news from Asia was still coming in, building up a more complete picture of what had happened. It was the talk of the office; people were following the updates and repeating the statistics in tones of bewilderment. The debris-choked waves had travelled at 500 miles an hour. A 100-foot roiling mountain of water had engulfed Banda Aceh in Indonesia, the nearest place to the epicentre of the earthquake, and killed more than 100,000 people. The waves rolled on to Phang Nga and Phuket in Thailand, killing another 5,400. On the southeast coast of India, the city of Chennai was engulfed, with 10,000 people lost there. Rushing on again, the tidal waves roared across the island nation of Sri Lanka, sweeping away more than 30,000 people and leaving hundreds of thousands homeless. It was beyond all the worst-case scenarios – the Indian Ocean had buckled and withdrawn, then the full weight of its power had been unleashed on Thailand, Indonesia, Sri Lanka, India, the Maldives, Malaysia, Myanmar, Bangladesh, Somalia, Tanzania and Kenya.

We were compelled to watch the devastation unfold just as the rest of the world was, but disaster relief didn't come under our remit at GNIB. We were lookers-on, donating money and prayers, but there was little else we could do. Unknown to us, the Department of Foreign Affairs was fielding phone calls from distraught relatives, who wanted help to find their loved ones who were in Thailand when it happened. Back then, mobile phones weren't as widely used; it was a time when you could still get happily lost if you wanted to. When people went to exotic locations on holidays, like Asia, they were largely out of contact, especially if they travelled around. There might be a weekly check-in call with home, but otherwise their families had to wait for their return to hear all about it. Now, those families were desperately ringing numbers, trying to get information, but none was forthcoming. And their loved ones hadn't called to say they were safe.

That was when I got the phone call I had never expected. The government had alerted the Garda Síochána to the possibility of Irish nationals being among the missing and the dead. There had to be a coordinated response. It had been decided that it made sense for an incident room to be set up at Dublin Airport, within the offices of the Immigration Bureau. I was used to GNIB being handed all manner of jobs – when you have an office at Dublin Airport, you become accustomed to being first in line when they cast about for someone to take charge of an international event – but it was still something of a shock that this was pushed under our remit. It was an absolute first for me on all fronts. I replaced the phone in its cradle and sat there staring at it, thinking: *How do we find people in the chaotic aftermath of a catastrophic disaster over 6,000 miles away?* We got to work.

The incident room was set up and staff were assigned to various roles. Our first step was to liaise with the Department of Foreign Affairs (DFA) to compile a list of all potential missing Irish citizens. We met the flights returning from Asia and talked to people on them, to get first-hand information and also to eliminate names from the list. Contact was made by families who had the blessed relief of a phone call to confirm their son or daughter was alive and well, and those names were crossed off the list. By this process of elimination, the DFA arrived at a final list of four people: Eilis Finnegan (born 1977) from Ballyfermot, Dublin; Lucy Coyle (b. 1975), from Glenageary, County Dublin; Conor Keightley (b. 1972), from Cookstown, County Tyrone; and Michael Murphy (b. 1981), from Blackwater, County Waterford.

That was when I received another unexpected phone call. Deputy Commissioner Fachtna Murphy instructed me to form an on-the-ground evaluation team in Phuket. The 'team' would comprise myself and Detective Sergeant Joseph Kinsella, a fingerprint expert with the Garda Technical Bureau. We would assess the situation first-hand, then advise on next steps. In short order, Joe and I got the appropriate vaccinations at Garda HQ in the Phoenix Park. We gathered the necessary clothing, masks and insect repellents, the cameras, satellite telephone and laptops. Most important of all, we quickly gathered as much information about the missing people as we could, packing medical and dental X-rays and charts, dental moulds and DNA information along with our bags. At 8.30 a.m. on Friday 7 January 2005, we departed from Dublin Airport on a journey which involved transiting London and Kuala Lumpur, Malaysia, before reaching our intended destination of Phuket, Thailand.

We disembarked to the humidity of early evening in Phuket, the complete opposite of the brisk winter air we had left behind in Dublin. Joe and I were booked into the Pearl Hotel, where the Irish ambassador to Malaysia and Thailand, Dan Mulhall, had established an emergency centre to help in the search for Irish citizens. We were met by officials attached to the Department of Foreign Affairs and brought straight to the hotel to deposit our things. I put all of the ante-mortem information into the room safe. Terry McParland of the Irish Embassy staff briefed us on where the search stood and I also spoke to Reidar Nielsen, Assistant Chief of Police and Commander of the Norwegian Disaster Victim Identification (DVI) team. He told us that the DVI teams met at the local police station at nine o'clock every morning to coordinate their efforts. That would be a welcome steer to myself and Joe in getting set up.

The acronym DVI was going to become extremely familiar to Joe and me, but we weren't aware of it to any great extent at that point. While it didn't feature in the work of the Gardaí, it was a significant part of policing in other countries. We discovered that there were dedicated DVI teams in the UK, Australia, Norway, Israel and many other countries, including EU Member States, trained and on standby at all times to respond to disasters where there were multiple fatalities and the deceased needed to be identified and repatriated. In Ireland, we do not have a DVI team of this nature, although it would seem to be an essential component of the state's service. That said, when Ireland was the site of a major disaster, the response was swift and excellent. It had happened back in 1985, when Air India flight 182 was brought down off the west Cork coast and plunged into the Atlantic, killing all 329 passengers and crew. No survivors. Sikh militants claimed they had planted the bomb that destroyed the plane. Ireland had to immediately activate a major accident plan, centred on the Regional Hospital in Cork. The state's various agencies and local people all pulled together to retrieve and identify the bodies and care for the grieving relatives who arrived. It was a mammoth task, but it was executed perfectly. Of course, I hadn't any involvement in that disaster, so I had no such experience to draw on. Joe and I were very much in unknown territory, in every way.

We were due to meet with Derek Ryan, the brother-in-law of Lucy Coyle, and Hugh Sweetman, the brother of her boyfriend Seán, who was another of the tsunami's victims. We met over dinner and they told us about Lucy. She was an accountant, holidaying with her boyfriend, staying at the Princess Resort on Koh Phi Phi island. The water had destroyed the resort and as many as 70 per cent of the people who lived on the island were dead. It didn't seem possible that Lucy could have survived, and Derek and Hugh had been searching for her body. They told us that there was a body, number 612, which could be Lucy, being of similar height and face shape and with a scar on the left leg, just like Lucy. Derek and Hugh now had to return to Ireland, but we promised that we would follow up on body number 612 and establish if it really was Lucy. If so, we would organise her return home to Ireland.

As Joe and I walked back to the hotel, I was struck by how surreal this experience was. Twelve days earlier, I had been watching the disaster on television, a disaster in a place thousands of miles away that I had never been to and of which I had little knowledge. Now here I was, standing in the scenes I had watched on television, feeling the heat on my own skin, experiencing the heavy sense of loss that blanketed the whole place and everyone we met. It was very hard to comprehend. We now had to find the bodies of three Irish people in this unfamiliar, unbelievable setting. It was a daunting task. I say three bodies because Eilis Finnegan had been identified and repatriated to Ireland. Her boyfriend and Dan Mulhall had searched for her in the immediate aftermath, and they did find her. Her best friend, Sinéad Ní Mhuircartaigh, a garda, flew out from Ireland with dental X-rays, and Eilis was formally identified from those. Eilis had made it home, but Lucy, Conor and Michael were still lost, and it was on Joe and me to help the ambassador and his team find them.

We woke to our first full day in Phuket, 9 January, and made our way to the police station for the DVI meeting. As we walked through the streets and got our first proper view of the area, we could see the devastation left in the wake of the tsunami. That day we would see the felled buildings and trees, the mud and debris, but there were also the people walking around in a daze, carrying photos of their loved ones, desperate for any scrap of information anyone might have or remember. They had to go through the traumatic experience of viewing bodies in the various locations where they were being stored, each time with the hollow dread that it might be their relative under the sheet. Joe and I weren't witnessing the immediate chaos, but we were witnessing the abject grief of so many people affected by the disaster.

At the police station, we squeezed into the room with the Disaster Victim Coordination Group, where the senior representatives of each DVI team were gathered. The focus of the meeting was on establishing a central location for processing and identifying the bodies, which would serve everyone better than the current piecemeal arrangement. The identification process was being co-managed by the Royal Thai Police and the Australian Federal Police and there had already been at least one error, when the body of a Thai national had been misidentified and sent to another country. This was always a possibility when rapid decomposition, due to the weather and storage conditions, made visual identification almost impossible after just 24–48 hours. The plan was that no more bodies would be released until a proposed disaster victim identification centre, which would become known as the Thai Tsunami Victim Identification Information Management Centre (TTVIIMC), was established, to be located on Chaofa Road, Chalfont Muang, Phuket. Any future repatriation of a body would take place only after identification had been established at the centre and approved by the Thai authorities. The outcome of the numerous post-mortem examinations would be lodged at the TTVIIMC, where an attempt would be made to find matching ante-mortem information and make an identification.

Luckily for us, the common language of the DVI conference was English. The DVI operation grew over the coming weeks to include people of more than thirty different nationalities as the international community came together to send experts to help. The Thai police had also asked Interpol for assistance and a team was sent to assist in setting up the process. Interpol is the only recognised authority on DVI and its protocols would guide all the work involved. It was immediately clear to me that the only prospect of making a positive identification of the Irish citizens would be to adhere to the rules laid down by Interpol and the new management centre, so I studied those to ensure I knew exactly what to do in every circumstance. I also registered myself as Ireland's liaison officer, which was mandatory for every country. It meant I would be responsible for lodging information at the centre and any finding would come to me first, and then I could pass it on. Joe put himself forward as a fingerprint expert to help in the post-mortem process. They were badly in need of expertise like his and his offer was gladly accepted. I was struck by the sense of allegiance and support among the whole group. It was my first time to see a truly international collaboration of this nature in action and it was heartening to see that we could work together so smoothly and effectively when the situation demanded it.

The meeting lasted about two hours, then Joe and I prepared to travel the three hours to Krabi, to meet with relatives of Conor Keightley. He was 30 years old, from Cookstown in County Tyrone, and he had last contacted his family on Christmas Day. Just as we were about to leave Phuket, I received an urgent request from Deputy Commissioner Murphy for a written update on our work. If I stayed to write it, I couldn't attend the meeting in Krabi. I was torn. But then I realised that I had equipment that would enable me to send an email on the move. I wrote the report in the car and sent it off. That was the first time in my career that I was able to send information from a remote location in an instant.

We met with Conor's two sisters, his uncle and cousin, and also present was Kyle O'Sullivan, First Secretary of the Department of Foreign Affairs. The family had to return home, but they were desperate to find Conor. We explained the identification process to them and they filled in an Interpol DVI document that I would need to observe the protocols. That was all we could do. It was heartbreaking to see them preparing to leave Thailand, leaving Conor behind. They trusted us to carry on their search.

The following day, 10 January, Dermot Ahern, the Minister for Foreign Affairs, arrived at the Management Centre with a delegation that included heads of Irish aid agencies and Ambassador Dan Mulhall. I introduced him to the senior members of the DVI team and he listened as the whole process was explained. I also briefed the minister privately on our efforts to find the missing Irish citizens. As I made my way back to the Pearl Hotel after the meeting, I was thinking for the umpteenth time in 48 hours how bizarre this situation in which I found myself was. I was briefing a government minister on the finer points of disaster victim identification, and yet just a few days earlier I had only the most basic knowledge of these matters.

In the afternoon, Joe and I had another talk with Kyle O'Sullivan and we sifted through information and realised there was one body that might be that of Conor Keightley: body number 467. We set off to travel to the Yan Yaw Buddhist temple in Takua Pa to investigate further. The Buddhist temple was being utilised as a morgue for hundreds of recovered bodies. At this location, foreign and local experts were undertaking post-mortem examinations on recovered bodies. Until now, we had seen the physical devastation of the tsunami. At Yan Yaw mortuary, we would see the human devastation.

The temple provided a contact point for the families and friends of all those who were still missing. There were rows upon rows of whiteboards outside the temple, covered with photographs of the bodies held inside. It was better to have the relatives look at those awful images than go inside and see the reality. There was a stunned silence around the temple, so many people milling about and yet no sounds, it was almost eerie. I remember there was an elderly woman sitting in a chair beside one of the boards and she was looking directly at me. I nodded slightly to acknowledge her, to give a sympathetic smile, but then I realised that although she was staring at me, she wasn't seeing me. She was in another world, here but not here, staring without seeing. I was struck by her and asked about her. She was a local woman, I was told, and her entire family had been swept away in the waters. It was deeply shocking and distressing to witness her unspoken grief. In fact, that is what stays with me most vividly from my time in Thailand – not the gruesome scenes inside the mortuary, but rather the muted, isolating despair of those broken people outside, searching the thousands of dead for their own unbearable loss to be confirmed.

There were foreign and local experts undertaking post-mortem examinations inside the building and Joe and I introduced ourselves to the UK DVI team. They were headed up by two British experts, Tim Peerless and Barry Philips, and in talking to them we realised they were extremely experienced. We asked to meet them after they had finished their day's work at the temple. A few hours later, we sat with Tim and Barry over some cold beers in a local bar and they described their work in DVI. They had assisted after a series of bombs had been detonated in Bali, for example, in 2002. They had an air of authority and knew exactly how to organise the DVI process. We told them about our mission, and particularly about our hope that we might have found Conor's body. They agreed to ensure that body 467 was on the list for examination the next morning. Joe and I booked into a hotel – the only time in my life I had two different hotel rooms booked at once, since we had to maintain our base in Phuket – and we got some sleep before rising early the next day to go back to the temple.

This time, we went past the boards and into the temple itself. As visitors to the mortuary, we had to don white hazmat suits and masks. There were 5,000 bodies stored there for examination, along with huge quantities of personal items.

There weren't enough freezers to hold the bodies, so some were buried until it was their turn to be examined. Joe and I were handed smelling salts, to help us cope with the smell in that heat, but I found the salts worse, so I opted to allow myself to breathe and acclimatise to the odours. In the examination area there were eight tables, with a body laid on each, and the examiners were bent to their work, concentrating and moving slowly and deliberately. There were 40 bodies lined up waiting their turn. This was how it was all day long: bring 40 in, move eight onto the tables, perform the examination, remove, bring the next eight, and on, and on. Those 40 bodies waiting were wrapped in material. Those being examined were sparsely clothed, closely examined for any identifying marks. It was an unsettling scene, but necessary to remain calm and composed. We responded to it by keeping our focus trained on our own body of interest, not staring or reacting in any way. It was the same respectful approach as at every post-mortem I had attended.

Body 467 had been brought forward and laid on a table. I had brought along the information I had for Conor – dental X-rays, etc. – and I handed this to the odontologist. She was an Israeli woman, very experienced in DVI, and I knew she had also examined the body that Lucy Coyle's family thought might be her. We watched now as the Israeli expert methodically went through the checks and there was a rising sense of hope as she got match after match. To our huge relief, she turned to us and confirmed that we had found Conor Keightley. We could organise his return to his family.

I took the opportunity to talk to the odontologist about Lucy Coyle, potentially body number 612. Matching features had been identified, but we still couldn't be fully sure it was Lucy. Her family had given me a piece of paper with a list of 12 or 13 reasons why the body was Lucy and if so should be returned to the family immediately, but we had to be sure. I knew it was asking a lot, but I put it to the odontologist that we now had more ante-mortem information for Lucy, and would it be possible to examine 612 again? To our immense gratitude, she agreed to examine that body once she had completed all her scheduled examinations that day. That would be hours later, so Kyle O'Sullivan along with Joe and I spent that time working to get the paperwork for Conor organised, so that he could be repatriated as soon as possible. Our foresight in getting the family to fill out the Interpol form would prove essential now, as we were the only team with the full documentation in place. It would ensure that Conor was returned home quickly.

We were called back into the temple later. The Israeli expert had spent the whole day performing examinations in the sweltering heat, in her hazmat suit and mask, but in that spirit of helping one another in a time of crisis, she prepared to examine body 612 for a second time. I gave her all the dental information I had and she began the methodical comparison.

We had thought that fingerprints would be the key identification tool but due to the ravages of the seawater and the heat, it was dental matches that were the most accurate. Of course, poverty was a factor in that. The poor are never well recorded and there were many Burmese who perished and there was no way to identify them. The same applied to younger victims – a child might not have had any dental work requiring X-rays or moulds. We were very lucky to have so much ante-mortem information about our Irish citizens.

The expert finished her examination and turned to us. She told us that she was one hundred per cent certain that this was not the body of Lucy Coyle. While I was glad that we had not misidentified Lucy and repatriated the wrong body, I was also gutted for her family, who wanted to have her home so badly. It was something that the examiners saw again and again – people who were so anxious to find their loved one that in some cases they forced the body to fit the person. It was completely understandable and desperately sad, but I was glad those protocols were in place to save us all from those very human emotions. It wasn't Lucy, and we had to keep searching for her.

Joe's job was very well defined, as a fingerprint expert, but mine was less so. Aside from my daily attendance at the TTVIMC, I felt it was important that I keep in touch with the relatives, regularly and in person. I made sure to call them and talk through our work and progress. I wanted to instil confidence in them that we were there when they couldn't be, that we were searching just as hard as they had, that we were just as focused and involved. It was a huge burden on them to be so far away and all I could do was try to lessen that load somewhat.

I also stayed in regular contact with the GNIB office and Sergeant Angela Willis in the incident room. She was working to gather any and all information about Lucy Coyle and Michael Murphy, to assist us if we believed we had found them. Michael's brother, Paul, had travelled to Thailand in the aftermath and searched tirelessly for Michael, but to no avail. He had provided buccal swabs and dental records before leaving to go back to Ireland. Michael's last known location was the Khao Lak area, so I waited until I was there to ring Paul Murphy. I explained what we were doing, the process we had to work within, and I promised him that we would continue his search for his brother. To that end, I deposited all the information we had gathered with the TTVIIMC, giving them a full and detailed set of paperwork and every piece of information possible to aid the identification process.

At the end of January, it was decided that Joe and I should return to Ireland. After a month in the aftermath of the tsunami, it was now surreal to be back behind my desk in Burgh Quay, looking out on the wintry light in Dublin. I kept up my liaison work with the DVI teams and Joe and I also travelled to meet the Murphy family in Wexford. It was upsetting not to have any further leads to share with them, but I remained hopeful that Michael's body was among those 5,000 being examined at the temple.

Throughout February I maintained regular contact with the DVI team, but there was nothing to report. In March, I returned to Phuket and deposited additional ante-mortem information with the TTDVIMC. As the weeks slipped by, it began to seem more and more likely that Lucy and Michael might never be found or identified. But it turned out that my hope was not misplaced. On 18 April 2005, 113 days after the tsunami struck, I got a call to give me the news that Lucy Coyle's body had been identified. They had used all of the ante-mortem information I had deposited and the match they now had was 100 per cent positive. The Coyle family were informed and finally, on 22 April, Lucy came home via Dublin Airport. Her funeral was held in Dublin on 26 April.

Just three days later, I was again in my office in Burgh Quay when the phone rang, and this time I received the incredible news that Michael Murphy had been identified. It turned out that, as I had feared for Lucy, Michael's body had been stored with those of local people, and that had greatly delayed the identification process. But all of the ante-mortem information had confirmed that they had found Michael. I rang Paul Murphy to let him know, and it was an emotional phone call. The family had held out hope that Michael had perhaps survived, but now came the terrible confirmation that he had died in Thailand. It was very difficult, but I was glad that we could at least give them that sense of closure to help them grieve.

It was one of the most extraordinary experiences in my career. There was simply no way I could ever have envisaged that becoming a garda would lead to being involved in an operation of that kind. It's not something you'd ever expect to be part of your job. But I was glad that Joe and I were able to be there and contribute to finding those Irish citizens. It was heartbreaking, but at least we got answers, especially when you consider that there are still 300 bodies in frozen storage in Thailand, unclaimed and unidentified, and other victims whose remains were never recovered.

When I returned from Thailand at the end of January, disappointed to not have found Lucy and Michael, my in-tray held a letter from the Keightley family thanking us for our work and for returning their beloved Conor to them. I was very touched that they thought to write and send that letter in the midst of their deep sadness. It remains to this day one of my most treasured possessions. We had to give the worst possible news to those families, but their gratitude was touching and heartfelt. It gave me that same sense I had attending post-mortem examinations or supporting grieving families after a fatal accident: when they needed us, we hadn't let them down.

CHAPTER 11

A CONVENIENT LOOPHOLE

The GNIB got steadily busier during the decade between 2000 and 2010. There were more people on the move worldwide, more conflicts and displaced refugees, more wealth being generated in Western Europe, including in Ireland, as we hurtled towards the Celtic Tiger years, and that all combined to keep the bureau extremely busy. We were contending with growing problems, two of the most pressing being human trafficking and bogus marriages. The GNIB staff had to continually update their knowledge of legislation and international law to keep up with the constantly changing immigration landscape we were trying to police. We had to become experts on so many different topics to do our job properly. It was hugely challenging.

I attended a number of courses on specific aspects of immigration controls and associated criminal offences. In September 2005 I went to the Czech Republic for a course organised by the EU's Agency for Law Enforcement on Trafficking in Human Beings and that November I was in Brussels for a course entitled European Training on Identifying and Providing Assistance to Victims of Trafficking. These courses were extremely helpful as it is essential to understand the indicators for trafficking. There can be red flags, but if you're not aware, you won't see them. For example, if you stop a car with five or six passengers, but only the driver speaks and answers questions, or the driver is holding all the passports, that suggests a level of control that should be investigated. As it had been since the start of GNIB, we were learning about a world that was new to us, so Europe-wide collaboration and pooling of resources was very useful and welcome.

The first trafficking cases in Ireland were uncovered through the immigration process, but not all trafficking falls under the immigration remit. This is why it has now been placed under the Protective Services Bureau, which was set up in 2015 to handle cases involving vulnerable victims, including human trafficking, child protection, domestic and sexual violence and missing people.

Our relationship with the UK was very important in working strategically to track any flagged individuals. There was one occasion when my colleagues Seán Cullen and Angela Willis came into my office to tell me that a senior officer in the UK wanted to meet to discuss trafficking issues. We flew over to London and had a meeting in a restaurant, where we were greeted by Chief Superintendent Nick Kinsella, who was soon after appointed as the first head of the UK Human Trafficking Centre and two assistant chief constables. The UK was involved in an important EU initiative on trafficking and the UK officers wanted Ireland to be involved as well. The only catch was that the initiative, known as Operation Pentameter, was already up and running, so we were late to the party. Nick Kinsella wanted to find out how best he could bring about Ireland's participation.

It was an excellent initiative and I could see it was essential that Ireland be involved in it, so as we sat there I grabbed a bit of paper and drafted the skeleton of a letter to the Deputy Commissioner Fachtna Murphy. To my surprise, the letter arrived on his desk a few days later, with only a few changes from my scribbled skeleton. Nonetheless, it achieved the desired aim, and I was instructed to attend a meeting associated with the initiative. Ireland agreed to participate and we took on the role of training and publicity. We developed a comprehensive training course that we ran regularly, and to his credit Nick Kinsella attended every one without fail. We devised a joint presentation and delivered it on a regular basis. It was symbolic of the need for and the benefits of cross-border communication, which became the cornerstone of our immigration operations.

In November 2008 I was promoted to chief super-intendent of GNIB, a key leadership role. The senior positions were very involved in the cross-border work and forging working partnerships across the globe. I remember one such task arising with regard to Beirut, where we had concerns about the visa-issuing process. There was a request for a delegation to travel to Beirut to investigate, which comprised a senior official from the Department of Foreign Affairs, another from the Department of Justice, and myself. We flew over to Lebanon and were put up in the St George Hotel in Beirut. I remember going into my room, laying my suitcase on the bed, then pulling back the curtains to take in the view. From my window I could see a huge crater in the road. I was later told that it was the spot where the Prime Minister of Lebanon, Rafic Hariri, had been assassinated. In one of those coincidences that so often occur during a long career, I remembered that a fact-finding exercise relating to the assassination had been conducted by Peter Fitzgerald, my chief super in the Store Street Drug Unit. He worked for the UN form time to time as a neutral investigator, and I knew he had brought Martin Donnellan, the first head of GNIB, with him on that mission. It was always interesting to see the unexpected places a career in the Garda Síochána might take a person.

There was no Irish ambassador in Beirut, which was served by the Cairo office, and we were invited to travel to Cairo to meet with the ambassador to brief him on the outcome of our investigations. We flew to Cairo and enjoyed a meal at the embassy. It was a brief overnight visit, which meant no time to visit the pyramids of Giza, which was very disappointing. I had never been, and it was frustrating to be in the vicinity and not get to see them. But after the meal, at about 8.30 in the evening, the ambassador suddenly asked if we would like to visit the pyramids. I had assumed they were in a remote location, miles from anywhere. But no, they were only about 25km outside Cairo and we were offered the embassy driver to escort us there. We leaped at the chance – even though we'd only have 45 minutes or so to explore them. The driver got us out there and I greatly enjoyed the visit – and watching the local police on camel-back patrolling and telling the visitors when it was closing time. It was certainly a long way from a Garda-issue bicycle.

The other striking and memorable thing about that visit was the abject poverty we saw on the streets of Cairo. It gave a glimpse into the kind of adversity that might convince a person to undertake a dangerous journey, to a country that was deeply foreign to them, in order to find a better life – or, at least, the chance of a better life for their children. It was a stark reminder that we can be a bit complacent in Ireland, forgetting how good we have it and how much we have, perhaps falling into a casual, ill-informed racism that doesn't recognise the nature of life for so many people in the world, and the fact that it isn't their fault. When it comes down to it, we all want the same thing – to be safe, to work, to be treated fairly, to raise families with decent opportunities.

The single most urgent issues throughout my time in GNIB were unaccompanied minors, child trafficking and child slavery. Children are, of course, uniquely vulnerable and we were often witnesses to the terrible outcomes they can suffer when separated from parents and family. With child slavery, which naturally is illegal in Ireland, we discovered that it was common for well-to-do people in some African states to have a child household slave. This was not something I would ever have known, but colleagues in the Netherlands had warned us to be vigilant about this among the diplomatic corps, in particular.

We staged a joint operation with the Police Service of Northern Ireland (PSNI) with regard to a particular family, and it culminated in a house search in west Dublin. There was a husband, wife and several children in the house, but we noticed that all was not right with one of the children. This was where the training proved invaluable because even with very few clues, we could now quickly ascertain if there was something amiss. We investigated further and discovered that all the documents relating to this child were false, that the child was not attending school like the others and did not leave the house. It was as we suspected – this child was not a family member, but was serving the household, doing all the chores, cooking, etc. To the family, having a 'helper' was a normal way of life, but under Irish law it was illegal and an abuse of the child's rights. We were able to rescue that child from that situation, but the constant flow of people in and out of the country and around Europe's Member States posed a huge challenge in terms of tracing and tracking those who might be in danger.

The very first case of people smuggling to come before the Circuit Criminal Court was the result of an interception by GNIB. I was in the court that day, to give evidence against the accused, Olaitan Ilori, a Nigerian national who lived in Blessington, County Wicklow. Ilori had arrived in Ireland in 1998 as an asylum-seeker, but withdrew his application for asylum after marrying an Irish woman. He received full citizenship in 2002 and worked as a lawyer. He was on trial for the charge of smuggling 14 people – 12 adults and two children – from Mauritius to Ireland in 2006, to which he pleaded not guilty. As a result, the case was sent forward to the higher court, where the trial would last 12 days.

I was one of the members of the GNIB team to give evidence. We showed that Ilori had been paid by the 12 adults for their passage to Ireland and the jobs he would find for them there. He had told them that when they got to Dublin Airport, they were to say that they were tourists. Our officers had stopped Ilori as he came through the airport and found nine receipts for 'down payments for work visa application in Ireland'. The Mauritian nationals also gave evidence against him, stating that they had given him around €3,500 to secure permits and work for them in Ireland. The group of Mauritians were not given leave to stay in Ireland. Ilori maintained his innocence throughout, but the jury returned a verdict of guilty and he was sentenced to four years. The judge took into account the fact that none of the people had been harmed in any way, but it was still an illegal operation to bring them into the country on those terms.

When speaking about the Garda Síochána's role in immigration issues, I repeated that the issue of greatest concern to me was the vulnerability of children to exploitation by criminals. A minor identified as unaccompanied by an immigration officer is automatically referred to the HSE, which is responsible for unaccompanied minors. However, GNIB was discovering a greater problem was the extent to which minors were arriving accompanied, but in circumstances where the relationship with the accompanying adult was not clear, giving rise to concern about the minor's welfare. The minors concerned often do not know why they have been sent to Ireland, the motivation behind their migration being that of a parent or other adult. In each of my last two years as head of bureau at GNIB, we referred to the HSE about fifty children encountered in the implementation of immigration controls at Dublin Airport. The majority of unaccompanied minors travel to Ireland to be reunited with family, but it was clear the possibility existed that a number could be victims of human trafficking, destined to enter forced labour or prostitution.

My concerns led me to establish Operation Snow, a law enforcement initiative designed to prevent and detect the trafficking of minors into, out of and within Ireland, to ensure the welfare of suspected victims of such criminality is adequately provided for and to achieve prosecutions where criminal activity has been detected.

The Dutch had discovered the existence of a criminal group known as the Peter Group, which was suspected of trafficking Nigerian unaccompanied minor asylum-seekers from Nigeria to EU Member States, particularly Spain and Italy, where female minors would be sexually exploited by being forced into prostitution. The minors would arrive in the Netherlands, be placed in particular accommodation, from which a short time later they would disappear, suspected to have been taken to unknown destinations by the Peter Group.

Wednesday 24 October 2007 had been designated a day of action throughout Europe and in Nigeria in relation to the suspected trafficking of children from Nigeria, associated with the Peter Group. Law enforcement authorities in the US would also participate. A number of arrests had been made in the Netherlands and elsewhere; however, the man believed to be named Peter, who was suspected to head the group, had evaded capture by the police in the Netherlands.

On 28 September 2007, a man named Mr Sarfo entered the registration office at GNIB headquarters at Burgh Quay, seeking permission to remain in the state. He produced a Ghanaian passport, but concern was raised about the authenticity of the passport. The Intelligence and Document section at Burgh Quay were immediately on the case, and they worked closely with UK Immigration Service, who had a staff member in our offices. The operation by the UK and Ireland of a CTA was a complicating feature from the perspective of operating border controls at our ports and at the land border with Northern Ireland. But a specific operation put in place by the UK Border Force, Operation Gull, was implemented, with the cooperation of GNIB. It involved personnel from both agencies occasionally being jointly present at a port, with the visitor agency advising the other with regard to granting permission to enter or remain in the CTA. This operation resulted in the UK Border Force deploying personnel to Dublin Airport and, on other occasions, GNIB having a presence at an airport in Belfast.

The UK immigration officer present on this occasion had a handheld device that provided access to a UK immigration database of fingerprints taken during the UK immigration processes. By placing a single finger on the device, it revealed a person's UK immigration record. Mr Sarfo was asked if he had any objection to his fingerprint being checked, and he said no. He placed his finger on the screen and within seconds a hit on the UK system was revealed, indicating that the man had previously interacted with UK immigration while claiming to be Jackson Smith.

Meanwhile, a detailed examination of the Ghanaian passport revealed it had been altered. Sarfo was interviewed by Detective Sergeant Seán Cullen and later refused permission to remain in the state. Then he was arrested by Detective Garda Mervyn Minto, on suspicion of having committed fraud-related offences with regard to the altered passport. As the investigation progressed, contact was made with the Investigation Unit of the Royal Netherlands Marechaussee in Amsterdam. They strongly suspected that the man we had arrested, with a passport issued in the name of Peter Sarfo, was the elusive Peter who was head of the Peter Group. The Dutch quickly packed their bags and made their way to Dublin.

Peter Sarfo, aka Jackson Smith, was brought to the Cloverhill District Court and remanded in custody until 11 October. The Extradition Section at Garda Headquarters was busy ensuring that a European arrest warrant obtained by the Dutch authorities would be available before then. On 10 October Sarfo was brought before the High Court.

The planned day of action took place on 24 October. In total, 18 suspects were arrested in five countries. Thirteen traffickers were arrested in the Netherlands, while five of the main suspects were detained in New York, Madrid, Antwerp and Coventry, England. The Dutch authorities issued a press release revealing that a year-long investigation had discovered that since January 2006, the targeted traffickers had transported at least 140 underage Nigerian nationals, mainly young girls, to the Netherlands with false travel documents, instructing them to seek asylum on their arrival. When the day of action was being planned, it had not been anticipated that Peter, the main suspect, would already have been located and arrested.

After a number of appearances in the High Court, on Thursday 17 January 2008 Mr Justice Peart dismissed a number of points of objection and said he was satisfied that the person before the court was the person whose arrest was being sought in the European arrest warrant and was satisfied to make an order for Sarfo's extradition. Peter Sarfo was extradited to the Netherlands, where he was subsequently convicted on charges related to human trafficking.

As I sat in the High Court listening to proceedings, I felt great pride in the work that had been done by Seán Cullen and his staff in our Intelligence and Documents section. The proceedings also emphasised for me, yet again, the importance of effective cooperation between law enforcement authorities in the EU and further afield. The case against Sarfo was made possible by the tracing device used by UK Immigration – we had no such handheld units to enable us to perform an instant and accurate identity check and that shouldn't have been the case, to my mind.

Aside from my frustration, Operation Snow had a very successful outcome in the case of Peter Sarfo. It was an excellent result for all of the agencies concerned and we were very glad to have taken a man like Sarfo out of circulation. That said, it was one bright spark of success in a swathe of darkness, where traffickers operated under the radar, moving people around, exploiting them, causing untold misery. That was one of the difficult aspects of our work in GNIB – while we uncovered illegalities every single day at Dublin Airport and did rescue people, at the same time we knew that we were up against a vast network of wrongdoers who sought every opportunity to make money off less fortunate people, even children. But then, despair would be a pointless waste of energy. The only attitude was to be relentless – that was what I had told my colleagues in Store Street, and it's what I said now to my team at GNIB. No matter how much they keep coming over the hill, wave after wave, we have to stand firm and meet them every time. We had to be as relentless as they were, always working against them, always interrupting, intercepting, interfering.

That was why I gave a name to it – Operation Snow. We were already doing all that work every day, but I knew that by giving it an operation name, I was putting a name on the problem as well and thereby raising awareness of it. The media latched on to Operation Snow, it featured in crime reports, and I think that helps to make people more alert to what's going on around them. Operation Snow ensured the HSE and the government were fully aware that this was happening and alerted everyone, in every agency, to be aware of the potential for that form of criminality.

Another pressing issue that defined my time at GNIB was bogus marriages. This became a problem after a ruling at the European Court of Justice unwittingly created a loophole that a whole lot of people rushed to squeeze through.

A case was taken against the Minister for Justice, Equality and Law Reform by Blaise Baheten Metock, a Cameroonian national. He applied for asylum upon arrival in Ireland in June 2006 and his application was refused in February 2007. He was married to a woman who was also originally from Cameroon but was now a British citizen living in Ireland. Metock wished to live with his wife in Ireland, based on the fact that he was married to an EU citizen, but the Irish government countered that he did not fulfil the rule that required a period of time spent living lawfully in a Member State before applying for residency. Metock appealed the decision and it went all the way to the European Court of Justice, where the court ruled that the European Community was the authority to grant or deny entry to the EU, and that non-EU family members did have a right to join their EU citizen spouse and be granted citizenship.

The decision was hastily implemented in several states, including Ireland. The Metock ruling became particularly significant because, while it was enacted to recognise a lawful and genuine marriage, it created a new situation where a marriage of convenience could be arranged with the tantalising promise of the golden ticket of EU citizenship to the non-EU national who married into the benefits of the EU family. The implications of the ruling were quickly understood by those outside the EU looking on, and then quickly acted upon. It has to be said, they were far quicker off the mark than the Irish government, which took some time to realise what was going on. The state was as surprised as everyone else to realise that two people from two different jurisdictions, neither being Irish and neither being from Ireland, could come here and get married.

In GNIB, the Intelligence section noticed a significant uptick in the number of highly questionable marriages taking place. We weren't alone in noticing this. The General Registrar of Marriages, Kieran Feely, and his staff were alarmed by the couples who were coming before them for marriage ceremonies – they quite obviously did not know one another, very often didn't speak one another's language and an interpreter would be required just to get them through the service and the signing of the register. GNIB followed up and discovered that there were reports from embassies in other Member States expressing concern that young women were travelling to Ireland to get married, in exchange for sums of money of around €3,000. Their bridegrooms were generally from the Indian subcontinent and our research showed that many were illegally resident in Ireland or were subject to a deportation order.

The figures were indeed alarming. By August 2009, the Department of Justice estimated that as many as 4,600 non-EU nationals may have married into citizenship, with an estimated 30 per cent of those being failed asylum-seekers or visitors whose visas had expired. From an immigration point of view, one concern was that bogus marriages could allow terrorists to marry in and gain citizenship – it created the possibility of a security threat to Ireland and to the EU. I spoke with the Latvian ambassador as a high percentage of the brides came from Latvia. He expressed grave concern that these young women were vulnerable to exploitation and that some had not returned home after their trip to Ireland. The whole situation could lead to various types of criminal activity and it was clear to me that we had to get on top of it.

I began to work closely with Kieran Feely, exploring how we might tackle the problem. He was as committed to the necessity for this as I was and to seeing it all the way through to the courts, if necessary, which made all the difference. I studied all the relevant legislation and landed on Section 58 of the Civil Registration Act 2004, which set out provisions for objecting to a marriage on various grounds. It allowed for any person to object to any marriage – you didn't need to be a relative or connected in any way. Once an objection was lodged within the three months of the ceremony date, the registrar was obliged to investigate it.

I set up Operation Charity, which Peter Cullen and his unit undertook, to target any marriages that might be bogus. When we discovered forthcoming nuptials where the bride and groom did not speak the same language, or there were any other red flags, I would write a letter of objection and lodge it with the registrar beforehand, if possible. When that wasn't possible, GNIB officers would turn up at the ceremony, state their case and hand over the letter to the registrar officiating. It got to the point where the media made us a figure of fun, with cartoons showing GNIB officers pelting up the aisle and not 'for ever holding their peace' in order to prevent a marriage taking place. In all, I objected to about eighty marriages – and I made sure to sign every single objection letter personally, so that if any became the subject of a court case, I would be the person in the dock, not my staff. That was extremely important to me, to show that leadership and to protect the team. If anyone was going to be hauled over hot coals for this, it was going to be me. When it finally happened, I wasn't surprised.

A marriage was scheduled for 12 January 2011 in Cavan Registry Office that we suspected was bogus. Two GNIB officers turned up on the day, spoke to the registrar and lodged my letter of objection. The couple were a Lithuanian national, Ms Izmailovic, who had arrived in Ireland in May 2010, and an Egyptian national, Mr Ads, who had been issued with a deportation order in November 2010. He had failed to present himself at our office at Burgh Quay as instructed, at which point he became an 'evader'. This meant he had no entitlement to remain and was in the state illegally. The GNIB officers arrested Mr Ads at the registry office.

An application was subsequently made to the High Court, under Article 40.4.2 of the Constitution: *Izmailovic & Ads v. Commissioner of An Garda Síochána & Ors*. The matter was heard very quickly, on 31 January, by Mr Justice Hogan, and I was required to give evidence. In my testimony, I clearly outlined the issues posed by marriages of convenience and how the loophole had been created and then exploited. I also pointed out that the address provided by Ms Izmailovic was the same one cited by a number of other people being investigated by GNIB for possible bogus marriages. I put forward my view that my objections were on sound legal grounds and therefore correct.

The court did not agree with me. The judge started by saying that there would need to be a high degree of justification for arresting a person minutes before their wedding ceremony. He found that the two people were of full age and capacity, had given the statutory notice and neither had ever been married before. He concluded that under Irish law, the marriage would be valid – even if there were issues around

Mr Ads' immigration status. For that reason, he ordered the release of Mr Ads from custody and declared my letter of objection invalid, which meant I could no longer use the objection route to prevent marriages we were investigating as bogus.

The only silver lining was that the judge publicly acknowledged that the loophole existed and went so far as to note that it could be closed: 'If the law in this area is considered to be unsatisfactory, then it is, of course, in principle open to the Oireachtas and, if needs be, the Union legislature to address these questions as this decision in its own way illustrates, the problems encountered here are difficult ones and present complex questions of public policy in relation to marriage and immigration.'

The state didn't appeal the decision, but it did decide to introduce legislation to address the issues we had been tackling. However, that didn't come about until 2014, and then it didn't come into operation until 2015. It was frustrating, but I was very glad to see the new, tighter legislation in place to help us police marriages of convenience and prevent abuse of the immigration process in this way. Once the legislation came into effect in 2015, the new management team at GNIB lost no time in setting up Operation Vantage, based on these stricter provisions. Vantage was more focused on criminality associated with bogus marriages, which was now defined in law, giving us a reliable legal foothold for our operation.

In the years since Operation Charity, criminal gangs moved into the space created by the loophole and were creaming off profits by securing residency status for non-EU nationals through arranged marriages, charging up to €20,000 for the service. Vantage picked up where Charity had left off, and we uncovered a range of activities linked to illegal immigration and prevented a large number of fake marriages.

There was a final addendum to our work on Operation Charity. Three years later, in 2018, another High Court judge, Mr Justice Humphreys, disagreed with the conclusion reached by Mr Justice Hogan in the Izmailovic case; and he felt that Mr Justice Hogan's judgment had paid little attention to 'the damaging consequences that were going to be unleashed by the decision'.

Disagreements between judges illustrate the onerous responsibility placed on gardaí. We must make decisions based on the information available. Our actions might be found defective in a courtroom, only for the judges to later disagree with each other. The judiciary must be thorough and fair and neutral in their work, but this can lead to difficult positions for the gardaí who must uphold the law far beyond the walls of the courthouse. That must be acknowledged as well.

CHAPTER 12

THE HARD LESSONS FROM IMMIGRATION

In July 2013, while I was head of bureau at GNIB, I had an unexpected opportunity to experience immigration control from the perspective of those who fall foul of the process of scrutiny imposed by immigration officers at a busy airport. On a number of occasions in the years prior to 2013, I had travelled to the US, from Dublin airport, utilising the US pre-clearance facility. In doing so I experienced some delays because I was subjected to 'secondary' or additional screening for a reason unknown to me. As the problem was resolved on each occasion and I boarded the intended flight, I never thought much about it. However, when flying with my family, we usually opted to fly via Europe, for cheaper flights, which meant no pre-clearance at Dublin airport. On these occasions, the rest of my family always passed quickly through immigration control, while I would be required to sit in a waiting area while my passport was closely checked. The area I was placed in was usually behind a glass screen through which my family could wave at me and joke about how long I would be detained this time. In any event, each time this happened I had a short wait and then my passport was handed back to me and I was told I could proceed into the US.

In July 2013, I was preparing for another family holiday in the US, travelling via Madrid to Los Angeles. I received a telephone call from a member of staff at the US Embassy in Dublin with whom I was in regular contact. We discussed a particular security issue and at the end of the call I informed him that I would be travelling to the US the following day, jokingly adding, based on earlier experiences, 'that's if you allow me into the country'. The following day we flew from Dublin to Madrid and boarded a flight to LA. Upon arrival in America, an immigration officer examined my passport and then asked who I was travelling with. My family gathered in front of him and to our shock he said there was a matter to be checked with regard to my application to enter the US and that we would all have to enter a detention area until the matter was resolved. He did not reveal what the issue was or how long we might have to wait.

The room was crowded, filled mainly with Latino people who were all facing the same uncertain wait as ourselves.

Time crawled by, with no information and still no idea why we had been detained. It was an extremely interesting insight. Here I was, the head of the Immigration Bureau of Ireland, a senior police officer, law abiding, and I was being detained for an as yet unknown reason. Eventually, after hours of waiting, a new officer came on duty and he spoke courteously to us and revealed that not only did I share a name with a person of interest, but also the same date of birth. I realised that as far as the US immigration authorities were concerned, I had potentially lied on my security form and failed to mention 'my' criminal convictions. I was impressed, though; despite the thousands of travellers passing through a hectic airport, the system had worked. There was a John O'Driscoll they were interested in and there was good reason to believe that I was him. These are the sort of detections that can, in other circumstances, ensure there will not be a repeat of 9/11. I was not to know then that a few years later I would become even more impressed with the efficiency of US Customs and Border Protection, when they would provide exceptional assistance to the Garda Síochána in tackling organised crime.

Finally, having established my true identity, we were told we could leave. Later on, while sleeping in our hotel, my phone rang. It was my old friend from the embassy, needing to check something with me; it was daytime in Ireland. He got the whole story of my temporary loss of liberty and my struggle to enter the US – the irony!

At that stage, my time as the Head of GNIB was nearing its end. The writing was on the wall in June 2014, when Martin Callinan resigned as commissioner and Nóirín O'Sullivan was appointed acting commissioner and embarked on a major reshuffle of senior management. Initially, I was made head of the Garda National Drug Unit (GNDU), on a temporary basis, while remaining head of GNIB. It was a challenging workload, but there were many common strands between the two and of course I had plenty of experience in working the Drug Unit, so I had the expertise for both assignments. I could see there was potential that I would fill the role of Head of the GNDU on a permanent basis and leave the immigration role behind me, but the longer-term plan was yet to be revealed.

In September 2014, while I was head of bureau at GNDU, one of the biggest drug seizures at sea in Europe took place. Two Navy ships, the LÉ *Niamh* and the LÉ *Roisin*, boarded a 20-metre yacht, the *Makayabella*, off the southwest coast of Ireland. The yacht had been loaded with more than a tonne of cocaine off the coast of Venezuela. The cocaine was seized and three men on board the vessel were arrested and detained for questioning.

Reflecting the dual role I held at that time, I travelled to Rome to an immigration-related meeting while the three men were detained. Relevant legislation provides that detention periods can be extended on the authority of a chief superintendent, who must make an assessment as to whether the longer period of detention is necessary. I had to leave the immigration meeting in Rome to take phone calls in which I was fully briefed about developments back home in the drug case. I assessed the information provided by investigating officers and granted authorisation for an extended period of detention. In April 2015, the three men were convicted at Cork Circuit Criminal Court and given jail sentences ranging from eight to ten years after they pleaded guilty to drug trafficking. In the course of a later visit to Rome I would attend a human trafficking related conference at the Vatican and be provided with the opportunity of a brief meeting with the Pope.

Looking back across my years in Immigration from the vantage point of retirement, I can see that we tackled many problems very well, but there is still so much to be done – and, of course, the issues constantly shift and change, are quelled for a time and then re-emerge. The problems are also interlinked because when criminality enters into immigration, it can come in many forms, from false documents to labour or sexual exploitation to smuggling of goods or people. The job of policing the full network of interconnected issues requires collaboration, excellent intel and reliable resourcing. The problem comes at us from many different directions, and likewise the solutions require us to manage many different elements at once. It's a challenging task.

At the time of writing, immigration is headline news day after day, with various agendas being pushed into the public domain. Some areas have a sizeable migrant population who may not speak the language, and this can lead to them viewing themselves as outsiders. That is a dangerous situation to allow to develop and one that goes far beyond the remit of law enforcement. Although, in reality, social problems always stem from the same sources: unemployment, deprivation, absence of opportunity. That is a fairly usual experience for first-generation migrants. In Ireland before 2000, however, we didn't encounter that because those who migrated here were nearly all medical professionals, so by virtue of their work they gained an immediate status in society that allowed them to slot in much more easily.

Now we are seeing first-generation migrants arriving and that presents a different picture. These people are fleeing their own countries for some reason, and they come here and end up on the lower rungs of the social ladder. The problems that brings are actually the same old ones of social deprivation, but they are sometimes misidentified as a race issue. As we have learned so often before about social deprivation, the problem is not that people do not want to work, it's that they cannot work. When that happens, it can create ghetto conditions, as has happened in the suburbs of cities such as Paris and Brussels. Initiatives such as that of the South Dublin County Partnership, which has established a Migrant

Integration Team, are essential. The team was established to support foreign nationals in their attempt to integrate and to diminish the barriers to their social inclusion.

From the policing side, the Garda Síochána and the community policing unit have been particularly good at developing community relations among migrant populations. In fact, officers from other EU countries have visited to see our work in that regard. Through the Community Engagement section the Garda Síochána has made direct contacts with the mosques and within the Muslim community, for example, which has been very positive and generates a lot of goodwill. And it's often a simple matter of listening with an open mind and understanding the issue from the other person's point of view. For example, we had an incident one day in GNIB when Muslim women were coming in to register, and a change in our registration process required everyone to remove their headwear in order to be photographed. There was good reason for this request; some face measurements are crucial to facial recognition, and the ears are one such. Ears are unique to an individual much the same way as fingerprints. So we had good reason, but that did not make this request any less difficult for the women. They did not wish to be unveiled in our presence.

Dave McInerney, who headed an intercultural office in Community Engagement, had fostered excellent relations with some Muslim leaders, and he was contacted about this problem. Dave, in turn, got on to me about it. We went to meet representatives of the community in a local mosque. We explained our reason for the request, and they explained why this posed a great difficulty for the women, who did not wish to go against the official procedures, but who were very uncomfortable with them. Once we understood the nature of the problem, we were able to design a solution. I wrote a letter to the imam, explaining how the revised process, involving an adequate level of privacy, would be implemented and how it would no longer put the women in a difficult position. Problem solved. It did take time and communication, but it was solvable, once we all worked together. I remember meeting the imam later, and he told me that he had framed my letter and hung it on the wall in his office. To him, it was evidence that it was possible for us all to work and live together peaceably and respectfully.

At base, I think that is what the vast majority of people want – peace, being able to live in peace – and their ethnicity or creed doesn't change that fundamental need. I think we have been lucky in this country that since the Civil War we rarely, as a police force, faced a major outbreak of violence. I can think of two particularly violent outbreaks in my service. One was when the football hooligans came to Lansdowne in 1995 for an Ireland vs. England match and they stormed the stadium and the city with the sole aim of ripping the place apart. We stood there with our batons at the ready, poised for the onslaught, and it was terrifying and bewildering all at once because you're looking at this mayhem and thinking, Why would anyone choose to do this? The other was the attack on the British Embassy, when the gardaí were caught between the gates and the mob – never a nice place to be. That was in July 1981 and the protest was about the hunger strikes in Northern Ireland. Bricks were flying, people were arming themselves with metal pipes and cars were set ablaze. The gardaí couldn't let the British Embassy be burned down again – as it had been in 1972 – and were ordered to stand firm. It was a horrible experience. But those two events stand out in my mind because they were as rare as they were awful.

Part of this can, I think, be attributed to our political system of proportional representation. It is a reliable way to deliver a fair democracy. That means it allows for a change of government to happen in an easier fashion. Through PR, all voices are heard and get a chance to take a seat in the Dáil. I think this is why we have never had a problem with the handover of power, because there is a general respect for and trust in the election outcome, and that is extremely helpful to policing. This is also why threats to the system of democratic elections are so serious and require a new policing angle and imperative.

I think in Ireland there is a general respect for law and order, even if it gets stretched to its limit at times. And, of course, we saw it get broken during the Dublin riots in 2023. That particular event highlighted the new problems we are facing, as a police force and as a society. Watching the gardaí try to corral that crowd – which they did – I was very much reminded of the day the Accession States joined the EU in 2004. The ceremony was being held at Farmleigh and we expected protestors to be present, objecting to increased militarisation of the EU and taxation policies, among other issues. It was the first time that we borrowed water cannon from the PSNI. Our intel had suggested this would be an organised protest, which is usually very different from a more organic gathering of people. What we saw that day was very interesting. A number of the people at the front were from abroad and were clearly there with intent. They deliberately kicked things off by lobbing bricks at the gardaí – they were prepared to instigate violence. When the gardaí responded, the word rippled through the crowd that they were being attacked and had to resist. It's like Chinese whispers with the truth becoming distorted as it gets passed back through the lines. Once things got riled up, those at the front melted away into the crowd, then out of the crowd, and were gone. They left behind a pitched battle. When that sort of thing gets unleashed, people find themselves doing things they had never intended to do because they have been manipulated into that situation and groupthink has taken over.

We saw that again during the Dublin riots, which were posed as being about immigration and the 'Ireland is full' rhetoric, but that's not what happened on the street. If you had taken any of the lads clutching Footlocker boxes off to one side and asked them what 'far right' means, or indeed 'far left', they couldn't have told you. For those rioting in the streets, it was simply an opportunity for mischief, for thieving, for alleviating the boredom of daily life. I don't believe those youngsters had any political motives whatsoever. The actual problem exposed that night was the power of social media to create and manipulate a crowd. That's why it put me in mind of the Farmleigh protest, because at least there the perpetrators had to fly in and be there in person and look into the whites of our eyes. They had to lob a brick. They had to engage. During the Dublin riots, the 'bricks' being lobbed were false information and images on social media, purely designed to ramp up the violent atmosphere and goad people into action. Those responsible didn't even have to be there. They could sit at home, in comfort, watching and directing from afar.

Afterwards, I heard discussions around the question 'Are people more violent now?' There was a sort of despair, and within that grew the idea that times just are worse now, that people are worse now, that there's no way out. I wouldn't hold with that thinking at all. The appetite for violence has always been there, it's not new. But what is new is the ease with which things can be organised. All you need is a phone, and suddenly those disaffected youth with no particular agenda can be gathered, aimed and fired. The digital age makes it easy to create a mob mentality and manipulate it. When this is allied to the power of 'fake news', it can be devastating. Again, we saw that with those faked images of an Army vehicle on O'Connell Street during the riot – when no such thing had actually occurred. Stoking the flames has never been easier.

The truly sad and dangerous part of all this is that the minority who relish this sort of violence link it explicitly to immigration. The new type of vigilantism we have seen in 2023 and 2024 has become a real threat to safety. There are actions that cannot be allowed to happen – such as stopping buses and cars and demanding information from the people travelling in them. The law is not understood by the people undertaking such actions. It is illegal to disclose that a person is an asylum claimant, so asking someone to declare that status publicly on a bus or anywhere else is overstepping the mark. The reason it's illegal is because it can put people's lives at risk. There is a solid reason for that legal protection of the person seeking asylum. When the uninformed try to take the law into their own hands, it creates far more problems than it could ever solve. The air of fear and intimidation that these actions are designed to foment are entirely unhelpful. Immigration is a reality, and the immigration process is there to check and protect. If you burn down a building, that doesn't make the people, or the problems, evaporate into thin air. The only constructive way forward in any situation is to deal with the reality of it.

In my 12 years at GNIB, where I was specifically engaged with immigration issues – both on the ground and in the academic qualifications I acquired – what I saw and learned was that the vast majority of the people arriving in Ireland are decent, happy to obey the law, would like to work and want to give better opportunities to their children. They want to live in safety, for their families to be able to go about safely, to be left in peace and to leave others in peace. Their circumstances and reasons for choosing to live here can vary widely, but there will always be a good reason. That other small number must be identified, found and if applicable filtered out, whether through refusal of leave to land or deportation. The immigration process must do its job of protecting the wider community. Once those protocols are in place, resourced effectively and working, the population can trust in that. The key, as always, is consistency of approach, communication and consultation. In this way we can significantly contribute to deflating the blown-up proportions of hatred, outrage and violence that we are all being subjected to more and more regularly.

During my time at GNIB, I had become extremely well versed in immigration law and issues and enjoyed the work very much, so I knew I would be sorry to leave that posting. However, I was also looking forward to my next move, anticipating that it would see the leadership of GNIB dropped from my remit, replaced by a dedicated role at the GNDU. In February 2015, Nóirín O'Sullivan, as acting commissioner, continued her reshuffle, and I was in for an unexpected surprise. We got word that Michael O'Sullivan would become the new head of the Drug Unit, an excellent posting given his long track record. Then word came that Dave Dowling would become the new head of the Immigration Bureau. In a move I hadn't seen coming, I received word that my role would be head of the GNBCI.

I had spent my whole career avoiding the NCBI because it was the bureau my father had headed up and that had defined his career. It was the Central Detective Unit in his time, but only the name had changed – some of my father's colleagues would still be there and they still covered the same serious crimes my father had investigated. I had always wanted to forge my own path, so NCBI had been crossed off the list as far as I was concerned. Alongside that, after so long in GNIB I did wonder if my level of knowledge of other areas of crime would be sufficient for the role. However, the commissioner needed to make changes involving the restructuring of the various bureaus and units tasked with tackling serious and organised crime and for myself and others that meant adapting to new structures.

I started my new role as head of bureau at GNBCI in March 2015. As well as the criminal investigation bureau, I was also responsible for the Garda Technical Bureau (GTB). The GTB would soon face major changes as some of its long-held functions would be divested to Forensic Science Ireland, which would move out of Garda Headquarters to a new facility at Backweston, County Kildare. In the reshuffle, extradition and missing people were moved under the remit of NCBI, while domestic and sexual violence and human trafficking were taken away from the bureau and moved to a new bureau, Protective Services. An Organised Crime Unit moved to what would now be known as the Garda National Drugs and Organised Crime Bureau (GNDOCB). It was a huge reorganisation of people and responsibilities, and everyone had to adjust to it. Seamus Boland, my old Store Street friend, was reshuffled too, and he ended up moving out of CAB, and was replaced by Gearóid Begley, who had made the visit to Denmark with us many years earlier, and into a lead role at the newly formed GNDOCB. It was good to know that our work would overlap once more and that we would no doubt be working in tandem on some cases of serious crime.

My cases now changed from bogus marriages and trafficking to homicide associated with serious and organised crime, motor vehicle crime, extradition, corruption in the public service and intellectual property crime. I had to study a whole new raft of legislation. One of our key functions was to support the districts and divisions to investigate serious crime, particularly homicide, when their resources were too thin to support an in-depth investigation. That October, just four months into my time as head of bureau, we were called into an investigation that every garda dreads – a capital murder.

On 11 October, Garda Tony Golden responded to a domestic abuse allegation. A young woman was living in fear of her abusive boyfriend, and her father had encouraged her to report it to the police and leave the relationship. She agreed. That Sunday evening, she was going to return to the house to collect her things and move back to her family home. Garda Golden drove her and her father to the house in Omeath she shared with her boyfriend. He told her father to remain in the car, and then he brought the woman into the house, to make sure she was safe. Tony Golden was in uniform and unarmed. He had no idea the woman's boyfriend, Adrian Mackin, a suspected IRA terrorist, was in the house and in possession of a firearm. When they were inside the house, Mackin appeared. He was carrying a Glock 9mm semi-automatic handgun. He shot his girlfriend in the head, critically wounding her, then he turned the gun on Garda Golden and shot him dead.

We had received a similar chilling phone call just three years earlier, when Garda Adrian Donohoe was shot dead in 2013 during an armed raid on a credit union in County Louth. The news of the killing of a garda always reverberates through the force, from Templemore right up to the commissioner's office. We are an unarmed force, and a brutal killing of this nature is deeply shocking. As a garda, you walk into domestic situations all the time, we run to them, to quickly provide the help and protection needed by the women and children, and occasionally men, under threat. It would not have occurred to us that a domestic call could turn deadly in this way. We did routinely bring firearms to house searches, but not to a domestic call.

As soon as I received the news, I drove up to Omeath. The remains of Garda Tony Golden were still inside the house. I didn't go in, though, as I had no place or function in that crime scene. Those who did have a function needed to get on with their work unimpeded. So I remained outside, keeping a vigil with other colleagues, until eventually the forensics was completed and Garda Golden was removed. As I watched and waited, I was thinking about the circumstances that had led to this terrible killing, and how we could prevent it happening in the future. Later, the Protective Services Bureau would draft new procedures designed to ensure that any member of the Garda Síochána responding to a domestic incident would have access to all relevant information about the premises they would attend and the people they were likely to encounter. That was a dark day for the Garda Síochána. Garda Golden was the eighty-eighth garda to be killed in the line of duty, and it was a terrible loss for his young family and his colleagues. It was beholden on all of us to learn from any mistakes and ensure they weren't repeated.

As the year rolled to its close and we headed into 2016, I was very much aware that my retirement was on the horizon. I had four years left in the force. The day I would have to retire would come in June 2020. I hadn't foreseen that I'd end my career back in Harcourt Square, as head of the NCBI, but that was how it was playing out. I made my peace with that prospect and settled down to my final years making a contribution to the investigation of serious crime.

PART 5

ON THE CASE OF THE OCGs
(2015-2022)

CHAPTER 13

THE BULLET THAT CHANGED EVERYTHING

They served good coffee in the coffee shop at the top of Grafton Street, so it was a good spot to hold a meeting. I arranged to meet Seamus Boland there, him as deputy head of GNDOCB and me as head of the GNBCI. There were various matters we needed to discuss, restructuring resulted in him taking charge of an organised crime unit recently moved from GNBCI to GNDOCB. We were on to our second cup, deep in conversation, when my phone beeped, and beeped again. Seamus's phone started beeping in unison with it. A chorus of texts coming in. We reached for our phones and looked at the screens. We were both being alerted to the same event, the urgency clear in the fact that we were getting the news at the same time from different sources. It was

5 February 2016, and at the Regency Hotel on the Swords Road, David Byrne had just been shot dead in cold blood and broad daylight. And eyewitnesses were saying that it was men who looked like Emergency Response Unit (ERU) gardaí who had pulled the trigger.

Seamus and I looked at one another. Whatever was going on here, there was much more to it than the alerts could tell us. He walked back to his office at Dublin Castle and I went in the other direction, to my office at Harcourt Square. In that moment, we could have no idea that the gunmen at the Regency Hotel had just put in motion a chain of events that would alter the lives of so many people; criminals, gardaí, and myself. That murder would change the course of my career, and my future plans.

The response was immediate and robust. Various units of gardaí raced to the hotel, where David Byrne's body lay against the reception desk in the foyer, blood spreading on the floor around him. The hotel was the venue for a weigh-in before a boxing match to be held that evening. One of the fighters was managed by MGM Boxing, which meant he was managed by Daniel Kinahan. The first gardaí on the scene found Byrne lying dead. He had been shot six times. A second man had been shot in the stomach and a third in the thigh. They were both on the ground, writhing in pain. The Kinahan contingent were nowhere to be seen. Neither were the gunmen. As the terrified witnesses pieced together the scene, later confirmed by CCTV footage, we heard how six armed men had calmly entered the hotel, three dressed as ERU officers and one dressed as a woman in a dress, wig and makeup. They had AK47 assault rifles and opened fire inside the hotel, even though it was crowded with people. It was a crime that we really hadn't seen the like of before.

The shock of what had occurred was palpable. As the news filtered out, everyone from the Taoiseach down to the ordinary people on the street was appalled by the utterly brazen nature of the hit team. This was another level entirely – dressing as gardaí, sauntering about with assault rifles, picking out targets and firing into a crowd. It certainly spoke of a kind of criminal gang that felt untouchable, that was operating on its own terms without regard for anything other than their own agenda. We'd seen hits before, of course – drug gangs have a penchant for taking out the opposition in a way that makes a loud statement – but not like this, not so public, so planned, so risky, so absolutely absent of any care about who saw what and who got in the way. This was a gang that obviously felt nothing and nobody could stop them or catch them or put them away. It was chilling.

As investigators filtered through the witness statements, CCTV and gathered evidence, it soon became apparent that all the key people involved were known to us. The Kinahan OCG had gained considerable notoriety, allegedly going from two-bit heroin dealers around the inner city to major international dealers living in luxury on the Costa del Sol, safely distant from the alleged selling of their cocaine and all the crime that went along with it. We quickly surmised that the likely intended target of the gunmen was a key member of the Kinahan OCG, who had been protected by his security detail and had made his getaway via a fire escape. Sources were telling us that this was a revenge killing – that the Hutch crime gang had targeted a member of the Kinahan OCG in reply to the killing of Gary Hutch in Spain in 2015. It was an eye for an eye, but they had missed the target, and now the Kinahan OCG was well aware of their intentions and bent on revenge of their own. The Hutch gang had made a serious miscalculation, and as events unfolded in the aftermath of the Regency attack it was going to cost them dearly.

The GNBCI was called in to assist on the investigation, with Ballymun Garda Station set up as the investigation HQ. I had witnessed a number of seminal moments in policing already, including the kidnapping of Don Tidey and the shoot-out during his rescue that left a garda dead, and the two murders in quick succession of Detective Garda Gerry McCabe and the journalist Veronica Guerin. Both events had wide repercussions for policing and led to important and far-reaching changes, such as the setting up of CAB. This was now another seminal moment of my career. I remember speaking with Nóirín O'Sullivan during the investigation and saying to her that the Regency shooting, despite it being a terrible crime, had very positive impacts for Garda Síochána. Out of that terror assault came positive action. We were suddenly given significantly increased resources: the money was there; the will was there; the manpower was there; and all the institutions got behind the gardaí and did everything possible to help us tackle the organised crime gangs. There was simply no denying now that things had gone way too far. The shooting showed how the location of a crime can make such a difference; if that murder had happened down a laneway, no one would have registered it – just another gangland feud, another dealer struck down. But it had happened in a normal hotel, on a normal day, with lots of normal innocent people milling about. It was the public nature of it, the complete disregard for law and order and human life that made all the difference.

The key outcome was that it showed plainly what happens when OCGs feel they have the upper hand, when their wealth has grown to a point where they feel immune. The Kinahan and Hutch gangs had amassed a huge amount of wealth, particularly the Kinahan OCG, and it allowed them to feel safe to engage in their illegal trade and live off its proceeds openly. They had the ready cash to buy the best lawyers, the best legal advice, the most advanced security tech, and that lent them a sense of invincibility. Whatever the little people tried to do, they could crush them, be they rivals or gardaí. The world was theirs for the taking, and they were too powerful for anyone to be able to prevent them from taking it. That's what everyone suddenly saw clearly as the gun smoke drifted over the Regency – the very fabric of society was under threat from these reckless, audacious, money-insulated gangsters. It presented a bleak picture of how the future might look, if they had their way.

The killing was part of a tit-for-tat series of attacks that had started in Spain, where members of both crime gangs lived. Gary Hutch, a nephew of Gerry 'The Monk' Hutch, well known to us from our Store Street days, had decided to take a key member of the Kinahan OCG out of the equation. Unfortunately for him, the hit he organised went wrong and an innocent man was shot instead. Then, on 24 September 2015, a killer had stalked Gary Hutch at his apartment block near Mijas, on the Costa del Sol, chasing him while firing bullets, and eventually shooting him dead. The Hutch OCG were distraught – and enraged. It seemed their response had been the attempted assassination in the Regency, but that too had gone wrong. If there was any doubt this was a pattern of revenge killings, a personal vendetta, it was quashed three days later. On 8 February, Eddie Hutch, the brother of Gerry Hutch, who has since been acquitted on charges relating to the Regency incident and thus is entitled to the presumption of innocence, was murdered as he stopped his taxi outside his home in Ballybough, where armed men were waiting for him and shot him nine times. The whole country was fixated on the gang warfare, and the media was reporting that if the revenge killings continued apace, we could be looking at fifty to sixty murders in short order.

The murders continued. Among those killed would be Noel 'Duck Egg' Kirwan, one of the men I had encountered the morning after the riot in Summerhill, in 1996. He was believed by the Kinihan OCG to be an associate of the Hutch family and was shot six times as he sat in his car in Clondalkin, on 22 December 2016. Significant resources were expended on maintaining armed patrols at the homes of people identified as potential targets. Responsibility for this difficult task fell on the assistant commissioner, Jack Nolan, who also ensured that every murder that could not be prevented would be afforded a thorough investigation. A total of at least 16 murders would eventually be attributed to the ongoing feud between the opposing organised crime groups. Many of the murder investigations would subsequently yield spectacular results, with many important convictions, but that would be a slow process.

The aftermath of the Regency shooting also highlighted the new angles of attack of organised crime, which would demand new angles of defence with regard to policing. In a sign of the times, the Kinahan OCG resourced reconstructing the scenes at the Regency, to support their allegation that the government was behind the killing. They made a video, released on social media, in which they suggested the explanation for an alleged slow response to the event at the Regency and the lack of any prosecution was because the state was collaborating with the culprits. The allegations of delay did not stand up to scrutiny and, of course, prosecutions were undertaken, leading to one acquittal but a number of convictions. The Kinahans were trying to sway the court of public opinion in their favour. In an unprecedented move, they also put together and published online a book on law and order that included, among other things, fake Interpol documents. Again, this was to put forward allegations of corruption in the Garda Síochána.

The truth is, there will always be instances of corruption in every organisation, but that doesn't mean the organisation itself is corrupt. But it's extremely useful to those who truly are corrupt to tarnish everything, to destabilise everything and to make it seem as if nothing is real or trustworthy. We are seeing this all across modern political life now, with the words 'fake news' constantly ringing out, making people feel as if there is no solid ground beneath their feet. It's a clever ruse because the effect of it is to push the idea that if everyone is engaged in bad actions, then there are no bad actions, therefore each person is free to behave however they wish. It's a familiar, but deeply divisive, playbook. The Kinahan cartel was savvy enough to invoke it on their behalf. It showed the vastly shifting landscape the Gardaí now face when dealing with OCGs.

In the midst of this high-pressure and fast-paced investigation, in which I was investing a huge amount of time as head of GNBCI, there was another unexpected event. On 24 May, I was sitting in my office when I received a call from the commissioner, Nóirín O'Sullivan. I updated her on the Regency case and related matters, but then she said that was not the purpose of her call. At the time, it felt that our world had narrowed down to just the Regency, so I hadn't anything else in mind when she rang. But now she told me that she had news about my position. An interview board she had participated in had just greenlighted my promotion to assistant commissioner (AC), and she expected the Cabinet to ratify the appointment later that day.

It took a while for the news to sink in. A few minutes earlier the most likely outcome, with so few positions at the rank of assistant commissioner, was that I would never make that rank. Now I was only minutes away from holding it. Then the news got even better. The Cabinet had met and it was revealed that there were to be four new assistant commissioners. In an office one floor above mine, Eugene Corcoran, then chief bureau officer in CAB, was also promoted. We had shared a room in the training college almost forty years earlier, and now we were sharing the sense of achievement of being promoted to such high office in the Garda Síochána. Also promoted were Michael O'Sullivan, current head of bureau at GNDOCB, and Anne Marie McMahon, who was director of training at Templemore. My own role would eventually be AC with responsibility for serious and organised crime, but before that I remained assigned to GNBCI for a number of months while additional organisational restructuring took place.

My first task after the appointment was a controversial one that would place me under great scrutiny – a baptism of fire into the public-facing responsibilities of an AC. A political debate was raging around the question of reopening garda stations. There had been a programme of rationalisation after the economic crash in 2008, when the Garda Síochána was faced with the closure of 139 stations. There had been huge public outcry from residents in areas earmarked to lose their local station, but it was implemented nonetheless. Eight years on, there was growing demand for reopenings. In the general election campaign of 2016, Taoiseach Enda Kenny, as leader of Fine Gael, had been supported by independent candidates like Shane Ross in return for certain issues being written into the programme for government – one of those being the reopening of six garda stations.

The Minister for Justice asked the Garda Commissioner to identify six stations for reopening on a pilot basis. In the request, the minister set out the criteria for selection, which included local population and crime trends, and they had to be stations that were still in state ownership. That request was passed on to me, and I was to conduct a review and nominate the six stations. My own private opinion was that rationalisation was a good course of action. I had seen that in Copenhagen and how well it worked. Many garda stations had been built when we patrolled on bicycles, so they were set up at very regular distances for piecemeal policing. That was fine at the time, but it didn't suit the way we policed in the twenty-first century. So my private thoughts were that reopening closed stations was an unwise course of action, but my public duty was to assess it thoroughly and make the recommendations. I was aware, though, that one of the controversial aspects was a lingering suspicion that Shane Ross TD was motivated by a desire to see his local station, Stepaside, reopened, so people were watching carefully to see which six stations would be put forward.

For a long time, no one was looking for the report. I worked away methodically, studying census data on population figures and crime, taking into account weekly changes of population and passengers through Dublin Airport. I began to compile the final list, but also included potential locations for new or enhanced stations, such as at airports and seaports. Then one Friday in March 2017, there was suddenly an almighty clamour for the report. The government wanted it immediately. I worked flat out the whole weekend, and submitted it before opening of business on Monday morning, with the final list comprising Stepaside and Rush (County Dublin), Leighlinbridge (County Carlow), Donard (County Wicklow), Ballinspittle (County Cork) and Bawnboy (County Cavan). I accompanied the Commissioner and others into Leinster House, where an Oireachtas committee subjected us to a grilling on our choices, especially given that one of the six was Stepaside Garda Station. In fact, the criteria issued by the Minister for Justice meant that Stepaside really had to be chosen because it fitted those criteria exactly. But I made sure I wasn't being used by either side – I listed out the criteria that had to be taken on board, and I showed all my workings. I could stand over the list as an impartial, fact-based assessment.

In spite of my thorough and transparent research and reasoning presented in the report, there was a strong negative reaction from opposition politicians. It was, predictably enough, the inclusion of Stepaside that ignited their criticism. There were allegations flying about and aspersions being cast at the report. However, I and my colleagues had to simply grin and bear it because we had to remain neutral from a political perspective. That is a crucial element of policing. It can be a difficult cross to bear at times, but it is part of the senior roles in the organisation, and I had to accept that, particularly now as I moved into the highly accountable role of AC. If the then opposition parties were to win the following general election, the Garda Síochána would be just as committed to implementing their programme for government.

In early August 2016, I received my first appointment as AC when I was assigned to the Northern Region, which involved being based at Sligo Garda Station. In addition, I was assigned to simultaneously head up a new Community

Engagement section. This assignment would be short-lived, but long enough to witness a very tragic event in the Northern Region. Not even a month into my tenure, on 29 August, local gardaí in Cavan received a worrying call. A relative had gone to the Hawe home in Ballyjamesduff at about 10.45 that morning and found a note pinned to the back door, warning any caller not to enter the house but instead to summon the gardaí. The relative had done just that and was now anxiously waiting for the garda support to arrive and find out what the note meant.

The local gardaí made their way to the house immediately. Inside, they made the grim discovery of the bodies of Alan Hawe, his wife, Clodagh, and their three children, 13-year-old Liam, 11-year-old Niall and six-year-old Ryan. Alan Hawe was a local school principal and his wife was a local teacher, so the family were well known. The whole community was deeply shocked and saddened by their sudden and violent deaths. I was working in Dublin when the news of the finding came through, and I drove straight to the garda station in Ballyjamesduff to talk with the superintendent. The scene had been preserved and forensics were under way. The main challenge at that time was the level of media interest, with cameras and journalists turning up in their droves. It was understandable, given the level of shock and the brutality of the killings, but it had to be managed so that it didn't affect the investigation or cause more trauma to family members.

We held a press conference outside the garda station. I gave as much information as I could, while emphasising that it was a sensitive case and we had to speak to all family members before releasing all the information. I answered all questions as honestly and thoroughly as I could at that time. I am an absolute believer in the usefulness of a well-planned press conference. If you reassure the public that no one else is vulnerable, that the perpetrator is not likely to offend again, and that the investigation is well under way, it calms the situation. That was the aim in Ballyjamesduff, and I think we achieved that aim.

The case was an extremely difficult one for investigators because of the violent nature of the murders. It was a crime scene that no emergency response personnel could ever forget. Alan Hawe had killed Clodagh by hitting her with an axe and stabbing her with a knife. He had slashed his sons' throats, rendering them incapable of crying out. When all his family were dead, Alan Hawe had killed himself. It was incomprehensible – an act of sheer terror and terrific violence visited on those he was meant to love and care for, those who were meant to be able to trust him as their protector. For a father to do that was beyond understanding. It is difficult for others to appreciate the impact of such a horrific event on bereaved families, friends and neighbours. That also applies to gardaí and paramedics and scenes of crime officers. It's a nightmarish scenario, the kind that can haunt those who have to witness it. And as I've noted before, it's an act of mercy that the gardaí and medics perform for the family, to take care of their loved ones in death and afford them the respect and integrity that their murderer denied them.

The organisational restructuring was finally completed some months later, and on 1 November 2016, as assistant commissioner, I assumed the role of regional commander in charge of Special Crime Operations (SCO), based in Harcourt Square in Dublin. I would now have charge of all the crime bureaus dedicated to various aspects of serious and organised crime, from drugs to economic crime, cyber crime to organised immigration crime, human trafficking to allegations of corruption among state employees, and a lot more. I would also assume a more important role with regard to tackling criminality associated with the Kinahan–Hutch feud.

The key approach was still disrupting planned criminality, and we were starting to score more successes in that regard. In January 2017, the GNDOCB, supported by the ERU, entered a business premises in Greenogue in Dublin and uncovered an arsenal of weapons maintained by the Kinahan OCG. There were 17 in total, including pistols, revolvers, a sub-machine gun and an AK-47-style assault rifle. A number of handguns were armed and ready for use. This find would represent a major blow to the Kinahan OCG as it also involved the arrest of a number of significant crime group members.

There were a series of murders that we could not prevent, but we also intervened on about seventy occasions to prevent a loss of life. Based on our intel, we were regularly able to issue Garda Information Messages (GIMs) to those who were potentially next in line to be targeted. A GIM is a formal notification of a threat to life, which is served on the intended victim by the Gardaí. We warn them of the threat, and offer to discuss with them how to be vigilant about their safety.

When I took on the role of head of Special Crime Operations, I became convinced that it was necessary to include another strand to our strategy of intervening in threat-to-life situations. We recognised that criminal organisations exercise power over each other, and anyone else who interferes with their criminal enterprise, by showing that they can murder at will. The hierarchy of a wealthy OCG can, at a remove, make a payment, hire a hitman or team and provide whatever weapons are necessary. Job done. Our thinking was: if we seize a firearm, it will be easily replaced; if we prevent a murder today by warning a victim, the OCG will merely take their time and pick another day. However, we assessed that top-quality hitmen, the ones OCGs tend to use, are potentially regular killers and are scarce. The courts in Ireland do not impose very significant sentences on those arrested in possession of a firearm. However, if the weapon-holders could be found in circumstances where the state could prove they had an intent to murder, lengthier sentences would be imposed, one or more planned murders would be prevented, and the hitman or team would be out of circulation for a long time. Successfully implementing this strategy would, we believed, bring down the murder rate over a longer period of time.

To succeed, however, we would have to know when a murder was being planned and to discover who the hitman or team would be. OCGs would usually plan a hit over time, do their own surveillance, pick the best opportunity to make a hit. We would have to become efficient at knowing their every step and being there to intervene at the time of potentially greatest impact. We would need to get court authorisations to utilise surveillance-related legislation to track and record those involved in planned hits. It would be hugely labour-intensive and costly because it would require skilled surveillance teams and firearms experts.

A perfect opportunity to put our strategy into practice arose when we got word that a foreign gun for hire, nicknamed 'The Butcher', was flying in to take on some of the work and outmanoeuvre the Garda operation. He wasn't a person we would have expected the Kinahan OCG to employ, so it was a strategic move that could have proved extremely successful, but as it was, he never got the chance to pull the trigger.

On 3 April 2017, we placed an Estonian man called Imre Arakas, who had that day arrived at Dublin airport from Alicante, Spain, under surveillance. Arakas, a suspected contracted hitman, was observed travelling by bus from the airport into the city centre. Having got off the bus at O'Connell Street, he walked towards Henry Street, then up Moore Street. The surveillance team watched as he bought a wig in a shop there and some other items. It was suspected that Imre Arakas was in Dublin on cartel business and his every move would be closely monitored. He was picked up that night by a white Mercedes van and spent the night in Blakestown Cottages, near Blanchardstown. The GNDOCB made their move the next morning, bursting into the house and taking the occupants by surprise. When they rushed to the room where Arakas was standing, he was on his BlackBerry. One of the team quickly took photos of the thread of messages on the phone, knowing they would no doubt be deleted remotely within minutes – as they were. But we had the images. We also had a piece of paper on which was written the name of a Hutch associate and a sentence in Estonian. When translated, we found it was directions to where this man was hiding out in Belfast.

We had our hitman and our evidence of his intentions. It was exactly the strategy we were aiming to carry out, and excellent surveillance work had secured the arrest. Arakas was questioned for two days, then brought to Dublin District Court and charged with conspiracy to murder. The top-tier marksman and hitman had been taken out of the game before the whistle had even been blown. It was a remarkable operation and outcome for all participating Garda units and it denied the cartel what they had no doubt planned to be a significant secret weapon.

The arrest of Arakas felt like a watershed moment in the operation to subdue the Kinahan OCG, and there was a second hugely significant moment that November. This was when all of the intensive work culminated in a major successful strike. We had become aware that there was an active plan in train for the murder of Gary Hanley, a convicted criminal himself who was regarded as a Hutch associate. A hit team had been put together and were busy staking out Hanley's daily routine. While they were doing that, they had no idea we were staking them out, maintaining constant covert surveillance. The Garda teams were waiting, hoping to make their move at just the right moment. The hit team was made up of some veteran criminals who were feared and considered dangerous even by their own ilk. The Wilson family were known across Dublin and had been involved in criminal activity all their lives – Alan, his cousin Eric 'Lucky' Wilson, and Luke Wilson. They were joined by two others to fill the roles of getaway drivers. We were able to track their movements as they planned to murder Hanley. On the nominated day, at about 8 p.m., they made their way to the road where Hanley lived. We knew that in the van were the firearms and the hit team, about to put their plan into action. The order to go was given and officers of the Special Tactics and Operation Command leapt into action and surrounded the van in seconds, guns drawn. The hit team were caught red-handed, with firearms in their possession.

It was the perfect ambush from our point of view – we had hard evidence from our surveillance, we had their phones and all the evidence they contained, we had the key hit team members together in one place with loaded guns, and a life had been saved thanks to our intervention. A number of months later, in March 2017, in a similar operation and after a long surveillance, a hit team was arrested on Parnell Street as they were about to execute a plan to murder Patsy Hutch, another brother of Gerry Hutch. This was exactly the disruption we wanted to cause to the Kinahan OCG. Hit teams were being taken out of circulation and were becoming scarcer and more reluctant to be our next target.

Our approach was working. At the same time, these were expensive operations. That level of covert operation eats up time and money – but it delivered, with incredible swoops on the armed-and-ready hit teams. Significant numbers of guns for hire were taken out of circulation. There had been concern about the costs of these operations, the amount of public money being diverted into this work, and consequently not available for other policing demands, but there were huge benefits accruing from it. We always argued that there could only be so many hit teams at work, so there was significant potential that we were arresting criminals who had already carried out similar crimes – and it seemed safe to assume that we were preventing them from committing future crimes. There's actually a huge cost saving to preventing a murder. Despite the not unreasonable concern about the cost involved, my immediate boss, Deputy Commissioner John Twomey, placed his trust in our capacity to deliver planned results and ensured the necessary resources were available.

I would soon after be required to prepare a report for the Comptroller and Auditor General on the economics of our expensive intervention strategy. In doing so, I showed that our chosen approach of preventing murders was, in fact, the correct and most cost-effective use of resources. For one thing, a murder investigation may cost about €5–€8 million, so we were saving that money with each life we saved through intervention. There is also the time taken to investigate a murder, which takes resources away from other crimes and policing priorities. And there is also the fact that preventing a murder is a high-profile activity that generates support for the Garda Síochána and its future work. The strategy resulted in a significant reduction in gangland murders over the following years. It was a proper and high-return use of our resources.

Tackling OCGs necessarily requires cross-border collaboration because they are cross-border enterprises. The Kinahan OCG had a network stretching from South America to Africa, so a police force working alone wouldn't get very far. We had links with the Spanish police reaching back to the early 2000s, and we were forging more links as we worked on disrupting

Kinahans' shipments of firearms and cocaine. A particularly important partner in this regard was the UK's National Crime Agency (NCA), and we found great support from Robin Barnett, the UK Ambassador to Ireland. He held events occasionally at his residence at which law enforcement officers from both jurisdictions could meet and talk, and generally offered every assistance possible so that we could help each other in chasing down the Kinahan OCG operations.

There was one occasion that struck me as another sign of the times moment. A number of Garda representatives and I attended a gathering in a premises in Ballsbridge hosted by the deputy head of mission. As we were leaving, the suggestion was floated that we go for a pint. I knew Ballsbridge well and nominated Crowe's public house nearby, the pub where I'd had my very first pint of Guinness many years before. It was agreed and we headed in that direction. I turned to see Robin Barnett standing next to me. He asked where we were going and I told him about Crowe's. To my surprise, he asked if he could join us. We walked there together and then took the last two bar stools and enjoyed our pints side by side. We talked about Irish history and I told him about my family connection to Michael Collins. By the end of our conversation, we had agreed a plan for us to travel down to West Cork, to visit the Collins birthplace. Unfortunately, Covid put paid to that plan.

As we chatted and sipped our pints, I was struck by how the passage of time shifts everything in its path. Back in 1976, my father had been part of the investigation into the murder of the British ambassador, Christopher Ewart-Biggs, who was a victim of the Provisional IRA at a time when tensions were running dangerously high. The ambassador and the embassy were not safe then, as we had seen when the embassy was burned down in 1972 and again when protestors threatened its perimeter in 1981. And now here we sat, thirty years later, sharing talk of history and enjoying each other's company.

This very thought struck me again that May, when I had the unique opportunity to attend a very special historical event. The Glasnevin Trust was hosting Charles, then Prince of Wales, and his wife Camilla, then Duchess of Cornwall, for the unveiling of Victoria Cross paving stones at Glasnevin cemetery to honour all those who had died in the Easter Rising 1916, killed by the British forces. Commissioner O'Sullivan could not attend, and I was asked to be present in her stead. There was a particularly poignant moment during the ceremony, when Prince Charles stood near the grave of Michael Collins, as I was standing behind him, in uniform, in the company of Robin Barnett and Dan Mulhall, Ireland's ambassador to the UK. Given my family background, and my family's long dedication to public service, which we could trace right back to Collins himself, it was an incredible experience. I thought of my grand-father, Michael O'Brien, Collins's first cousin, neighbour and school pal, and wondered what his reaction would be if he could bear witness to this gathering – and my place in it.

It is good to receive those reminders that time does change everything, that nothing remains in stasis, that when you are facing an intractable problem – like policing a fast-changing society – you can trust in the fact that things will reach an end. You cannot control what exactly comes next or when, but when good deeds are sown, they do at some point push through and bloom into something new. We were seeing that now with the new relationships being forged between Ireland and the UK, and the security relationship was part of that. When history is honoured and understood, that allows for new perspectives. As we moved onto the second angle of attack on the Kinahan crime organisation – targeting the wider enterprise in order to dismantle the many networks and revenue streams – those relationships and collaborations would prove to the cornerstone of that endeavour. There would be a new level of cooperation that would reflect the new level of criminality we all had to take on, together.

CHAPTER 14

THE BROAD REMIT OF
AN ASSISTANT COMMISSIONER

There might have been a perception that my time as AC was spent solely on the Kinahan OCG investigation, but that was not the case at all. It was a constant thread running through my working day, but it ran in tandem with many other important and challenging undertakings. The remit of any AC is extremely broad, and we have to oversee a huge number of investigations and cases. I was kept exceptionally busy at this time – I had one eye on retirement, which was now not long away, still slated for June 2020, but I also focused on getting through as much of my extensive workload as I could before that day arrived.

One of the very enjoyable aspects of being a senior officer is the opportunity to attend various ceremonies. I had been honoured to attend that historic ceremony at Glasnevin, and in June 2019 I was equally honoured to attend a Kinahan investigation-related award ceremony. The Spanish Guardia Civil and the Garda Síochána had established a very successful working partnership over the previous twenty years, dovetailing our investigations into the Kinahan cartel. One particular success was the investigation of the murder of Trevor O'Neill, who was shot dead near Santa Ponsa, Mallorca, in a case of mistaken identity. The gunman mistook him for a member of the Hutch family who was on the hit list – but Trevor O'Neill was in fact an innocent man on holiday with his family and had no connection whatsoever to the gangs or the feud. The Gardaí, particularly GNDOCB, and the Guardia Civil had worked together very effectively to deliver an arrest and conviction in that and other cases.

The Guardia Civil was hosting a ceremony to mark the 175th anniversary of its foundation, to be held at its HQ on the island of Mallorca, and in a most unusual move its chief officers decided to recognise the contribution of the Garda Síochána to policing in Spain. They invited my old friend Seamus Boland, now head of GNDOCB, and Detective Sergeant Kevin Duggan, our liaison officer in Spain, to receive their most prestigious award for service, the Merit Order Cross. It was an incredible honour for both men and it reflected the depth of the collaboration between the two jurisdictions and the impact of that collaboration. To my delight, I was invited to attend the ceremony, which I did, along with the two medal recipients, in uniform. As I watched my colleagues being recognised and awarded, I felt it was a wonderful testament to how far we had come in our efforts to undermine the power and the intent of the Kinahan cartel. At the same time, there was much work still to be done.

The OCGs needed to have people in the right places doing the wrong things to enable their shipments to pass through borders and customs checks unimpeded. At an international level, law enforcement was aware of this, and of the need to bring as many private companies as possible on board, to ensure we were all pulling in the same direction and working to stop the flow of contraband. This will get easier in time, as technology takes over certain jobs from humans, such as loading and checking containers. No matter how much money you have, you can't bribe a robot. But for now, that remains a concern, both in private enterprise and in state agencies. This was reflected in the appointment of Patrick Sullivan as one of three ombudsman commissioners at the Garda Síochána Ombudsman Commission (GSOC). He had a background in the US Secret Service and federal agencies in the USA and brought that wealth of experience with him into the role. When he contacted me looking to meet, I was very interested to talk with him and hear about his career.

He came to my office at Harcourt Square, and we discussed his new role and my new role and the work being done in Ireland to tackle OCGs. He had extensive experience of oversight in US federal agencies and he remarked that in his new role he intended placing a particular focus on any incidents of corruption of gardaí by association with organised crime. I was thinking to myself that it wasn't a problem we had encountered much and I didn't think he would have much to deal with in that regard. As with any organisation of its size, the Garda Síochána has discovered wrongdoing among its employees, often associated with personal problems, such as alcohol addiction, but we had rarely had cases of serious corruption. But then his words also made me think about the threat assessment documents from Europol, which frequently referenced the extent to which OCGs were targeting public officials across Europe. It struck me that it would not be wise to consider the Garda Síochána immune to this and that it might be an area that could potentially become a much bigger problem and that would need to be monitored carefully.

As we talked, we exchanged stories about cases we had worked on, and he told me he had worked on a case with an Irish link back in his Secret Service days. The US Secret Service was responsible for investigating all dollar counterfeits, and in 1989 they noticed that there were high-quality fake $100 bills in circulation. An investigation ensued, and it eventually led them to Irishman Sean Garland, one-time general secretary of Official Sinn Féin and later president of the Workers' Party, and also a former leader of the IRA in the late 1960s and early 1970s. The US lodged an extradition warrant and Garland was arrested by the PSNI in 2005. He was released on bail and headed south of the border. He was later arrested by the Garda Síochána, but much to the annoyance of Patrick Sullivan and his colleagues, the High Court dismissed the USA's extradition application.

I listened to this with great interest, then I said, 'Let me show you something.' I went over to a drawer where I kept personal items, took out a photograph and handed it to him. He looked at it, then looked at me in puzzlement. It was a photo of a crime scene. I explained that it had appeared on the front page of the *Sunday Press* in March 1975. In it, my father and his boss, Detective Chief Superintendent John Joy, were standing at the scene of an attempted murder in Ballymun. The victim? Sean Garland. He was returning home from the theatre with his wife when the Irish National Liberation Army (INLA) tried to assassinate him. They fired eight bullets at him, and he only survived because he protected his head with his hands. So in his hands Sullivan was holding a photo of my father investigating a murder attempt on his counterfeiter. He was fascinated by the coincidence – and by the story. I told him how the photographer, a neighbour, had arrived at our family home and given us a copy of the photo, because he thought we might like to have it. I had kept it safe and, lo and behold, almost half a century later, a man from the US Secret Service walks into my office and begins to talk about Sean

Garland. Another of those many interesting coincidences in my career.

The words Patrick Sullivan spoke in my office that day, those warning words about corruption always going hand in hand with the huge financial power of organised crime gangs, would prove, in time, to be prophetic. The GNBCI would experience a significant increase in the number of criminal investigations it would have to initiate with a Garda employee as a suspect. It was an expanding problem. We had cases of gardaí allegedly assisting criminals in obtaining passports, a civilian staff member selling information from PULSE (the Garda computerised information system) and a number of gardaí being the defendant in cases of coercive control pertaining to their personal lives. In response, a new internal affairs unit was set up at Garda HQ to take on all investigations of this nature as a centralised unit. Of course, GSOC would also have an important role to play, its function being to deal with matters involving possible misconduct by members of the Garda Síochána in an efficient, effective and fair manner. The fact that, in 2022, a retired superintendent was charged and convicted of possession for sale of a significant quantity of cannabis served to highlight the need to be proactive in preventing corruption in the organisation.

As an AC, you are overseeing so many bureaus and there is a constant stream of information to contend with, but it does also give you the chance to shape policy and organisational change. During my tenure as an AC, I would be tasked with developing policy with regard to the introduction of an Investigation Management System (IMS). This is an electronic solution designed to regulate and support the administration and control of an investigation and specified operations undertaken by the Garda Síochána arising from a crime incident. The IMS was designed to augment the management of all investigative assignments, allocation of roles, and documentation relating to the conduct of an investigation and operation. The IMS rollout, which was in progress when I retired, will track a full history of the chain of events relating to an investigation or operation, and information and evidence gathered along the way. This initiative will help ensure proper governance of an investigation and prevent many of the faults that haunted investigations undertaken in the past.

My role as AC also involved chairing a group assigned an oversight role with regard to training detectives in the Garda Síochána. In my time as an AC this role would include an opportunity to implement recommendations made at an earlier time relating to ensuring the process of interviewing suspects would be done in a way that would be above reproach, and unrecognisable compared to the way it was done in earlier years, when it was the focus of considerable controversy. One initiative involved the appointment, on a full-time basis, of a member at inspector rank who would be responsible at a national level for oversight of the process of interviewing suspects. The first person to assume the role, on a full-time basis, was Inspector Karen Clifford, who would be based in an office in Special Crime Operations. Her role would include attending at locations where suspects were being interviewed and, by way of monitor in another room, ensuring that the interviewing was being undertaken in a lawful and appropriate way.

The teaching and practice of interview techniques has, thankfully, changed markedly in the course of my career. It was a much-needed change, to my mind. Until the 1980s, gardaí had no power of arrest solely for the purpose of interviewing a suspect. This would have been the way it was when my father was policing Dublin city – you could ask someone to voluntarily come down to the station, but there was no power to arrest them for the purpose of interview. That changed in 1984, when power of arrest was granted for interviewing, although it isn't a blanket power and doesn't apply to summary offences that are dealt with in the District Courts. In my father's time, that meant that solving crimes was highly dependent on an admission of guilt. That was a problematic situation because it could lead to miscarriages of justice, whereby an admission of guilt was secured under duress or alleged to have been so derived. It didn't help matters that interviews were not recorded at that time.

A tradition of tough, uncompromising interviewing had grown up in particular units. After the 1974 Dublin bombings, the government had enacted the Emergency Powers Act and it was alleged that a certain cohort of gardaí saw that as a 'get results at all costs' instruction, one where the end justified the means. The Murder Squad, a unit based in Garda headquarters that was dispatched throughout the country to investigate serious crime, had acquired a negative reputation in this regard. Allegations of improper investigative practices were a feature of the 1980s and associated with such investigations such as the Kerry Babies case. The alleged approach was one of heavy-handed interrogation with a view to securing a confession. The Murder Squad were controversial for their methods and eventually disbanded, with their role transferring out of Garda headquarters to the GNBCI. That sort of interview style is, thankfully, no longer a feature of crime investigation.

In early 2022, RTÉ aired a series called *Crimes and Confessions* which looked at three of the most notorious miscarriages of justice from the 1970s and 1980s and posed questions about how it appeared particular gardaí were able to continue over a number of years to use the same alleged tactics to get false confessions and convictions. The commissioner accepted a request from RTÉ to participate and respond to the questions posed; he delegated that task to me. The final episode has an interview with me, in which I responded to some of the questions the series had raised. In doing so, I accepted it was incorrect for anyone to persist in justifying some of the investigative techniques of the time, but highlighted that they had occurred almost half a century earlier. I went on to describe how the investigation of crime and interviewing of suspects had radically changed since then. The day after the programme aired, I received a call from the Policing Authority thanking me for my 'important' contribution. An ability to acknowledge that policing did not always adopt best practices in the past tends to engender a greater level of belief that lessons have been learned and faults are being rectified.

Nowadays, there is no longer a dependence on an admission of guilt. Instead, investigators are looking for hard evidence because a court case demands a high level of provability. That said, the ability to conduct an effective interview is a necessary skill, which is why training is so important. The garda interviewers operating today are highly skilled and highly trained. They undertake a special course, studying either basic or advanced interview techniques. Only a certain number will pass the course. Those who fail tend to do so because of an inability to grasp the concept of a leading question, some for unintentionally offering induce-ments, saying things like 'We can talk about bail later,' and still others for being overly aggressive in their manner. Those who do pass have excelled in all the techniques and can be trusted to conduct lawful and effective interviews.

This is very important because any sort of misbehaviour or misstep during the interview process can leave the door open for a defence barrister in court to suggest that investigators had not adhered to correct procedures, which could compromise the evidence procured. However, it can be frustrating to hear lawyers brag about their skills at winkling information or admissions out of a witness on the stand, to celebrate having managed to get someone to say something they had not intended to say, but suggest that an investigator doing the same thing must have done so in an illegal manner. It has been a positive step for all concerned – gardaí, criminals, victims, the judiciary – that every interview is recorded in full, usually both audio and video.

The most high-profile and extraordinary and, I think it's fair to say, unexpected interviewing of my career came when I was responsible for an investigation in the course of which it was necessary to interview then Tánaiste, Leo Varadkar TD, who was former Taoiseach and likely to be the next Taoiseach. We had to tread very carefully because there could potentially have been an element of 'fake news' involved – the Gardaí receive regular calls from citizens to complain about politicians without a scintilla of a basis for the complaint, so we are always wary about jumping to any conclusions. In this case, however, the allegations had been supported by two senior counsel, who naturally would be expected to know which actions would constitute a potential breach of criminal law. It was an undoubtedly sensitive case and all of its various aspects had to be managed carefully.

The allegations that arrived in a report on my desk regarded actions of Mr Varadkar in 2019, while he was Taoiseach. There were negotiations between the government and GPs, represented by the Irish Medical Organisation. On Tuesday 9 April, a memorandum was brought to Cabinet by Minister for Health Simon Harris, informing them that 'engagement had concluded' with the Irish Medical Organisation. A number of days after this, Varadkar posted a copy of the agreement, from the Office of An Taoiseach, to Dr Maitiú Ó Tuathail, president of the National Association of General Practitioners. Over a year later, on 13 November 2020, Michael Smith, editor of *Village* magazine, forwarded an email to the Garda National Economic Crime Bureau (GNECB) in which he alleged that this action was a breach of the Official Secrets Act and of the Criminal Justice (Corruption of Offences) Act 2018 and also, potentially, a breach of data protection legislation. That email was immediately passed to me.

I replied by letter to Michael Smith, informing him that we would examine the issue with a view to establishing if a criminal investigation was in order, and that the initial assessment would be undertaken by the GNBCI. That correspondence would end up being published in the March/April 2022 edition of *Village*. When the allegations became public, the Taoiseach made a statement in the Dáil, acknowledging that the informal communication channel he had used was not good practice. He accepted sole responsibility and apologised. He also defended his position, denying that any criminal wrongdoing had been involved in his actions.

As could be expected, the media interest in this case was colossal. The investigation would be under spotlight scrutiny from first to last, which always adds a layer of pressure. But we had one clear focus: had there been a breach of criminal law? It was not for us to question the motive of anyone who would make such an allegation; we only had to find out if there were grounds to launch a criminal investigation. We consulted regularly with the DPP's office, which is normal procedure during a complex case. This helps to ensure that the investigation remains properly focused on the salient aspects of the case and also facilitates the quicker issuing of a direction when the file is eventually submitted. As a result of our initial assessment, it became clear that it would be necessary to commence a criminal investigation and to send a file to the DPP at its conclusion.

That decision meant we had to interview Mr Varadkar as part of the criminal investigation. He was called for interview on two occasions and gave comprehensive statements both times. From my point of view, it was crucial to ensure there were no leaks to the media during this process. Obviously I was aware that journalists were clamouring for any snippet of information, but we had to follow the process assiduously and not compromise a fair trial, should the case end up in court. I made sure that no one could leak information about the time and location of those two interviews, so that Mr Varadkar would not be observed arriving or leaving. The detectives in GNBCI had considerable experience of sensitive investigations involving government departments and employees and they went about their business with their usual efficiency, remaining quietly in the background.

One of the big challenges of the investigation was that it took place during Covid-19 restrictions, which added extra time to the whole process. We were occasionally criticised in the media for the timescale involved in conducting the interviews. It did take longer than everyone wanted, which we understood, but it had to be carried out properly, and I would not rush an investigation to suit other agendas. Journalists occasionally published claims that the file had been forwarded to the DPP, but each time they were incorrect. I knew they were pushing for access to team members, but I was satisfied they weren't gaining any traction on that front, and I was able to reassure Commissioner Drew Harris that the investigation was being progressed in an appropriate manner and that I was certain there were no leaks. He was asked about it regularly, too, and ultimately would have to take responsibility if the case was in any way mishandled. I remember one day a journalist asked Drew Harris about the Varadkar investigation and he replied that he had recently been fully briefed about its status. I smiled as he said that, because I was thinking of the nature of that briefing. We had been in

Washington just days before, at high-level meetings regarding the Kinahan OCG investigation and other matters. One day we had a break between meetings and took the opportunity to visit Arlington cemetery. At one point, it was just the commissioner and myself, side by side, and as we walked among the graves I discreetly gave him an update on a number of sensitive matters, including with regard to the Varadkar investigation. That was the briefing he was referring to when answering the journalist's question. Again, a nod to the number of significant cases we were attending to at one time.

When the investigation was fully concluded, in April 2022, we submitted a comprehensive file to the DPP, seeking direction as to whether criminal proceedings should be commenced. The decision was issued that a prosecution would not arise based on the evidence. That concluded the matter. Varadkar had admitted wrongdoing, but it did not give rise to a criminal prosecution. There was no charge to be answered.

While there was criticism aimed at us during that investigation, I felt proud of how we had undertaken it and I felt that it reflected very well on our democracy. We had investigated the allegations impartially, proving that our justice system did not favour anyone. The Tánaiste was treated as a citizen, like any other. It was an onerous task, to undertake an investigation of a person in high office, but the criminal law applies equally to everyone. It was essential that no person, irrespective of the position they hold, would be seen to be above the law when the subject of a criminal allegation. Our work in response to this allegation proved that this was the case, which I feel was an extremely important outcome.

As mentioned, that investigation took place during the pandemic and its associated lockdowns, which afflicted the country – indeed, the world – from February 2020. The virus reached Ireland just days after I had submitted my application seeking an extended retirement date. The compulsory retirement age was 60 years, and I had mid-2020 pegged as my retirement date since passing out from Templemore. Now that year had arrived, and I found myself in no way ready to leave – the Kinahan case was becoming more and more complex and I felt it could deliver in a big way, and I wanted to remain in place to guide it through. I drew on the provision in the retirement regulations that allow for a member with special qualification or experience to apply for an extension, which could only be granted by the consent of the Minister for Justice.

I didn't have to wait long for a reply. On 26 March 2020, Charles Flanagan TD, Minister for Justice, wrote to the Commissioner to confirm his consent to my request. My new retirement date was set at June 2022. I had requested five more years, so there was some disappointment at not receiving the full quota, but I was nonetheless delighted to have an opportunity to provide another two years of public service. Looking back on it now, I am extremely grateful that I was permitted to continue in my work. If I had retired in 2020, I would have been launched straight into a tiny life, adhering to that holding pattern of walking 2km this way and 2km that way. I would have found that extremely frustrating. As it was, those new final two years of my career would be incredibly eventful.

There is no chapter in the Garda manual on how to police a country during a pandemic. All we had at the start were questions, and no answers: How do you police in a pandemic? Will policing be needed? What type of policing? Where should we deploy people? What roles should we give them? We had to learn the answers in real time, on the job. We quickly realised that, yes, we were still needed because crime wasn't going to stop. And then we came to realise that we had a whole new range of crimes to tackle – online criminality went through the roof, with scams being constantly dreamt up and launched. It soon became apparent that cyber crime was going to present us with a huge set of challenges. My father couldn't have imagined such a problem, or such a bureau to tackle it – indeed, I couldn't have imagined it at the early stages of my own career. There was a huge learning curve to ascend and everyone in the Garda Síochána had to work around the clock dealing with the consequences of the pandemic and catching up with the fraudsters and hackers.

For some time we had been developing a cyber-related investigation capacity. There was a unit in the GNECB, headed by Detective Superintendent Pat Ryan, who had shaped it into a very capable unit, albeit inadequately resourced. Just as had happened with regard to drugs, fraud and immigration in earlier years, it had reached the point where it was necessary to establish a separate, dedicated bureau for cyber-related matters. In 2021, I was successful in getting permission to establish a Garda National Cyber Crime Bureau (GNCCB) and I was delighted when Paul Cleary, who had worked with me in the Store Street Drug Unit and who had been promoted to the rank of chief superintendent in 2019, was appointed as the first head of the new bureau.

It also became clear that the organised crime groups were not resting. In particular, drug trafficking was only slightly disrupted, so we could not afford to reduce the resources we were deploying in this area. It also meant that we needed to be able to move, so an early vaccination programme was organised that key members, myself included, could avail of. Many of our own meetings migrated online and we became adept at Zoom and Teams, like the rest of the country who were working from home. The senior management team held online meetings a number of times per day, updating each other on the issues as they emerged.

For my own part, I was constantly scanning the global policing scene, looking for clues as to what we might expect.

Ireland entered into the Covid landscape a little later than some of our fellow EU Member States, so I was looking to them to find out what sort of problems it was causing their law enforcement agencies. This was how, from the earliest days of the pandemic's arrival into Ireland, I was advising the senior management team of an emerging trend of increased levels of domestic abuse and violence. There were extremely worrying red flags and we knew we would have to confront this potential upsurge quickly. At least we were working from a better basis than in the past; that was one advantage. In my younger years, there was a definite division between men and women, one that religious belief and practice upheld. Women were seen as the possessions of men, and wives had few rights under the law. The state and the Church both reinforced that status and it made women extremely vulnerable. In my early career, I'd sometimes go to prosecute a man for domestic abuse, only to have his wife drop the charges. I'd do all I could to encourage her to pursue the process, but often she refused. It was disheartening, but I understood that those women were vulnerable, both socially and financially. Every year, we'd see an increase in domestic abuse over the Christmas period – when people were drinking at home, the levels went up. And that was a huge part of what happened during Covid lockdowns – people cooped up together day and night, often drinking every evening, and then the tensions would blow up – and the women and children would come out the worst of it.

The Garda Síochána had to develop strategies to protect those families who were facing domestic abuse. The newly established Garda National Protective Services Bureau (GNPSB), which came under my remit, took the lead role on this. We set up Operation Faoiseamh (Relief) to ensure court orders were being adhered to and to offer support and monitoring to vulnerable families. This was one of the welcome changes of our approach to policing domestic abuse – that we were victim-focused. Along with GNPSB, it was planned to establish a local protective service unit within every Garda division, resourced by personnel who would receive training to enable them interact in an appropriate manner with victims of crimes such as those involved in domestic abuse. This initiative arose from the *Future of Policing in Ireland* report produced by a group chaired by Kathleen O'Toole. Progress of the initiative was monitored closely by both the Taoiseach's Department and the Policing Authority, to whom I was required to provide regular updates. My job in that regard was to ensure those protection services were available and working effectively. The organisation's work in this area was subsequently commended by the Policing Authority for having 'a lasting impact on the quality of people's lives and [it] will save, already [has] saved, lives'.'

Protective Services was, unfortunately, one of the busiest bureaus during the pandemic, but another very busy section was the economic crime bureau. The criminal activity they had to contend with ranged from the individual level to national security, but all these activities delivered crippling losses when they hit their target. A significant and constant threat was invoice redirecting. This was an online scam whereby a company would receive an email from their bank outlining changes in processes, the company would send the money according to the new process, but the email was not from their bank and their payment would be redirected and all the money would disappear into the virtual hole created for just that purpose by the scammers. It always put me in mind of jumpovers – that's what we called the once-prominent crime of leaping over a shop counter to rob the till. This was going on since my father's time and shop owners lived in fear of it happening to them. The lad would jump over the counter, you might get a belt of a gun, and the money would be gone, the till drawer left empty. When I met the victims of invoice redirecting, I often found myself thinking how they would probably have preferred an old-fashioned, eye-to-eye jumpover and its relatively small losses than this scenario where they could be put out of business at the touch of a button, potentially losing a week's or a month's payroll, rather than the contents of one till.

We found that company owners were often too embarrassed to come forward to us and admit what had happened. They'd waste precious hours wringing their hands, kicking themselves for not copping it, and trying in vain to fix it somehow. But these situations are time critical – if you don't report and act immediately, get your bank to try to block the transaction, then the money is gone for ever. I received a phone call one day from a retired garda who had been contacted by a desperate friend who had been the victim of invoice redirecting and it had cleared out his account. I put him on to Pat Lordan, head of bureau at the Economic Crime Bureau. They knew to work fast and Pat got on to the transaction immediately, utilising his international contacts. So when two fellas turned up in a bank in Turkey the next morning, eager to withdraw the huge sum of money redirected from this man's account, they found their account frozen and the money irretrievable. The speedy reaction had saved this man from financial ruin and the loss of his business.

It's the nature of the digital world we all inhabit now, when we are all living online in so many ways. The reality is that an email is like a skeleton key – it can unlock so many doors. You can sequester yourself behind steel walls and gates, CCTV monitoring every entry point, doors locked and bolted, but an email can slip through any defence you care to put up. The whole world realised the extent of that during the Covid years when so many were duped by people they never laid eyes on. I remember one jumpover criminal saying to me, 'If I could only read and write, I could do cheque fraud.' That was the limit of his ambitions, because he knew the return on a cheque would be multiple times that of a jumpover and yet the cheque fraudsters only ever got suspended sentences. I thought of him again during Covid, how he could only have dreamed of cyber scams and their vast potential – the huge sums of money all robbed from a safe distance.

At the other end of that spectrum were the cyber crimes that posed a threat to national security. The potential for major disruption was made very clear by the cyber attack on the HSE. In the early hours of Friday 14 May 2021, the HSE's IT systems were infiltrated by Conti ransomware. The HSE's critical incident process was activated, which began a sequence of events that culminated in the decision to switch off the entire IT system. Healthcare professionals lost access to all HSE-provided IT systems, including patient information, clinical care and laboratory systems. It was a grim illustration of how a whole system could be taken down – and also of the price that might have to be paid for relying on old systems. There were huge weaknesses in the HSE system because of a lack of updates being carried out and an absence of upgrading. The hackers had exploited that vulnerability expertly.

This presented a huge challenge for the nascent cyber crime bureau, which was so new that it was yet to be properly resourced with the equipment and personnel needed to take on an operation of that nature. But under the leadership of Paul Cleary, assisted by Pat Ryan, the bureau personnel assigned to the HSE investigation made huge headway over the coming months. Again, international collaboration was essential to the operation and the outcome. After months of skilled work, they discovered the stolen data on a commercially available server in the USA and then invoked a mutual legal assistance treaty to request the US Department of Justice to seize the data and return it. This successful outcome was greatly assisted by the cooperation of the FBI, Interpol and Europol. The GNCCB didn't stop there, though. They went after the group behind the infiltration and, while they were not able to prosecute them, tracked the gang down to Russia and Eastern Europe. When Poland later suffered a similar attack, Polish authorities contacted their Irish counterparts for advice. We had learned quickly – and now could offer an experienced role in that all-important international collaboration.

Throughout this extraordinary time, I never stopped working on the Kinahan OCG case. It was one of a number of tasks that fell within my remit that required a hands-on approach. This is difficult to do at AC level because you are occupying an overseeing role across so many operations. But the Kinahan OCG case required constant attention and a guiding hand, and I wanted to provide that. We had watched with disappointment back in 2010, when Operation Shovel fell apart and failed. It was spearheaded by the Spanish Guardia Civil when the Kinahan OCG were based in the Costa del Sol, and was hugely successful in some regards, but had fallen at the final hurdle. They had arrested senior figures in the Kinahan OCG, but it just wasn't possible to gather sufficient evidence to get convictions in court. Not only did particular members of the Kinahan OCG walk off into the sunset, but they took with them a sense of being untouchable – they had been targeted, they had withstood the volley of fire, and they had walked away unscathed. It could only leave them feeling emboldened, beyond the reach of law enforcement, and they returned to their businesses and grew them even bigger, generating even more wealth from their new luxury base in Dubai.

We were achieving significant success in our targeting of the Kinahan OCG. In Ireland: gangland murders had practically stopped following the successful intervention in threat-to-life incidents and the associated arrest of hitmen and teams; firearms were being seized on a regular basis; significant quantities of drugs associated with the Kinahan network were being seized and the traffickers arrested; we were regularly seizing large sums of cash identified as the proceeds of the Kinahan drug trade, often as it was being prepared for removal from Ireland and about to enter the international money-laundering systems. Meanwhile, detective units in the Dublin Metropolitan Region tasked with leading investigations arising from feud-related murders were making impressive progress that would later lead to a significant number of convictions.

In April 2017, Paul Cleary, while a detective superintendent in Dublin's South Central Division, led a team that searched a premises in the city centre and arrested a man whose identity would be revealed as Naoufal Fassih, a Dutch citizen of Moroccan origin, having found him in possession of fake passports and identity documents. It was believed he was an associate of the Kinahan OCG who was in hiding from Dutch authorities. He would later be extradited to the Netherlands, where he would face charges of attempted murder, assault, possession of fake documents and money laundering. He was convicted and received a jail sentence of 18 years.

Collaboration with law enforcement entities at international level was also yielding impressive results. Following our liaison with the UK's National Crime Agency, Thomas 'Bomber' Kavanagh, identified as the head of Kinahan OCG operations in the UK, was arrested and subsequently sentenced to 21 years at Ipswich Crown Court. The NCA told the court that they had estimated that the cartel had imported drugs with a street value of more than £30 million (€36 million) into the UK. Others linked with the UK operation would be arrested and receive lengthy sentences. Gary Vickery, who was 'immediately beneath' Kavanagh, was jailed for 20 years, while Daniel Canning, who was 'subordinate to Vickery', was jailed for 19 years and six months. Our liaison with the Spanish police had resulted in additional prosecutions, including for murder.

The international collaboration would also include a US dimension. The US Drug Enforcement Administration (DEA) had become invaluable partners in pursuit of the target of dismantling and disrupting the Kinahan OCG's criminal enterprise. Much of the Kinahan OCG's drug trafficking was being undertaken far removed from Ireland and the DEA was better placed than the Garda Síochána to pursue criminal prosecutions in such circumstances. The DEA had worked closely with the Gardaí in the past and was eager to assist us again.

CAB was also contributing to the plan to dismantle the Kinahan OCG. It achieved vital successes in a number of important cases. In one case, CAB provided evidence, in April 2022, to a High Court hearing that in 2009 a senior figure in the Kinahan OCG had handed James Mansfield Jr two suitcases full of cash, amounting to €4.3 million. CAB subsequently seized a luxury gated home in Saggart, County Dublin, from the Mansfield family, having satisfied the court that it was under the control of members of the Kinahan OCG. The High Court granted CAB orders allowing it to seize the luxury residence and cash and remit the assets to the Exchequer.

However, despite the great success story CAB had become as a tool in the state's armoury to tackle serious and organised crime, it had its limitations. Europe's big players in the world's drug trafficking trade, which now included the Kinahan OCG, had taken up residence in Dubai, potentially putting themselves and their ill-gotten gains outside the reach of the, perhaps not so long, arms of the law enforcement authorities in Europe. From the time I assumed the role of AC in charge of Special Crime Operations and undertook a more pivotal role in tackling serious and organised crime, in particular with regard to that associated with the Kinahan and OCGs, I would often recall the success I participated in at an earlier time in my career, when we attempted to deprive criminals, such as the Felloni family, Roly Cronin and Derek Dunne, of their crime-related wealth. I remained in no doubt that while pursuing criminal charges against crime gangs remained an essential element of success, the demise of an OCG would only be achieved if you hit them hard in their bulging pockets. However, it was one thing to be taking possession of the contents of bank accounts in Dublin, Belfast and even London, tackling wealth that was located in Dubai and further afield was potentially an impossibility. But then one day, as I sat in my office at Harcourt Square, I received an unexpected phone call from an officer at US Customs and Border Protection (CBP). I had learned my lesson all those years ago in Store Street, when I took a call from UK Customs and it ended up leading to successful collaboration on the Derek Dunne case. So I took the call, interested to hear what it was about. The voice at the other end said, 'I was told you were the person to talk to, to get business done' and that was the moment it all began to fall into place.

Our conversation centred on our mutual interest in the Kinahan OCG. The US CBP plays a significant role in the US effort to tackle serious and organised crime, including drug-related crime. The Border Agency works hand in hand with the US Drug Enforcement Administration (DEA) and both were aware of the Kinahan OCG and the extent to which they had developed as a large-scale drug trafficking cartel, at a global level. Because of the Kinahan OCG's Irish origins, the US CBP officer who contacted me wished to discuss the efforts being made by law enforcement at an international level to tackle the criminality involved. We had an interesting conversation and I assured him that I welcomed the potential to collaborate with the US CBP in bringing about the demise of those at the apex of the Kinahan OCG.

As I questioned the CBP officer about the US approach to tackling significant drug cartels, he referenced work undertaken by the Office of Foreign Asset Control (OFAC), a section within the US Department of the Treasury, with regard to the imposition of financial sanctions on drug-selling cartels operating between the US and South and Central America. It then struck me: OFAC could have the potential to address the limitations on CAB to pursue assets in the hands of an OCG like the Kinahans, of Irish origin but conducting its financial affairs far removed from Ireland. My questions revealed that OFAC had never imposed financial sanctions on a Europe-based OCG, but I informed the person I was talking to that I would be very interested in joining him in exploring the potential for an OFAC involvement in an attempt to dismantle the Kinahan OCG. We agreed to hold a conference call a few days later, at which I would arrange to be accompanied by Detective Superintendent Seamus Boland, who was leading on Kinahan OCG investigations within the GNDOCB. That meeting took place and it was agreed we would, as soon as possible, host a meeting at Dublin Castle at which representatives of both the US CBP and the DEA would attend, where we would set in train a process of coordination with regard to gathering evidence of the nature required to make a case to OFAC for it to consider imposing financial sanctions on the Kinahan OCG. While all the other strands of activity in play designed to bring about the demise of the Kinahan OCG would continue without interruption, another was being added and, if it worked, it would be a game-changer.

CHAPTER 15

OFF-GUARD

After the Regency attack, while the Kinahan OCG organised armed assassins to bring terror to the streets of Dublin, those at the apex of the OCG were far away, living a life the people on those streets couldn't even begin to imagine. The hierarchy of the group relocated to Dubai from Spain in the months following the murder of David Byrne at the Regency, and their key associates followed suit. They moved into luxury homes and joined the elite society who are the hallmark of Dubai's ultra-high-net-worth lifestyles. In making this move to a place that is high on wealth but low on regulations, they were joining many other drug lords and gangsters, who had realised that Dubai provided a safe haven from which to conduct business operations, beyond the reach of extradition warrants.

Back in 2010, when Operation Shovel targeted members of the Kinahan OCG, their wealth was thought to stand at about €100 million. That in itself is a staggering achievement – to have come out of the south inner city, from street deals and prison sentences, and to have built up an organised crime network that had amassed that kind of wealth. But in the decade since then, the Kinahan OCG had branched out, made new contacts, entered new markets, and were now estimated to be worth as much as €1 billion. They were awash in money, particularly as they had joined forces with some other of Dubai's criminals to form what became christened a 'supercartel'.

This was very much in evidence in reports received about who was present at Daniel Kinahan's wedding in 2017, in the famous seven-star hotel, the Burj-al-Arab. Guests at the wedding included Raffaele Imperiale of the Italian Camorra, Ricardo 'El Rico' Riquelme, a Chilean drug boss, Naoufal Fassih, a Dutch-Moroccan drug boss, and Ridouan Taghi, a Dutch drug-trafficker. It was a blow to realise that these high-level criminals may have joined forces, and that they were living carefree lives of opulence out in Dubai, another world entirely from the worlds inhabited by many of the people who bought the drugs they sold. It was obvious from that information that no single jurisdiction could tackle the supercartel and that law enforcement entities would need to band together across various jurisdictions to undermine this wealth-generating machine they had built up.

The benefits to the criminals of pooling resources were huge – they increased their market share, taking over about one-third of the entire European cocaine market. They could negotiate lower prices for their massive shipments. They could share shipping channels and personnel. They could set prices to control the market even more in their favour. This collaboration opened them up to a market worth billions of euro per year. Of course, the critical factor in wealth generated by organised crime is the ability to 'clean' their money by laundering it. The cartel needed to launder a vast amount of money constantly, setting up front companies and offshore accounts and 'clean' businesses to enable them to filter through their ill-gotten gains with the legit-gotten gains. Money laundering is key to being able to use the money made from criminality and in this, too, the supercartel could pool its contacts and 'clean' channels.

To my mind, we were facing the same setup as we had in our Store Street days, where money is the motive and money buys power, and often immunity. It was just like the heroin dealers of 1990s Dublin, but on a vast, global scale. But at base, it was the same motive and pay-off. And just as it had been in Store Street, the response had to be to deprive them of their motive and their power by taking away their money and assets. The whole enterprise was worth nothing if it didn't make them wealthy. We had taken away the drug money of people like Tony Felloni and Michael 'Roly' Cronin, and now we had to find a way to do it with the multinational, multi-million euro Kinahan OCG empire. It was a huge challenge, I knew that, but anything can be unravelled if you pick at the right threads.

From the time of my appointment to the role of AC, I was working on the case, making contacts with other police forces and law enforcement agencies, figuring out how to target the Kinahan network of wealth. I made trips to Washington on a number of occasions, to meet with counterparts in the Department of the Treasury and other agencies. The key crime that got me through those doors and into those offices was the money laundering engaged in by the cartel. The US agencies had never before gone after a European cartel, but they did understand only too well that money laundering had a knock-on effect on the economy, fostered other criminal activities and that the money it created was often used for things like financing terrorists, people who might want to attack America, if they had the wherewithal to do so. It was this angle of the cartel's business that caught the attention of the US crime agencies.

The phone call I had received from a contact in the US CBP in March 2018 had brought a new sense of purpose to the plan to dismantle the Kinahan OCG. Thereafter, over the following weeks, the team assigned to the Kinahan OCG investigation in GNDOCB would be in regular contact with the US DEA and the US CBP. A few weeks later representatives of the

DEA and CBP flew to Dublin for the first in-person meeting. It was held in the offices of GNDOCB at Dublin Castle. In September 2018, Drew Harris was appointed commissioner of the Garda Síochána. In the course of the first briefing I provided to him, I outlined the current position with regard to tackling criminality associated with the Kinahan/Hutch feud and informed him of our plan with regard to the US imposition of sanctions on the Kinahan OCG, ambitiously estimating it could be done within 12 months. I emphasised to the commissioner how few of the team had any knowledge of this aspect of our targeting of the Kinahan OCG, as its success would depend on the element of surprise. It had been planned for some time that myself and Seamus Boland would travel to Washington to have our first in-person meetings at the offices of the various US participating agencies.

The opportunity arose in March 2019 when the commissioner was travelling to the city on other business. We arrived in Washington and were warmly welcomed by the DEA and CBP, who hosted us at their headquarters. The commissioner took the opportunity to express his gratitude to the US authorities for the extent of collaboration that been achieved and the level of progress that was being made. Between meetings, one of the DEA team arranged for myself and Seamie to visit Capitol Hill, which included an opportunity to be on the floor of the House of Congress. I sat in a seat of one of the elected members, to see what it looked like from that privileged vantage point. As I did so, an electrician who was doing maintenance work on the electronic voting system, shouted down at me to press a button as if casting a vote, to test the system. I obliged. As I did so, I smiled to myself, thinking that I had now spoken on the floor of the Dáil chamber, back in 1996, and had cast a vote in the US House of Congress, without ever having been an elected politician.

We were also invited to attend a gathering at the residence of the Irish ambassador to the USA, who was at that time none other than Dan Mulhall, who I knew well from my time in Thailand in the wake of the tsunami. As ever, Dan was the consummate host, allowing people to meet each other socially and discover how they might be useful to one another. This particular gathering turned out to be memorable. At one stage, having spoken to a number of people in one room, I headed into the room where a buffet was laid out and began choosing food for my plate. As I was doing so, a man came and stood beside me. I turned to find it was the former Vice President Joe Biden. We greeted one another, I revealed my law enforcement background and we chatted about Ireland and, in particular, a visit he had made to Westport. Then I returned to the other room, where I bumped into Ruairi Quinn, who was talking to a senior member of the Irish Defence Forces, who was in full uniform. We were talking – about the setup of CAB, as it happened – when Biden walked into the room, came up behind us, put his hand on my shoulder, raised a finger to the Army officer and jokingly said, 'If I was you, I'd do as he says!' We laughed, the two in my company perhaps thinking I was an acquaintance of Biden, who soon went on to the next group. The Army commander asked if Biden was going to declare a run on the presidency. I said confidently, 'Yes, he's going to declare next week.' I had read that in the newspaper, but I got a kick out of declaring it, further adding to the impression Biden and I were on friendly terms.

In October 2019 I represented the Commissioner at an EU Chiefs of Police conference in the Netherlands, at which I spoke about Ireland's experience in civil seizures of the proceeds of crime. I opened my address by stating that there were convicted criminals in detention in prisons in the EU, serving lengthy sentences, who continued to manage their criminal enterprise through surreptitious means and who would eventually be reunited with the financial gain of their criminal activity, which was totally unacceptable. I went on to repeat my mantra about the appropriate means of evaluating success when tackling OCGs, referencing quality over quantity and the need to remove their power by separating them from their wealth. Of course, while I spoke I had the OFAC plan in my mind, but I would not be revealing that closely guarded secret.

The Covid pandemic impacted significantly on the financial sanctioning aspect of our attempt to dismantle the Kinahan OCG. Across the globe law enforcement entities, like everyone else, were in survival mode, with priorities and agendas greatly altered. However, meetings regarding our ambitious project, albeit not in person, did get back up and running again. As time moved on, though, I became very concerned that our project was no longer on OFAC's list of priorities and potentially might never again feature on it.

After Ireland's experience of lockdown, relief greeted the arrival of the Covid vaccines. The Commissioner informed me that he believed it appropriate to recommence essential foreign travel, for areas such as extradition and removal of persons refused leave to land, but he also included travel associated with the security of the state and serious and organised crime. For me, it was perfect timing. I immediately made contact with Seamus Boland and told him I intended to make arrangements for him and his deputy, Detective Superintendent Dave Gallagher, who had assumed a key role on the team, to travel to Washington DC along with me.

By June 2021, the US had opened up to a greater extent than Ireland, but there were still no direct flights to DC, so our trip involved a stop in Boston en route to the capital. It was also necessary to acquire visas as the visa waiver programme was suspended. When the DEA office in Boston became aware of our plan, they insisted we pay them a visit, too. We had developed an excellent and productive rapport with the Boston team over a number of years. We were collected at the airport by our DEA friends and brought to their offices for an operational briefing. Later, we boarded one of their vessels and toured the harbour, and travelled with their aerial wing by helicopter to receive a display of other capabilities.

Before we retired for the evening, they insisted on taking us to a local pub, where other members of the Boston DEA team and the wider Boston law enforcement community had gathered to join us. As we were about to enter the premises, we were stopped, and instructed to wait a moment. To our astonishment a number of the Boston Irish bagpipe unit came around the corner in full regalia, playing with gusto as they guided us inside to a round of applause. It was a strange experience, particularly since pubs and restaurants in Ireland were still closed. Photographs were taken and soon made their way, via social media, back to our colleagues in Ireland. They must have been surprised. We had all been so careful not to breach Covid regulations in Ireland, and now here we were, in a licensed premises, not breaching any law, having a pint and meeting the law enforcement community of Boston. It was a far cry from lockdown.

Next morning we headed for Washington to meet with the various US entities who were involved in our project. We continued to receive the full support of both the DEA and CBP, who were doing all they possibly could to ensure that OFAC would undertake the desired financial sanctioning of the Kinahan OCG. The fact that the Kinahan OCG involvement in money laundering was potentially contributing to the financing of international terrorism was a particular focus for the US authorities. This visit to Washington had one important purpose from my perspective, and that was to get to meet those in the US Department of the Treasury who would ultimately make the decision about the sanctions. By this time the Garda Síochána had placed Enda Mulryan, a full-time liaison officer, at the rank of superintendent, in Washington. He had made the necessary arrangements for a meeting at Treasury before we travelled to Washington.

We arrived at the Department of the Treasury and were ushered into a conference room, where we were joined by Gregory Gatjanis, OFAC's associate director for global targeting, and his officials. I was accompanied by Seamus Boland and Dave Gallagher, two of the best operational police officers you could encounter, and they would answer any questions about the evidence gathered to support OFAC in pursuing financial sanctions against the Kinahan OCG. I thanked Mr Gatjanis for meeting us and we discussed the level of progress achieved to date. I then spoke passionately about the importance of international collaboration in targeting OCGs, and about the power of OCGs to interfere with the democratic processes in particular countries, and also their huge impact on vulnerable communities, such as those in inner-city Dublin. Mr Gatjanis looked engaged and interested, but I knew he had many priorities. There had been a change of administration in the US – Biden was now

President – and a new president always involves the setting of new priorities.

As I spoke to Mr Gatjanis, I recalled my first encounter with ICON, at a meeting in Croke Park almost thirty years earlier, and the impassioned call from its chairperson, Fergus McCabe, to the state agencies to assist the communities he represented who were being devastated by a heroin epidemic. It felt like I had, in a sense, taken the baton from Fergus McCabe and, astonishingly, I was now sitting in a room in the US Department of the Treasury, attempting to hand that baton over to Gregory Gatjanis, who had the power to make a decision that would assist in bringing about the demise of an OCG that had wreaked so much havoc in Ireland and further afield.

Before departing for Dublin the following day, I received an indication from the Department of the Treasury that the previous day's meeting had been productive and that OFAC would impose sanctions on the Kinahan OCG in the not-too-distant future. We returned to Dublin with definite arrangements regarding Dublin being the location where the Department of the Treasury would make the announcement and tentative arrangements with regard to the date it would take place. Four years after the plan was first hatched, it would soon become a reality, but it was as important as ever that the US plan to impose financial sanctions on the Kinahan OCG remained secret.

It was incredible to know that we were on track to deliver on this crucial aspect of dismantling the Kinahan OCG network. This was building up into a very significant moment of my career. When you've been doing a job for forty years, you do tend to feel that nothing more could surprise you, that there's nothing new left for you to do. My career had turned that expectation on its head. In the role of AC, in my final year as a garda, I was tackling some of the most high-profile and far-reaching cases of my career. And yet I was struck again by the thread connecting my four decades in uniform, from those days on the beat in Store Street to the high-level stakes involved at AC level. I could see that everything I had learned, everything I had thought, the conclusions I had reached, my experiences, my approach based on those experiences, all of it was coming to fruition now, coalescing into a knowledge base that would frame and define my work on the Kinahan OCG. My long career had been broken into different roles and time periods and places, but that didn't matter. Now I understood it was a working whole, everything feeding into and nurturing everything else, a continuum, with all the parts connected and moving together. Just when I might have been expecting to be winding down and passing on knowledge to the next generation of gardaí, to my surprise I found myself on an even wider stage, deploying every bit of policing knowledge I had ever gleaned in order to plan a strategy to outwit an organised crime gang that had grown into a network of wrongdoing that stretched across many borders and raked in millions of illegal euro every year. I was a long way from Store Street, but I carried it with me still, and it would be those lessons that would prove to be the very tools I needed to crack a major criminal gang.

Buoyed by the sense of making a real contribution to policing and to society, which had always been the guiding light of my work as a public servant, I was eager to stay on and do more. There would be so much more work to undertake to truly break down the Kinahan cartel, and I wanted to do that work. So in February 2022, four months shy of my retirement date, I again wrote to the Commissioner and requested another extension, to give me three more years. The application, if approved, would be passed to the Minister for Justice; all I could do was wait for the decision to be handed down.

In the meantime, the time was approaching to bring our background endeavours into the light, and that would require very careful planning. We had managed to keep everything under wraps for four years, which was a minor miracle in itself, but now the pieces were in place between Ireland, the USA and the UK. It was agreed at all levels – the very first such action of this nature to be taken by the powerful US security agencies against a European cartel. Now I had to design the announcement of this extraordinary measure so that it would have maximum impact.

My strategy whenever I was planning an operation or an event was the same – I presented a fully worked-out plan and said: This is what we're going to do. The first step was to have clear objectives, to know exactly what this event was about. I had two objectives: one, to show we could reach all the way to Dubai and beyond, that nowhere was beyond the scope of the Garda Síochána and CAB; and two, to show that we were effectively tackling the motive – wealth – and that we had stepped up to the OCG level by involving the US entities. The next crucial decision was the venue. My first choice was Dublin Castle, but in the event it was unavailable. I got the team working on an appropriate alternative and, by chance, one of them had a contact at City Hall, next door to Dublin Castle. The Rotunda Hall there became a possibility, but we had to reassure the authorities at City Hall that this event would not be of a political nature, even though some politicians might be in the audience.

I was extremely pleased that we had secured the City Hall venue because it was in south inner-city Dublin – we would make our announcement in the heart of the Kinahan OCG's home territory. That held important symbolism. And there was the fact that City Hall was the place from which much of the cityscape had been planned, where the vision for the city had been articulated. We would be articulating a vision for Dublin city, too – one where the drug dealers did not hold sway, where the community had the gardaí at its back, supporting and protecting.

The date for the press conference was set for 12 April 2022. It would take place in front of a live audience of journalists and other interested parties, and it would also be live streamed. I was extremely careful in choosing the name for the event, so that it did not give away what was coming. I needed a title that would slip under the radar and wouldn't raise eyebrows. So we released the information that on 12 April a press conference would be held under the title 'Cooperating at an International Level in Protecting Communities from Organised and Serious Crime'. That was vague enough not to raise red flags.

On the day before the event, the media were advised of its title and the venue. Despite an embargo on revealing the fact that the event was taking place, a number of journalists wrote about it and included speculation about its purpose. By now, the journalists knew something was up, despite all our efforts to disguise the event. Their nose for a story had sniffed out that there was something a bit different about this press conference, so, on the day, as the starting time drew closer, the room swelled with people. Our panel assembled in front of the banners and screen: Commissioner Drew Harris; US Ambassador to Ireland Claire Cronin; Deputy Commissioner and soon-to-be Commissioner for US Customs and Border Protection Troy Miller; Associate Director for Global Targeting at OFAC Gregory Gatjanis; Special Agent in Charge of the DEA's Special Operations Division Wendy Woolcock; Deputy

Director of Investigations at the UK NCA Matt Horne; Head of the Serious and Organised Crime Centre at Europol, Jari Liukku; and myself.

I performed the role of MC, and as I made my way to the microphone to get proceedings under way, a hush fell across the room. There was expectation in that silence; they were still with listening, with curiosity. I listed our positive achievements. I told the room about our 70 threat-to-life interventions, 49 of which directly related to the Kinahan–Hutch feud. On the screen, the positives were emblazoned in symbols: €20 million of drugs seized, 48 firearms seized, 79 convictions to date, €7.5 million in cash seized. We were targeting the wealth, and we were making ground. Those statistics had the same effect as always – they boosted confidence in our work, connected with our audience, put our work front and centre. We had their attention.

I introduced Drew Harris and he referenced the consequences of a crime network like that operated by the Kinahan OCG – drug-related crime, addiction, corruption – and the fact that the Kinahan cartel had now grown to such an extent that we needed international cooperation to tackle all those issues. But our audience were much more interested in hearing from our guests. I introduced US Ambassador Claire Cronin. I was watching the audience as she spoke and I remember in particular the journalists who were seated in the front row. As Claire Cronin spoke, I saw the moment they realised what was happening – their faces were a picture, eyes wide with shock as they stared at the screen in near-disbelief.

Claire Cronin announced a reward of $5 million for information leading to the arrest of Christy Kinahan Sr. Then she went on to offer the same amount for information on Christy Kinahan Jr and Daniel Kinahan. On the screen beside her, stark red-and-white posters came up, one of each man. In the centre of each poster was a photograph of each Kinahan, their poses and smiles contrasting markedly with the fact that what Claire Cronin was saying had just made them three of the most wanted men in the world. They were now quarry, and all financial institutions across the globe would be hunting them out, careful not to do business with anyone with these sanctions on their heads. The US Office of Foreign Assets Control had placed the three Kinahans on a Specially Designated Nationals list, which was used globally to screen and potentially block financial transactions. The world as the Kinahan OCG knew it had just ceased to exist.

The journalists were still reeling from those staggering figures of $5 million per head when I introduced Gregory Gatjanis. It was his office that administered sanctions, and this was the first time they would extend their reach to a European cartel. His was a powerful presentation, listing the major OCGs in the world and ranking the Kinahans alongside them in terms of terrible impact – and terrible consequences, for them. He said that the USA viewed the major Kinahan drug and crime network in the same bracket as the Camorra, the Yakuza and the Russian mafia. The Kinahan OCG had wanted to hit the big time, and now they certainly had.

Gatjanis described the effect of the sanctions on the crime group. Serious and organised crime relies on the ability to carry out safe and effective money laundering on a massive scale, without interruption in that supply. This money was kept away from all of the oversight instruments of the legal financial system. It was that money that eventually made its way into the cartel's bank accounts and funded their luxury lifestyles – and further crimes. It was a cycle of criminality that would keep rolling on, gathering more and more into itself, unless it was stopped. The effect of sanctions was essentially to put a spoke into those wheels. The sanctions placed on members of the Kinahan OCG would prevent them entering into any financial transactions in the USA and would block all their property and interests in property. They would suddenly find that their financial world had shrunk to the notes in their pockets. They were ruled out of money transfers, property purchases, setting up companies, operating companies and generally engaging in business and finance. They had seen themselves as untouchables; now no one would want to touch them, for fear of running foul of the sanctions and being caught up in the law enforcement web along with them. It was unprecedented, it was far-reaching and it could not fail to massively destabilise the carefully constructed network that supported the Kinahan empire.

Gregory Gatjanis finished his presentation by thanking me for persevering in getting the operation to this point. I was honoured and grateful to be recognised in this way. It had taken great perseverance – by all in the small, dedicated team who had put in such huge work over the past four years. In fact, it was thanks to every garda who had ever dealt with the fallout of Kinahan OCG criminality. It was thanks also to the dedicated teams in the US DEA and CBP and the UK's NCA. Every moment in that long battle had led to this moment. It had required bravery of vision to see that this could be possible, and then it had required focused effort to make it happen. As I nodded in thanks to Gregory Gatjanis, I felt a huge sense of pride in our organisation, the Garda Síochána, which achieved so much, year in, year out, from what was in international terms a relatively small base of budget and staffing. We had stepped up to meet our responsibilities in every way possible, and it had resulted in this incredible moment that would provide a template in policing for those coming after us.

When it was my turn to speak, I had a final surprise to land on the Kinahan OCG, and on our audience. We had secured a European arrest warrant for alleged Kinahan OCG member Sean McGovern. Up on the screen came an image of Sean McGovern – Wanted on Warrant. This was the announcement of our intention to reach the long arm of the law right into Dubai and hopefully return McGovern to Ireland to answer alleged criminal charges in Ireland. I saw it as a test case, because Ireland has no extradition agreement with the United Arab Emirates, so we have to negotiate on a case-by-case basis. Here was the first case, and that meant we could open negotiations and try to establish a common understanding and a sense of cooperation. (I am sorry to say that at this point, in 2024, the warrant still stands, but Sean McGovern has yet to be extradited to Ireland to answer alleged criminal charges.)

In conclusion, I spoke of success, knowing full well those parameters hadn't changed since my Store Street days. Wealth grants power, and organised crime gangs are all about power. They wield it through force and they protect it through force. It is that power that must be removed from them, which we do through removing their wealth. The key to the entire plan being laid out that day was to break the drug-trafficking revenue model. In that way, we would remove their power to keep investing in criminal activity at all levels. The Kinahan OCG had considered themselves above and beyond the law, but we had matched them. When the state intervened with its full power, it could smash organised crime – that was the very important lesson for everyone to take away from our press conference.

The repercussions from that day are still occurring. In the immediate aftermath, the financial world was astounded by the imposition of sanctions. It has huge consequences for banks when sanctions are laid because they have to be extremely careful not to inadvertently breach any of the conditions and end up with a penalty being levied on them. The sanctioned person will find it hard to get legal representation as well as banking facilities. In the case of the Kinahans, it was not just the three family members who were the subject of the sanctions; they were also placed on associates Sean McGovern, Ian Dixon, Bernard Clancy and John Morrissey; and on three companies, Nero Drinks Company Limited (owned or controlled by, directly or indirectly, John Morrissey), Hoopoe Sports LLC (owned or controlled by, directly or indirectly, Ian Dixon) and Ducashew General Trading LLC (owned or controlled by, directly or indirectly, Daniel Kinahan). All relevant financial institutions had to respond to this and apply the law of the sanctions to all those entities.

In May, one month after the press conference, I returned to Washington for a debrief and brought some members of my team with me. We met up with our key contacts once more and reviewed the state of play at that point. At my final meeting in the Department of the Treasury, Gregory Gatjanis gave me a letter from Brian E. Nelson, under-secretary of the Office of Terrorism and Financial Intelligence. The letter thanked me for my work and leadership during the operation. It was a thoughtful and much appreciated gesture and a testament to the relationship we had built up with our US counterparts.

It was important for us to see that the US commitment to dismantling the Kinahan network was unwavering and they were in it for the long haul. It was a fantastic illustration of the mutual benefits of a strong cross-border relationship and collaboration.

The aftermath for the Kinahan OCG is still in train. They may still be in the UAE, but there have been reports that they wish to move to a new location, perhaps in Africa or Russia. One of their alleged key money launderers and a subject of the sanctions, John Morrissey, was arrested in Spain in September 2022. Their associates in the supercartel, Raffaele Imperiale and Ridouan Taghi, were arrested and extradited to their own countries to stand trial. This channel is still being worked on by the Irish authorities. The Garda Síochána has placed a liaison officer, at superintendent rank, in Abu Dhabi, where they will work as a full-time liaison with law enforcement in that region. It is a slow process, but it is progressing.

On 9 June, a letter arrived for me from the commissioner's office. It expressed an apology for being unable to support my application for an extension to my retirement date, and that this request would not, therefore, be forwarded to the Minister for Justice. It was the response I had expected and I accepted the fact that my 41-year career with the Garda Síochána would end in 21 days' time. The end date had been set, and there was nothing I could do to change it. I focused on getting through as much work as possible in the time left to me.

The weeks flew by, as of course they always do when you want time to stand still. I felt there was still a mountain of work to scale, but time was against me now. There were cases to review, reports to write up, instructions to leave behind, meetings upon meetings, and all the while I had to compartmentalise my own inner thoughts and feelings about retirement so that I could devote all my time and energy to the tasks in hand. In truth, there were mixed emotions. On the one hand, I felt it would be very enjoyable to spend time with friends and family without work pressures, to be able to travel at my leisure. On the other hand, the last two years had been among the most exciting and fulfilling of my career and I felt energised by that and ready for more. I wasn't tired or weary of it all, none of those things that would let me slip away gratefully. Instead, I felt full of purpose and vigour – that made the thoughts of stopping a little harder.

In 2021, Donal, my younger brother, decided to retire from the Garda Síochána after almost 38 years' service. His career in the Garda Síochána had a similar start to mine and our father's, pounding the beat in Dublin's north inner city. However, after that, Donal, similar to a significant number of our colleagues, took a career path that would see him removed from the public eye. The rest of his career, with only one brief promotion-related return to uniform, would be discreetly served within the Security and Intelligence section of the organisation. When he retired Donal was a detective inspector attached to the organisation's Special Tactics & Operations Command. His career involved participation in numerous high-risk operations that helped protect the state from the threat of terrorism and heavily armed organised crime groups. He and his colleagues also ensured that visitors to the state, including many heads of state, remained safe and unharmed until their departure. Donal's career, similar to my own, would involve travel abroad. For him, this would include a year-long deployment in 2010, with a number of his colleagues, to Afghanistan, where they would participate in an EU police mission. Following his retirement from the Garda Síochána in 2021, Donal went on to serve with European Union Missions in Iraq and Moldova, providing government-level advice on crisis management and civilian security sector reform.

My last day was 28 June 2022. I was working at my desk from early morning, determined to finish a few important outstanding reports before leaving the office. There were some cases that I particularly wanted to push forward before leaving, so that they didn't fall into the gap between me and my successor. My door was open, and colleagues were dropping in throughout the day, wishing me well, asking if I'd be available for a parting pint at close of business. However, it was looking like that would have to wait another day.

The first task was to order a review of the murder of Sophie Toscan du Plantier. The Serious Crime Review Team within GNBCI had put a lot of time into assisting a new investigation team in West Cork and were recommending a full review of the case. I agreed, and was anxious that it would not be delayed any longer. The du Plantier case is probably the most investigated in the history of the state, but it still merits further examination. Over time, advances in crime investigation techniques, including those relating to DNA, can provide the prospect of advancing a long-stalled investigation. Also, in this case, a person had indicated, by way of sworn affidavit, that they could offer additional relevant evidence. It is necessary for the Garda Síochána to be open to reviewing work previously done: we owe it to the victims and their families and friends. That review is ongoing and, although chief suspect Ian Bailey died in early 2024, it is making progress. I look forward to its final report.

Reports written and filed, I glanced up at the clock. I also had to clear out my belongings, so I decided to get that job done next. I gathered up the personal items in my office – letters, photographs and other belongings. My custom-made formal uniform was mine to keep as well, and it would hang in the wardrobe at home alongside my father's. I gathered the uniform and the box of items and brought them out to the state car that was provided to me as AC and stashed them in the boot.

Back in the office, I knew there was one item I was obliged to surrender and leave behind, albeit it would be very difficult to part with. I took my Garda badge out of my pocket and opened it. John O'Driscoll, 22317D. Your Garda ID is a constant – always on your person, always ready to show at any moment to identify yourself and verify your police powers. By this stage, it felt like a part of me. This was who I had been for the past 41 years. But I was ready now to hand it back and begin a new phase in my life.

It reminded me of my father's early death. He and my mother had plans for a long retirement they saw stretching out ahead of them, but it didn't turn out like that. He died a few short months after retiring. A garda from the local station turned up at the front door, looking to collect his Garda ID. We couldn't put our hands to it right at that moment, so I promised to find it. Eventually, our searching uncovered it and I put it in my pocket and walked up to the station and handed it in. And now here I was, forty years later, holding my own ID, and it was now time to part with it, too. I placed it on the desk, ready to be collected by Inspector Michael Griffen, who had so efficiently managed my office for a number of years.

I turned my attention to writing my final report on the fatal shooting of Garda Gary Sheehan and Private Patrick Kelly in Ballinamore during the rescue of kidnap victim Don Tidey. That was a seminal moment in Irish history, when the IRA shot dead a serving member of the Irish Defence

Forces for the first and only time. It had shocked the nation to its core and shook my own family deeply. Now, I had the responsibility to ensure that the history books could not be rewritten, to place on record the fact that the firearms that delivered the fatal shot were held and fired by members of the IRA. Garda Gary Sheehan and Private Patrick Kelly had not died from friendly fire, as some had argued, and it was essential that was officially recorded.

By the time I'd finished everything on my desk, it was 11.30 p.m. If my colleagues had managed to enjoy a farewell pint, they had enjoyed it without me. At midnight, I would become a civilian, therefore not permitted to drive a state car. I would not break that rule, even if no one else knew or minded. I stood up from my desk, neck stiff, and I looked around my office. I had what I was taking with me, I had left what I must leave behind. I walked out and closed the door softly, hearing the click in the almost empty office.

I drove home through the dark-bright of a summer's night. I parked the state car outside, where it would be collected first thing in the morning. I let myself into the house, walked down to the kitchen and looked up at the clock: 11.59. In another minute, I was no longer a garda.

It is so peculiar how four decades can pass so quickly. I could picture myself in Templemore, a new recruit, eager to prove myself. I remembered the questions put to myself and my fellow recruits by Stephen Rea, editor of the *Garda*

Review, who a number of years later profiled the class that passed out in 1981. He asked each of us what we wanted for our future careers. He later told me that my answer had stayed with him because it was different; typically, people referred to the rank they aspired to achieve, but as a callow 22-year-old, I'd said that I wanted to influence policy in the Garda Síochána. I smiled to think of that now, as I'm sure he had then.

And I remembered, too, later on, when, after a number of enjoyable years on the beat and as a detective in Fitzgibbon Street Station, I felt the need to move on to some other role. Colleagues asked me what I wanted to do, and I said to them: 'I just want to be a busy policeman.'

That was indeed what I had always wanted – to be busy, to be in the middle of intense problem-solving with likeminded people, to be working hard, to be making a difference. Looking back on it now, I realised that the thought of who I wanted to be, the sort of garda I wanted to be, was there from the start, long before I knew how to be it. I'd had to learn it the hard way, over decades, figuring out how to be a good productive officer and public servant. Forty-one years later, a civilian again, no Garda badge in my pocket, I could at least say that, yes, I had always been a busy policeman.

EPILOGUE

WHAT COMES NEXT?

I spent my childhood summers around Sam's Cross in West Cork, the land of the O'Briens, my mother's family. In 1966, a monument was unveiled there to commemorate the life and legacy of Michael Collins and his service to Ireland. That monument stands beside my grandfather Michael O'Brien's home at Sam's Cross, where my mother grew up in the same house where Collins's mother had grown up, a generation separating them but joined by the same strong beliefs. Those same beliefs were passed down the generations, giving us youngsters a sense of duty and responsibility from the start.

In February 2020, I was in West Cork to attend a funeral and I decided to pay a visit to my father's homeplace, Ahiohill House, in Enniskeane. My father would have been 100 years old that month and I was pleased to have the chance to visit the place he started from. He was born and reared in Ahiohill, he had joined the Garda Síochána from that house, and it was good to get that sense of him there, after being without him for so many years.

I drove up the driveway and parked and walked inside the house. It was now called Carra Lodge. My uncle had sold the farm about twenty years before, but had donated the farmhouse for charitable purposes. The woman who managed it was there at the reception desk, and I explained my story and my father's story and she welcomed me in and invited me to ramble around. The house was now the main treatment centre in Cork for teenage male drug addicts. I took the opportunity to walk about downstairs, but I didn't go upstairs. I was worried that a recovering addict might get a nasty shock to see Garda John O'Driscoll who tackles drug trading suddenly appear in his room – that might not be good for the nerves.

It was another of those interesting coincidences, that the home of my father had become a refuge for those trying to find a way out of drug addiction – reflecting my own career and the ways I had tried to help communities find a way out. For me, it was part of that thread woven across the years, connecting me and my choices to those of my family line, each of us taking up the mantle of public service, embedded in that sense of duty and responsibility with which we had been imbued.

Added together, my father's career and my career span 82 years of Irish social history. In that time the country has been engulfed in a maelstrom of change. It has changed the face of crime, and continues to do so, and that has necessarily changed the parameters of policing. But within the maelstrom, there are points that hold fast, that do not get swept away. As with my own family, the roots still feed the branches – there is a set of core values that holds us steady through time, that anchors us in what is good and right. As long as the Garda Síochána remains steadfast in those core values, it can weather any storm.

The qualities that make a decent and effective garda do not change, even as the job widens to encompass the modern world. A good garda has a strong sense of empathy, but it is always in service to the police work that must be undertaken and completed. They have perseverance, the ability to stay the course no matter the obstacles along the way. They have an informed understanding of who the victim is and why they are a victim. We all know there are two sides to every story, as the saying goes, but there can be many more sides than that. A good garda has the curiosity and the sensitivity to uncover all the sides. They have an innate sense of purpose, and that purpose is anchored in a core belief of what public service is and should be. These things do not change.

While 41 years seemed to go by very fast, it is a long time, and that sort of investment of time does bestow experience and insight and deeper understanding. I learned that there are four key pillars to policing, and that every operation, no matter how major or minor, must be founded on them.

First, the evaluation of success. As became clear to me in Store Street, policing must have an impact on the problem, not on the statistics. You only achieve success when it aligns with what the community sees as successful – and they will deem an operation successful because it has answered a pressing need. I have been honoured to receive a number of awards in the course of my career, but the one that means the most to me is the Respect for Law award that I received in 1997. That particular award was special because it matched my own idea of success. It acknowledged that we were trailblazers in Store Street. It might have been given to me, but I saw it as a team award, a recognition of our new and different approach to drugs policing. We established taking assets as a new measure of success, a means by which we could achieve what the community needed us to do. The award was given for cultivating respect for law, which recognised the huge impact our work had on community relations. How we choose to measure success is a crucial factor in effective policing.

Second, accountability and the desire to be held accountable, to have no fear of that because you are safe in the knowledge that you have observed correct procedure and covered all bases. I remember my interview panel for the job of assistant commissioner asking me about the increased level of accountability that would come with the post. I replied, very honestly, that I loved and wanted accountability. As gardaí, we provide a service to the people of Ireland, and being accountable to them for that is an important part of that service. This is why I never shied away from speaking in public, no matter how nerve-racking it was.

Third, communication. Leading directly on from accountability, the ability to communicate effectively is a cornerstone of good policing. From the pulpit in Seán McDermott Street to the worldwide broadcast of the press conference on the Kinahan OCG, I took every opportunity to talk and explain what we were doing and why. My rule was that if I was invited to speak anywhere, I would accept that invitation. It is a mark of respect to those who want to engage with you, and it quickly teaches you to think on your feet, speak carefully and arm yourself with solid information. It should be a prerequisite to holding any senior position in the Garda Síochána that you are readily available to explain and provide information about matters that fall within your remit. This role cannot be left solely to a few or mainly the commissioner. I think it is imperative that gardaí learn to communicate at all levels, from individual conversations on the street to media appearances and press conferences. It is part of our job to inform, to explain and to calm situations with good and reliable information.

Fourth, consultation. Policing cannot happen on its own, it relies on intel, insights and insider knowledge that can lead and support operations. Listening to and interacting with the community is essential, which is why community policing is essential. Sometimes there is a tendency in some quarters to sneer at it as a 'soft' form of policing, but it is the basis on which everything else is built and rests. Again, a garda is a public servant, providing a public service, and the public are necessarily central to that.

When those four pillars are present, the core values of good policing will be upheld. The young gardaí of today might perhaps feel that they are facing a wildly different landscape, more violent and volatile than the world of the past. But those gardaí of the past also dealt with public disorder and violent mobs. We had to provide armed escort to politicians during the Troubles – and it looks like things might go that way again. There were gruesome murders and tragic deaths and grieving families. It has always been this way.

The one thing that truly separates modern policing from the past is the digital revolution. It is social media. That is challenging the Garda Síochána in new and pervasive ways. Indeed, it is challenging the very fabric of democracy in new and pervasive ways. There is a line of gunpowder that you can trace from the riots on Capitol Hill in the US in early January 2021 to the explosion of the Dublin riots in late 2023. The common denominator is the mob mentality, and that is created and fed by social media, misinformation, disinformation. Today's young people are living in a totally different universe online, and it can take shape in the real world in sudden and unpredictable ways. Tackling this mentality will require legal deterrents, long sentences and charge sheets for high-profile people. The red flags for democracy are flying high, and policing has a role to play in de-escalating the situations that arise.

In terms of the future of the Garda Síochána, I am very optimistic, but I can of course see elements that would benefit from examination and review. From my vantage point, now outside the gates looking in, a recommendation I would make is to look at retired officers and how they could be used within the organisation. I remember one of the training courses that I gave with Nick Kinsella, where a member of his staff was retiring. At the end, I said a few words about that person, only to be corrected and told that, yes, he was retiring from the force but would return to work as a civilian, still helping with the training so that the organisation did not lose that expertise. For now, senior Garda managers go to the UK for training, but that could take place here, utilising the experience and expertise of the retired cohort. Because if it doesn't happen, all those skills and knowledge are simply lost when a garda retires. It's wasteful in the extreme. There is an opportunity there that is not being taken up, but could provide huge benefits.

Since my own retirement in 2022, people have been kind enough to express their gratitude for my work over the years, which has been a true and unexpected delight. I am also often asked what I miss about my job, having lived it for 41 years. Most of all, I miss my colleagues and all the everyday interactions. Being a garda is a very people-oriented occupation and I enjoyed that very much. When I look at the work-from-home culture that has mushroomed since the pandemic, I don't think I could ever have done that. I loved working in a station, in an office, being part of a unit, and interacting constantly with the public. I also miss the energy of the work – being part of a team working on finding solutions. I loved being in the middle of that. And I miss – as I'm sure all retired people do – the sense of pride in having an input and making a contribution. I miss the busyness.

I remain optimistic because I know the calibre of the people in the organisation, the dedication, the skills and the commitment. I worked with the very best and was impressed by them every single day. It is a hard job, but the people who want to do it tend to be people of principle, and they must be sought out and encouraged at every level. The new capabilities of the Garda Síochána, across cyber crime and international policing and forensics, are powerful tools, providing new methods for tracking and cracking crime. When my retirement was announced, not long after that unprecedented press conference on the sanctions being imposed on the Kinahan OCG, one newspaper quoted a security source as saying that my departure 'should not lead to champagne bottles being popped in Dubai'. This was because, as the source said, there were so many other gardaí working away quietly, capable and resourceful, getting results. This is exactly right. Those coming after me have the ability and the potential to achieve so much more than I did. The house doesn't fall down when you leave, because you built it with others. That's the aim, that's the legacy. As I said in my post-retirement interview, paraphrasing the criminal Larry Dunne: *If you think I'm good, wait until you see what's coming next.*

ACKNOWLEDGEMENTS

My career in the Garda Síochána extended to over forty-one years, one consequence of which is that I owe a debt of gratitude to many people who made that achievement possible. I am particularly grateful to my now deceased parents for ensuring I was equipped to embark on the career I had chosen and supporting me in that endeavour throughout their lifetime.

I must express my deepest gratitude to my wife for the endless support she has provided to me throughout my lengthy career, despite the burden she endured as her spouse frequently worked unsocial hours and at times was transferred to, or was otherwise required to work in, a location far removed from our family home. My children also deserve a big thank you for the manner in which they accepted the inconvenience they experienced as a consequence of the career path I had chosen.

In the final years of my career a number of people expressed a view that I should make a written record of the many interesting and varied experiences that featured in my long career. However, I never anticipated that an opportunity would arise to undertake such an adventure. I am very grateful, therefore, to Teresa Daly of Gill Books for contacting me and suggesting that the writing of a memoir was a viable project worthy of pursuit. A special thank you also to Rachel Pierce, who through her vast editing skills made sure the book would be of appropriate quality and the story I wished to tell would be presented in a way that has the reader in mind.

I undertook a career in the Garda Síochána as a means of providing public service. However, I owe a vast debt of gratitude to that public, who through my many interactions with them, ensured I experienced such a sense of fulfilment and enjoyment over my 41-year career. The residents of Dublin's north inner city deserve particular mention in this regard.

More than ever the Garda Síochána require the assistance of their colleagues in law enforcement in other jurisdictions, in tackling a vast range of criminal activity. I am very grateful to the assistance I received in my career from many law enforcement entities in other EU Member States and from agencies such as Europol, Eurojust, Interpol and Frontex. That gratitude extends also to UK law enforcement related entities, particularly the UK National Crime Agency, UK Border Force, UK Immigration Enforcement and the Police Service of Northern Ireland. The transnational dimension of serious and organised crime that impacts on Ireland is reflected in the fact that I am also so grateful to the US Drug Enforcement Administration, US Customs & Border Protection, US Department of Treasury and the US State Department, for the extent of assistance they provided to the Garda Síochána and to me personally in tackling drug trafficking and associated money laundering. I am also grateful to the US Secret Service and US Federal Bureau of Investigation for their assistance in tackling such issues as cyber crime and online-related child exploitation.

Throughout my career in the Garda Síochána I had the privilege of working with the best of colleagues, many of whom became personal friends and whose friendship continues into my retirement. The events that I recall in this memoir involve many of those colleagues and friends whose professionalism and sense of duty, I hope, is properly reflected in my description of those events. I am forever grateful to them for the part they played in making my career so interesting and rewarding.

I am grateful also to the public servants in the many government departments and state agencies, particularly the Department of Justice, that I interacted with, and received great support from, throughout my career. The dedicated staff of the many NGOs and charitable organisations that I encountered, who provide support and assistance to so many vulnerable people, deserve a particular word of thanks also.